UNCOMMON
SENSE

UNCOMMON SENSE

CREATING BUSINESS EXCELLENCE IN YOUR ORGANIZATION

STEPHEN GEORGE

John Wiley & Sons, Inc.

New York ➤ Chichester ➤ Brisbane ➤ Toronto ➤ Singapore ➤ Weinheim

This text is printed on acid-free paper.

Copyright © 1997 by Stephen George
Published by John Wiley & Sons, Inc.

Library of Congress Cataloging-in-Publication Data:

George, Stephen, 1948–
    Uncommon sense : creating business excellence in your
organization / Stephen George.
        p.   cm.
    Includes index.
    ISBN 0-471-15377-X (cloth : alk. paper)
    1. Total quality management.   2. Quality assurance.
   3. Success in business.   4. Organizational change.   I. Title.
HD62.15.G464   1997
658.5'62—dc20   96-42474
                                              CIP

Printed in the United States of America
10 9 8 7 6 5 4 3 2

Contents

Chapter 3: Focus through Shared Vision   55

Chapter 4: Engage Employees   83

Chapter 5: Know Your Customers   115

Chapter 6: Organize to Optimize   135

Chapter 7: Think Process   151

Chapter 8: Manage by Fact   169

Preface

If you're unhappy with how your organization is running—whether the organization is a department, division, or company—you're probably looking for solutions. Read on. *Uncommon Sense* is filled with solutions from some of the best thinkers and practitioners in the business.

It is also filled with *one* solution, and that is gaining control of your management system. If you're wondering where to start making changes, you're probably wading through the many options that are available. Read on. *Uncommon Sense* presents proven options that any organization can learn from and apply.

It also promotes *one* option, and that is a systematic approach to change. Every successful change initiative has four ingredients:

1. A clear understanding of where you are
2. A clear vision of what you want to become
3. A comprehensive plan to get from where you are to what you want to become
4. The will to change

The best way to know where you are is to assess your management system using a proven, comprehensive tool. I recommend the criteria for the Malcolm Baldrige National Quality Award. You will find a simplified assessment based on these criteria in Appendix A. It is not meant to replace a rigorous assessment, but its careful completion will give you a snapshot of where your organization currently stands.

The eight basics of business excellence described throughout the book present a vision of how leading experts view management and how world-class organizations are doing business. You can work with their ideas and insights to develop a vision of what you want your organization to become. Just don't get carried away and assume your vision is the organization's vision (see Chapter 3).

At the end of each chapter, you will find strategies for improvement that will help you translate ideas into action. The strategies are divided into three levels: Jump Start, for organizations that have done little or nothing in that area; Tune Up, for those that have plans or processes in place but improvement has stalled; and Pull Away, for those organizations that have mastered the basics and are ready to put some distance between themselves and the competition. The strategies are intended to stimulate thinking and offer options to consider as you develop a comprehensive action plan.

The last chapter discusses the will to change, which is the moment of truth. If you do an exceptional job of assessing your current condition, creating a vision, and developing an outstanding plan, but the will to change is missing, you have probably done more damage than good. You have encouraged people to imagine a better organization. You have led them to believe that a new way of doing business is at hand. You have given them hope that they can rid themselves of the old, ineffective, frustrating management system. When nothing changes, the people who must work within the old system will lose hope. Good people will leave. Those who stay will become more cynical. They will feel deceived, disregarded, disrespected. And the old system will become even more entrenched.

This is no time for tinkering. *Uncommon Sense* is about exploring the complexities of a management system, understanding how different elements of that system affect each other, and initiating changes that will make the entire system more efficient and effective.

It requires a willingness to change, both personally and organizationally. If that's something you are committed to, read on. *Uncommon Sense* offers myriad ways to make broad, fundamental changes to your management system. Changes that will produce immediate benefits and long-term success, transforming your management system into a competitive advantage. Changes that will energize employees, please customers, and satisfy owners.

Which, for an organization, are the only kinds of changes that make sense.

Acknowledgments

One of the few facts I remember from high school was a quote by Sir Isaac Newton: "If I have seen further it is by standing upon the shoulders of giants." Looking for the exact words in Bartlett's *Familiar Quotations,* I now learn that Newton's insight was not original; Lucan wrote something similar 1600 years earlier: "Pigmies placed on the shoulders of giants see more than the giants themselves."

At six feet five inches I'm no pigmy, but I have enjoyed the view from the shoulders of giant thinkers in the business world. I thank them for sharing their insights and experiences; you will find their works listed in Appendix B. I've also seen how their insights and experiences work in the real world through the organizations featured in this book. For their many contributions I thank Jeff Pope, Judy Corson, Diane Kokal, Ray Marlow, Chris Witzke, Jay Schrankler, Larry Welliver, Bruce Woolpert, Bob Gower, Don Wainwright, and Mike Simms.

I also want to thank my wife, Ellen, and my children, Dan, Kate, Allie, and Zachary, for their love and support.

Stephen George
June 6, 1996

UNCOMMON SENSE

$Chapter$

1

Learning the Basics

Leading an organization today is like walking the deck of a ship barefoot in the rain: You'd die for sure footing.

After you fall a few times, slide farther back, watch others negotiate the same deck with fewer problems, and fear you will never find a way to proceed, you look for help. You develop techniques for sliding rather than stepping. You watch others to see if you can learn their tricks. You form a team to explore the property of slipperiness and discover that the best solution is a dry deck. But it's raining. You get rid of the deck. You get rid of the pilot. You switch ships. You discover they're all slippery.

In times of constant, rapid, unexpected change, leaders crave sure footing. Old approaches to leadership hold no sway. Old methods of management fail. Leaders—whether they lead organizations, departments, work groups, or initiatives—seek a proven path through the deluge of customer demands, competitive pressures, employee needs, and shareholder expectations.

This book offers a proven path.

Unlike other authors of management books, however, I make no claim to a revolutionary breakthrough in management thinking. Too many books boast about a unique approach that is *the* way to manage your organization. *The* way does not exist. How you lead your organization depends on your customers' requirements, your market's demands, your organization's culture, and your leadership team's commitment. This book offers an approach that helps you get your arms around the many elements of your management system. An approach you can tailor to your needs. An approach that draws from the best contemporary management thinking and practices, with documented positive results for organizations of all sizes and types. An approach that will give you the sure footing you need to lead with confidence.

This fundamentally sound, holistic approach involves understanding the basics of business excellence and learning how to master them for competitive advantage, customer satisfaction, and profitability. Each of the basics connects to the others; you cannot isolate one without seriously diminishing its power, any more than you can build a high performance automobile with great tires and a poor engine or win a baseball title with great hitting and poor pitching. The fundamentals—*all* the fundamentals—must be mastered for the organization to have a chance at achieving its potential.

■ EIGHT BASICS OF BUSINESS EXCELLENCE

The basics of business excellence bubble up from current management thinking, expressed in the most incisive management books and articles and through the best practices of world-class organizations. The organizations I define as world-class have been finalists for or have won the Malcolm Baldrige National Quality Award. You can argue with this definition, but I challenge you to find any other criteria anywhere in the world that allow you to measure excellence with the same breadth and depth as the Baldrige criteria. The organizations featured in this book embody the core values of the Baldrige criteria, many of which are reflected in the basics of business excellence.

The eight basics of business excellence are:

1. Lead by serving
2. Focus through shared vision
3. Engage employees
4. Know your customers
5. Organize to optimize
6. Think process
7. Manage by fact
8. Align through planning

Not flashy, but effective. And frankly, the leaders and managers I talk to are tired of flashy. They're tired of the management solution of the month. They're buried in information and it keeps piling up and they know some of it has value, but finding the value takes too long. Deciding how best to manage is like deciding which computer to buy: You hate to commit to the latest model when it's likely to be obsolete within months. And there are too many options to know what's best, anyway.

That's where the basics of business excellence come in. Once you've grounded your organization in the basics, you are free to evaluate new management approaches on their long-term benefits, rather than their short-term promises of salvation. With the basics mastered, you can assess new management approaches based on their fit with your system, not on a desperate need for the quick fix. You can act rather than react. You can achieve order and success—but only if you let go of the old management model and the common sense it seems to represent.

In her insightful book *Leadership and the New Science,* Margaret Wheatley observes, "In many systems, scientists now understand that order and complexity and shape are created not by complex controls, but by the presence of a few guiding formulae or principles." A growing number of leaders are coming to the same conclusion. Their guiding principles are the basics of business excellence.

➤ Lead by Serving

To excel, organizations must be flatter, faster, and more flexible, with high-quality processes, products, and services. That can happen only with fewer layers of management and with employees who are completely engaged in improving quality, reducing cycle times, and meeting customer requirements. And that cannot happen when you lead by command.

Servant leadership is not the best term I've seen, since few leaders possess the humility to see themselves as servants, but it accurately captures an effective new uncommon sense approach to leadership. As we'll discuss in Chapter 2, leaders are finding it increasingly difficult to develop a high-performance organization using command-and-control techniques. The best among them are redefining their roles to help them achieve their goals. The new definition includes teaching, coaching, supporting, listening, designing—and serving.

➤ Focus through Shared Vision

If you cannot move an organization toward its goals by command, how do you do it? The world-class companies featured in this book do it through a shared vision. A shared vision has three qualities that make it an ideal focal point for an organization: (1) It reflects a sense of the organization that the people in the organization support; (2) it states what the organization is working toward, giving its members a guide by which they can validate their decisions and actions; and (3) it focuses all decisions and actions in one direction, producing a collective strength of purpose that makes it possible for an organization to be flat, fast, flexible, and focused.

Chapter 3 looks at how to create and communicate a shared vision. It presents the shared visions of many of the organizations featured in this book. It also introduces the use of strategic thinking as a means of exploring who you are as an organization and who you want to be ten years from now.

➤ Engage Employees

Engaging employees is about respect, trust, and responsibility. In organizations where employees are guided by a shared vision, people are engaged in interpreting that vision when they complete a task, make a decision, or initiate an improvement. They are high-performance employees, self-motivated, self-directed, responsible, productive, and satisfied—all of which influence customer satisfaction and business results.

In Chapter 4 we'll look at the changes in attitude necessary to engage employees. We will also discuss *how* to engage them: individually and through teams, by aligning compensation and rewards, and by recognizing their achievements.

➤ Know Your Customers

This is the one basic of business excellence where uncommon sense is desperately needed. Almost without exception, people believe they know what their customers require. They hear customers complain. They design products and services they expect will respond to customer requirements. Marketing and sales departments have daily contact with customers. How could they not know their customers?

An organization exists to serve customers. To do that effectively, it must know exactly what its customers require, and it cannot know that intuitively or by assumption. It can know only by asking customers often and in different ways, by verifying requirements at every opportunity, and by seeking requirements that the customer has difficulty articulating. In Chapter 5 we will look at ways to identify customer requirements, opportunities to provide value, methods of bringing the voice of the customer inside the organization, and the benefits of measuring and improving customer satisfaction.

➤ Organize to Optimize

Flat, fast, and flexible suggest the need for new thinking about organizational design. For most of this century organizations organized as hierarchies without much thought. Hierarchies are well suited to serve managers, leaders, and owners, but they are not designed to serve customers. And unless an organization commits to serving customers first, it will endanger its source of revenues and dim its prospects for long-term success.

Chapter 6 strips the hierarchical design of its allure, then digs into some of the alternatives that successful organizations are using.

➤ Think Process

The functional nature of hierarchies opposes process thinking, yet processes are how work gets done. As a result, one function handles one step in a process, then throws the job over the wall to another function, which does its thing, then over the wall again and again until the process is complete. Such functional thinking helps managers control what their people are doing, often at the expense of speed and quality.

Process thinking is different. It supports many of the basics of business excellence. It engages employees who work the process in improving it. It focuses on the customers of the process. It makes flatter organizational designs possible. It demands management by fact. Chapter 7 shows how you can identify your organization's core processes, then provides guidelines for improving or reengineering them.

➤ Manage by Fact

Most people think they're already doing this. Most people are wrong. Managing by fact means identifying exactly what your customers require. It means creating a system of measures that best represent the factors that lead to improving performance. It means collecting and graphing the data at every reasonable opportunity. It means analyzing the data to manage processes, improve quality and speed, reduce costs, make decisions, and align all activities with the organization's goals.

In Chapter 8, we'll look at what managing by fact really means.

➤ Align through Planning

If your organization is like most, you're already familiar with budget planning. That's not what we're talking about. Strategic planning is a means of translating a shared vision into measurable objectives for the organization, work units, and individuals. It involves key employees, customers, and suppliers in a process that considers a broad range of issues—customer, supplier, competitive, organizational, financial, technological, etc. The strategies and plans that come out of this process are translated into key business drivers, requirements, and measures that are used to align the efforts of everyone in the organization.

Chapter 9 describes how successful companies turn their vision into reality through strategic planning.

■ HOW MASTERING THE BASICS BOOSTS PROFITS

Now before you start thinking, "Oh, those basics sound nice, but we're a bottom-line kind of organization," consider this: If you bought the stock of publicly traded companies on the day they won the Baldrige Award, your money would be reaping the rewards of these fundamentally sound businesses.

To quantify the financial performance of Baldrige Award winners, the National Institute of Standards and Technology (NIST) "invested" a hypothetical sum of money in the Standard & Poor's 500 and in each of the publicly traded companies (five whole companies and nine parent companies of subsidiaries) that have won the Baldrige Award since 1988. The investment was tracked from the first business day in April of the year the winners received their awards or the date they began publicly trading. As of February 1996, the fourteen organizations soundly outperformed the S&P 500 by greater than four to one, achieving a 248.7 percent return on investment compared to 58.5 percent for the S&P 500.

The "pure plays"—the five whole company winners—performed even better: 279.8 percent to 55.7 percent.

NIST also performed a similar investment study for the forty-one publicly traded applicants that have received Baldrige site visits. The group outperformed the S&P 500 by greater than two to one.

Such stellar performance can be attributed to mastering the basics of business excellence. None of these organizations is perfect. They all make mistakes. What separates them from the rest of the S&P 500 is their ability to anticipate, recognize, and learn from their mistakes at all levels of the organization: individual, work unit, division, and company. They excel because they are driven to improve and compelled to learn.

■ TWO REQUIREMENTS FOR MASTERING THE BASICS

Excellent organizations display a passion for learning. Many acquired this passion over time. In the course of mastering the basics, the people in these organizations had to accept that they didn't have all the answers. They had to ask for help. They had to appear—to customers, competitors, and coworkers—ignorant. In return, however, they got to enjoy the freedom of pursuing knowledge without the burden of always being right. They had permission to be curious. They were rewarded for learning.

Peter Senge, a leading proponent of systems thinking and author of *The Fifth Discipline*, has written that the outstanding leaders he has worked with "instill confidence in those around them that, together, 'we can learn whatever we need to learn in order to achieve the results we truly desire' " (Senge 1990). Whether you lead a company, division, department, or work unit, you can be such a leader. But you must be open to learning.

Senge's statement suggests two requirements for achieving success: Leaders must learn how to participate in a shared journey, and everyone in the organization must be able and willing to learn.

■ LEARNING TO LEAD

Organizations operate on assumptions. People assume they know what their customers require. They assume they know how well they are performing. They assume that if they correct enough problems, the number will eventually diminish. And they assume that their leaders have all the answers.

Seldom are any of these assumptions based on facts. You cannot know what customers require unless you ask them, in myriad ways, repeatedly, all the while comparing what you learn and running it past the customers to verify its accuracy. You cannot know how well you are performing unless you are tracking trendable, actionable measures of quality and timeliness. You cannot eliminate problems without systematically improving the processes that produce them. And no leader has all the answers.

We grow up believing that people in authority have the answers. We expect our leaders to know what to do, what to say, what to decide in every situation. Followers expect it. Leaders accept it. No one wins.

While followers grumble about leadership's need to make every decision, they conveniently ignore the benefit of not having to make decisions: They don't have to be responsible. They don't have to wrestle with complex issues. They don't have to weigh advantages and disadvantages of different positions. They don't have to take the time to learn.

While leaders strain under the burden of having to be omniscient, they conveniently ignore the benefit of getting to make decisions: They don't have to share their power and authority. They don't have to expose their needs, weaknesses, and fears to anyone. They don't have to explain what they want, build consensus, or encourage participation. They don't have to change how they lead.

As a result, everyone loses, because while the hidden benefits may seem appealing, the visible damage is not. Organizations that believe only leaders are qualified to make decisions construct layers of decision makers. The hierarchy restricts speed and flexibility, stifles innovation and creativity, breeds fear and mistrust, and discourages involvement. That's a heavy price to pay for getting to be right all the time.

The alternative is learning to lead an open, changing, horizontal, learning organization. Such an organization demands a new set of characteristics of its leaders. Like leaders in any situation, they must be self-confident, knowledgeable, honest, and determined. Unlike traditional command-and-control leaders, they must also learn and practice new characteristics including:

➤ *Curiosity:* The leader who must know everything cannot afford to ask questions because it would look as if he or she didn't know everything. In contrast, the leaders of fast, flexible organizations exhibit a constant curiosity about how their organization and others work. They participate in industry associations and conferences. They scan business books and magazines for new ideas. They ask their peers in other organizations about leadership and management. They ask their coworkers how they do their jobs and what prevents them from doing their best. They question. They wonder. They open themselves to new ideas, new thinking, and new approaches.

➤ *Willingness to change:* The leader who must know everything cannot afford to change because it would look like he or she may have been doing something wrong all along. In contrast, the new leaders embrace change as the natural course for them as individuals and for their organizations. They not only invite new ideas, thinking, and approaches, the leaders use them to facilitate positive change. They distrust the status quo. They never coast.

➤ *Sincere trust and belief in people:* The leader who must know everything cannot afford to trust people because he or she knows that no one else is as vested in the organization's success. In contrast, the new leaders recognize that every person in the organization can, given the responsibility, training, and tools, find ways to make the organization better every day. In Chapter 5, we'll look at how one company built its transformation on the idea of a sincere trust and belief in people.

➤ *Ability to listen and communicate:* Leaders who must know everything cannot afford to listen because they're too busy telling everyone what they know. In contrast, the new leaders see listening as an opportunity to learn and communicating as an opportunity to spread learning. Robert Galvin, retired chairman of Motorola, once said, "My job is to listen to what the organization is trying to say, and then make sure that it gets forcefully articulated" (Spears 1995).

➤ *Constancy of purpose:*   Leaders who must know everything cannot provide constancy of purpose because they will, at some point, be forced to admit they do not know everything, then accept a new course of action they hope will get the organization back on track. In contrast, the new leader finds the organization's purpose in the will of its people, creates a shared vision that captures that will, then holds the organization to it through times of prosperity and adversity. Constancy of purpose requires patience, commitment, and tenacity. It builds integrity. It provides security.

These characteristics are not about style. They are not about leaders having to be handsome, witty, charismatic, or dynamic. The most effective leaders in today's most successful organizations are those who see themselves as key players in a larger system, uniquely positioned to focus that system on satisfying its owners and customers.

To accomplish these goals, an effective leader must learn to lead in a variety of challenging roles:

1. *The leader must help create and communicate a shared vision.* Don Wainwright, chairman and CEO of Wainwright Industries, showed up at an offsite vision meeting of fifty managers with a five-page vision for his company. The managers promptly told him his vision wasn't what they thought the company was about. They threw it out. Two months later, they had created a shared vision that Don now proudly communicates to customers, suppliers, employees, and those curious about his Baldrige Award–winning company.

2. *The leader must facilitate empowerment.*   When Jeff Pope and Judy Corson formed Custom Research Inc., they had two choices: "You either do it yourself and everyone is helping you," Jeff says, "or you give everybody a way to fulfill themselves and you will be successful that way." CRI has used the latter approach to make it one of the most profitable marketing research companies in the country.

3. *The leader must focus the organization on its customers.*   For Ray Marlow and Chris Witzke, leading with a customer focus is a matter of preaching Marlow Industries' corporate mission, which is to make its customers successful. They believe the company will be successful as a result, a belief

rooted in performance. Since 1991, every key measure the company uses has improved: customer satisfaction and retention, on-time delivery, productivity, profitability. And it wasn't that bad in 1991, the year Marlow Industries won the Baldrige Award.

4. *The leader must produce results.*   When Bob Gower stepped in to lead Lyondell Petrochemical, it had lost $200 million a year for three straight years. Four years later, it ranked first in sales per employee among all industrial companies in the United States. Bob achieved the turnaround by employee involvement, and he achieved employee involvement by training managers and supervisors in ten key management behaviors that Lyondell values, including quality, responsibility, teamwork, and communication (George and Weimerskirch 1994).

5. *The leader must provide a systems perspective.*   When Bruce Woolpert decided Granite Rock Company should apply for the Baldrige Award, he wasn't sure how the company's approaches would hold up under the scrutiny of the evaluation process. It held up: Granite Rock won the award. Recognizing the value of the process and the systems perspective inherent in the Baldrige criteria, Bruce became an active participant in the award process, serving first as a Baldrige examiner, then as a judge.

6. *The leader must share information.*   Larry Welliver was put in charge of Honeywell Solid State Electronics Center's total quality management program in 1986. Two years later, he was put in charge of the entire organization. Larry spearheaded the development of SSEC's Quality Star, which identifies the five stakeholders for which SSEC creates value, and of the training program that shares information about the key requirements of these stakeholders with all employees.

7. *The leader must lead and institutionalize change.*   You institutionalize change by institutionalizing learning. "In a learning organization," Senge writes, "leaders are designers, stewards, and teachers. They are responsible for building organizations where people continually expand their capabilities to understand complexity, clarify vision, and improve shared mental models—that is, they are responsible for learning" (Senge 1990).

■ SIX FEATURED ORGANIZATIONS

The leaders of the six organizations featured in this book are designers, stewards, and teachers. All excel at far more than the single role for each mentioned above. I chose these leaders and their organizations because they exemplify the basics of business excellence outlined in this book. You will read more about each of them in the chapters that follow. This is what they do:

Wainwright Industries manufactures stamped and machined parts at its headquarters in St. Peters, Missouri. The privately held company, which was founded in 1947, has 275 associates. It won the Baldrige Award in 1994.

Custom Research Inc. (CRI) conducts marketing research for Fortune 100 industrial, consumer, medical, and service companies. Also privately held, CRI has 100 full-time employees at five locations, including its headquarters in Minneapolis, Minnesota, and 125 part-time employees. A finalist for the Baldrige Award, CRI won the Minnesota Quality Award in 1995.

Marlow Industries is the worldwide manufacturing leader of thermoelectric coolers. The privately held company, based in Dallas, Texas, employs 225 people. Marlow won the Baldrige Award in 1991.

Lyondell Petrochemical produces a wide variety of petrochemicals at four sites in the Houston, Texas, area. It has approximately 2,300 employees. Lyondell has consistently ranked among the leaders in sales per employee in the United States, has been identified as one of the 100 best companies to work for, and has been a Baldrige Award finalist.

Granite Rock Company manufactures high-quality construction building materials for road and highway construction and maintenance, and for residential and commercial building construction. The company, based in Watsonville, California, employs 400 people. Granite Rock won the Baldrige Award in 1992.

Honeywell Solid State Electronics Center (SSEC) develops and produces integrated circuits and solid state sensors to improve the performance and cost effectiveness of control products. It is a leading supplier of integrated circuits for external aerospace and military markets as well as internal Honeywell divisions. The division, which is located in Plymouth, Minnesota, has approximately 470 employees. It has been a finalist for the Baldrige Award.

You'll notice the size of the organizations. I intentionally focused on smaller companies and divisions because their experiences are relevant for the broadest audience of leaders and managers. I realize that none of the six may be directly relevant to your organization's situation, but I also know that you can learn from them. Every organization is unique, yet every organization shares key characteristics that allow the transfer of knowledge to occur, such as understanding customer requirements, designing products and services, collecting and analyzing information, managing processes, and leading and managing.

■ A SYSTEMS PERSPECTIVE

Learning to lead in times of rapid change requires knowledge of these shared characteristics, the elements of an organizational system. W. Edwards Deming defines a system as "a series of functions or activities . . . within an organization that work together for the aim of the organization." He emphasizes that "management of a system . . . requires knowledge of the interrelationship between all the subprocesses within the system and of everybody that works in it. Management's job is to optimize the entire system" (Latzko and Saunders 1995).

Understanding interrelationships and optimizing the system require a systems perspective, something for which few leaders and managers are trained. One goal of this book is to show how the basics of business excellence work together to optimize the system. If you want proof of the need for a systems perspective, just look at all of the failed change initiatives over the last decade, whether those initiatives involved reengineering, TQM, restructuring, downsizing, teams, mergers, or any other attempt at improving a part of the system without understanding how the entire system operates. "Because we see the world in simple, obvious terms, we come to believe in simple, obvious solutions. This leads to the frenzied search for simple 'fixes' " (Senge 1990).

You won't find any simple fixes in this book. No short-term salvation. Mastering the basics of business excellence requires leaders who are willing to wrestle with complexity, who are wary of get-rich-quick promises, and who welcome the responsibility of managing the system. These astute leaders understand that most problems in an organization can be traced to problems in the system, not to problems with people. They believe Dr. J. M. Juran when he says that at least 85 percent of problems in a system can be corrected only by changing the system, and that less than 15 percent of the problems are under a worker's control. The leaders control the system. Therefore, at least 85 percent of the problems in an organization are leadership's responsibility.

At issue is the way your organization functions, the management system in place to translate customer requirements into products and services that meet those requirements. Learning to lead means acquiring this systems perspective. It means doing double duty for a while, reacting to today's pressing problems at the same time you're attending to systemic issues in the belief that systematic, continuous improvement will lift the organization out of firefighting mode and will serve the organization best in the long run. As the authors of *Product Juggernauts* write, "In seeking continuous improvement rather than a knockout, an organization can achieve two overriding objectives for the future. The first is to replace conflict with balance and harmony among the three important stakeholders of a company: customers, employees, and owners. The second is to create the self-improving organization, in which recognition of the need for change and improvement, the desire for it, and the effort to create it permeate the organization" (Deschamps and Nayak 1995).

To produce continuous improvement and change, an organization must learn to learn.

■ LEARNING TO LEARN

Learning is one of the words that races from our eyes to that file cabinet in our brains filled with childhood memories, messages, and impressions. We see the word and think memorization, drills, tests, and grades. Learning feels formal, structured, boring. Put a bunch of workers in a conference room instead of a classroom and teach them what you think they need to know. That's the first perception of a learning organization, a perception that keeps us from recognizing its benefits.

Learning is not about acquiring information as much as it's about asking questions. It's not about learning one piece of information before moving to the next as much as it's about learning the tools and skills needed to improve, then applying that knowledge daily.

Charles Handy describes the learning process as a wheel of learning that begins with questions. The questions prompt a search for possible answers or ideas, which must then pass rigorous tests to see if they work. People reflect on the test results to determine if they have identified the best solutions. If so, the solutions are implemented—then questioned, moving the wheel of learning another turn. According to Handy, "Organizations that have acquired the learning habit are endlessly questioning the status quo, are forever seeking new methods or new products, forever testing and then reflecting, consciously or unconsciously pushing round that wheel" (Chawla and Renesch 1995).

Quality professionals will recognize the wheel of learning as Deming's Plan-Do-Check-Act (PDCA) cycle. Plan what you're going to do and how you'll know if it works. Carry out the plan. Evaluate the results and learn from them. Take action.

The PDCA cycle is a systematic approach to continuous learning. As Brian Joiner writes, it is "the essence of managerial work: making sure the job gets done today *and* developing better ways to do it tomorrow." The degree to which the PDCA cycle is effective depends on the degree to which it is understood and applied. "To be effective, the entire PDCA cycle must become the basic mindset of every employee, every department, every function" (Joiner 1994).

Turning the learning wheel makes it possible for organizations to get everyone thinking about how to improve. Rather than relying on a few leaders and managers to initiate change, the learning organization taps into its intellectual capital, its capacity to generate knowledge. A force of few becomes a force of many. Employees who serve customers learn how to serve them better. Employees who design and produce products or services learn how to design and produce them better. Employees who support these core processes learn how to support them better. The organization's intellectual capital grows. Communication increases. The organization becomes faster and more flexible. Results improve. Learning accelerates. And the organization makes systematic, productive, profitable change a characteristic of its culture.

■ CREATING A LEARNING ORGANIZATION

Creating a learning organization means creating a climate in which learning is encouraged, assisted, applauded, and rewarded. For most leaders, it requires a dramatic change in thinking, from viewing employees as commodities to be managed to seeing them as resources to be leveraged. "The essence of such leverage," according to C. K. Prahalad, "is learning, sharing knowledge, redeploying knowledge, and bundling physical and intellectual assets in new and creative ways" (Ashkenas, Ulrich, Jick, and Kerr 1995).

The *first step* in creating a climate for learning is a commitment by leadership. The commitment must be more than words, however. Leaders must make it part of their jobs to turn the learning wheel for their areas of responsibility. They, too, must learn. They must measure, benchmark, and track learning. They must invest in learning. They must communicate the importance of learning, sharing stories and successes with employees at every opportunity. And they must persist in their commitment, knowing that changing a culture takes time.

The *second step* is to create a shared vision the organization can use to guide the change. "Without a pull toward some goal which people truly want to achieve, the forces in support of the status quo can be overwhelming" (Senge 1990). The status quo does not promote learning. To break its bonds, an organization needs a vision everyone can embrace, a vision that demands learning if it is to be achieved. We will discuss how to create a shared vision in Chapter 3. From the vision comes a blueprint for change that includes strategies, goals, and action plans.

The *third step* in creating a learning climate is to engage employees in the learning process. As Senge says, "People learn most rapidly when they have a genuine sense of responsibility for their actions. Helplessness, the belief that we cannot influence the circumstances under which we live, undermines the incentive to learn, as does the belief that someone somewhere else dictates our actions" (Senge 1990). Charles Handy describes this as an assumption of competence, meaning the expectation that people will perform to the limit of their competence with minimum supervision. An assumption of competence "is supported by four other qualities or characteristics: curiosity, forgiveness, trust, and togetherness" (Chawla and Renesch 1995). We will explore the assumption of competence and the delegation of responsibility in Chapter 4.

Engaging employees is very hard for hierarchical, command-and-control organizations. But it must be done. You cannot create a learning organization if people don't want to learn, and they won't want to learn if they are feeling helpless, untrusted, and afraid. It is the leaders' responsibility to create a climate where competence is assumed, where people feel responsible for their actions, where everyone is encouraged to experiment and innovate, to test and fail.

Fortunately, leaders have a bag full of tools and methods for creating a learning organization, including

➤ *Cross-functional teams or task forces,* which help people see broader processes and issues and how others within the organization work

➤ *Job rotation*—what Handy calls "horizontal fast-tracks"—rotating the best people through a variety of jobs in various parts of the organization

➤ *Work-outs,* a GE term for bringing groups together for an intensive problem-solving experience that lasts roughly three days

➤ *Mentoring programs,* through which leaders and others take responsibility for helping novices learn and grow

➤ *Training,* by which an organization can provide people with the approaches and skills they need to learn most effectively

➤ *Town meetings and other communication vehicles* that help employees understand how their work relates to the bigger picture

➤ *Subsidiarity,* another Handy term, which means giving power to those who are closest to the action

➤ *Self-enlightenment,* by which employees who are given the power are motivated to turn the learning wheel

➤ *Incidental learning,* in which employees look at every incident as an opportunity to learn

➤ *Managerial practice fields,* similar to the practice afforded athletes and performing artists, by which operational managers learn through interactions in a transitional medium. Fred Kofman and Peter Senge describe the concept in *Learning Organizations* (Chawla and Renesch 1995).

You will need all these tools and methods plus large doses of commitment and perseverance to overcome the obstacles to creating a learning organization. Perhaps the greatest obstacle is an ingrained belief that we already know what we need to know. Chris Argris calls this skilled incompetence, meaning people are skilled at protecting themselves from the threat and pain that come with learning, so they remain incompetent and blinded to their incompetence. To create a learning organization, leaders must acknowledge their own skilled incompetence and expose it in others. The malady is especially pernicious in organizations that have been doing things the same way for years, preventing people from distinguishing between assumptions and facts.

Another obstacle is a misunderstanding of what learning means, the tendency to relegate it to certain groups of employees or a few formal training programs. As I noted at the beginning of this section, learning is an attitude, not a task. Being curious, asking questions, planning, measuring, comparing, testing, improving—these are all part of the learning process. Their repetition turns the learning wheel.

The work environment can also inhibit learning. Hierarchical, command-and-control structures block communication, breed fear and helplessness, and discourage learning. So does not listening. I've worked with companies where listening is a forgotten skill, and it's like watching a United Nations conference with no translators: Everybody is attentive, but nobody could tell you what anyone else said. Just as listening is a valuable skill for leaders, it is an essential requirement for a learning organization.

The obstacles to creating a learning organization are also obstacles to achieving business excellence. Those organizations that master the basics of business excellence have used these basics to effectively eliminate the obstacles. They have learned in order to change, changed in order to improve, and improved in order to succeed. In the process, the people in these organizations have rediscovered what it means to be curious, to wonder, to learn.

In contrast, Fred Kofman and Peter Senge describe what we give up when the joy of learning is absent:

> *Building learning organizations is not an individual task. It demands a shift that goes all the way to the core of our culture. We have drifted into a culture that fragments our thoughts, that detaches the world from the self and the self from its community. We have gained control of our environment but have*

lost our artistic edge. We are so focused on our security that we don't see the price we pay: living in bureaucratic organizations where the wonder and joy of learning have no place. Thus, we are losing the spaces to dance with the ever-changing patterns of life. We are losing ourselves as fields of dreams (Chawla and Renesch 1995).

■ STRATEGIES FOR IMPROVEMENT

One of the problems people face when they read books about management issues is how to translate the ideas into action. To address that problem, I decided to summarize some of the strategies available to help you master the basics of business excellence.

I've divided the strategies into three categories: *Jump Start*, for those organizations that are just beginning to look at a systematic approach to management or that need a boost to the next level of performance; *Tune Up*, for those organizations that have embraced the concepts but are having trouble getting things to run smoothly; and *Pull Away*, for those organizations that have a sound system in place and are poised to excel.

The danger in offering strategies is the same danger that exists with any new initiative: applying one strategy without thinking about its effects on the rest of the management system or the effect of the system on the strategy. The best way to minimize the danger is to develop a systematic approach to improvement and change, then to choose strategies that serve your plan. To accomplish this, you will need to develop a systems perspective and to understand all of the basics of business excellence.

➤ Jump Start

➤ Learn about the basics of business excellence. Read books (including those listed in this book's bibliography) that provide a systems perspective of management. Talk to leaders and managers in organizations that excel at the basics, most notably Baldrige Award winners, and site visit companies. Get a copy of the criteria for the Baldrige Award, read it, and consider how your organization would respond. (You can obtain a free copy from MBNQA–NIST, Route 270 & Quince Orchard Rd.,

Administration Building, Room A537, Gaithersburg, MD 20899-0001, or on the Web at http://www.nist.gov.)

➤ Identify the characteristics of effective leaders that your organization will need to succeed. For example, Corning's Chairman Jamie Houghton has identified five key leadership traits: honesty, vision, caring, strength, and willingness to change; ten key traits a person must have to be a leader at Corning (including strategic thinking, risk taking, being a catalyst for change, and listening); and ten personal traits he or she should have, including different work experiences, financial proficiency, and being a contributor to the local community (George and Weimerskirch 1994).

➤ Assess your organization's learning climate: how well it encourages and promotes learning; how well the organizational structure and communication processes facilitate learning; to what extent leaders demonstrate a commitment to learning.

➤ Tune Up

➤ Develop an organizational philosophy of management. Include leaders from all levels of the organization in the discussion. The philosophy may be reflected in a vision, mission, purpose, goals, and objectives. It may be captured in a strategic plan. Or it may be stated as a philosophy of management. Articulating the philosophy will give leaders and managers valuable guidance in their day-to-day activities.

➤ Institutionalize a systems perspective by adopting the Baldrige criteria as your management model. Assess your organization using the criteria. Explore state-sponsored award and quality programs based on the Baldrige criteria (more than 80 percent of states now have such a program).

➤ Commit to becoming a learning organization. Identify what that will mean for your organization. Develop measures of progress toward the goal. Engage employees in the learning process by assuming their competence, making each responsible for changing and improving, providing the necessary training, and recognizing and rewarding learning. Communicate successes at every opportunity.

➤ Pull Away

➤ Identify obstacles to learning and develop strategies to break them down. Look carefully at communication and behavioral issues that can inhibit learning. To compare what you are doing with the efforts of other leading companies, identify and benchmark organizations that exemplify a learning culture.

Chapter 2

Lead by Serving

I see our institutions changing, from hierarchical chain of command groups with rigid rules led by superior, elitist bosses who direct the activities of subordinates seen as inferior to a whole new approach. I see an open, participative, entrepreneurial environment with loose, flexible teams. I see a core set of values being well understood by everyone. I see a common venture with clear linkages to a shared vision, where value is created for people, where they can grow and realize more of their innate potential. I see organizations with trust and caring, where work is a meaningful part of your life experience. And, most of all, I see servant-leaders guiding these institutions, servant-leaders at all levels throughout them.

ROBERT VANOUREK, President and CEO
Recognition (Spears 1995)

I could work for Mr. Vanourek. I share his vision, the sacred view of people and the work we do, the basic needs common to us all: for trust and caring, to grow and serve. I, too, see our institutions changing. Not all. Not even a majority. But enough to show us a better way.

Several years ago, during one of those phases when I felt compelled to reexamine my purpose in life, I enrolled in an *est*-like workshop. I joined a diverse group of thirty men and women in a three-day assault on the walls that keep us from knowing more about who we are. During one session, each of us sat knee-to-knee with another member of the group. One person asked, "What do you want?" and the other answered with the first thing that came to mind: "A million dollars." "A new car." "Chocolate." As soon as one answer was out, the same question was asked again, and again, until a minute had passed. Then we switched roles. After both people had asked and answered, we changed partners and repeated the exercise.

It was the minute that did it. The first answers tended to be thoughtful or funny or convoluted. But the question nagged at you and you had no time to think and inevitably you got at a deeper truth. "I want to be happy." "I want to be loved." "I want to be healthy." "I want meaning in my life." I gave those answers. You would give those answers. But what struck me was that everyone I faced in that session gave those answers. Young and old. Rich and poor. Black and white and brown. Leaders and followers. Well-educated and barely 'educated. Everyone.

I know that probably shouldn't have surprised me, but I don't think I had ever really understood what connects us as human beings. Our needs are the same. We may prioritize them differently. We may add a few. But at a very basic level, we have the same needs. And the same fears. And our common needs and fears unite us in ways far stronger than our economic, social, religious, political, cultural, ethnic, and racial differences divide us.

That's why Vanourek's vision rings true for me. It speaks to unity, not division. It respects the needs of all employees, leaders and followers alike. It sees work not as putting in time to get a paycheck but as "a meaningful part of your life experience." And it advocates servant-leadership.

I realize that the servant-leader part may be disturbing, and with good reason. We've grown up in a command-and-control world. Our parents commanded us to act according to their rules and controlled our behavior (or at least tried to). Teachers used command-and-control tactics to enforce discipline and guide learning. And remember the first "real" job you had? The one where you were told exactly what to do and when to do it, to follow the rules or suffer the consequences?

It's no wonder command-and-control is the leadership model of choice. It's what we know. We know it so well it's hard to imagine any other form of leadership taking its place. Especially not a leadership model based on service. Yet that is exactly what many of today's experts on leadership—including some of our most effective leaders—are advocating.

The idea of servant-leadership is not new. Around 600 B.C., Chinese philosopher Lao-tzu wrote, "A leader is best when people barely know he exists, not so good when people obey and acclaim him." His ideal conflicts with the American image of business leaders as heroes, even if our heroes turn out to be, in Vanourek's words, "superior, elitist bosses who direct the activities of subordinates seen as inferior." That attitude is a legacy of command-and-control leadership, an attitude that some of us are better than most of us because of titles, knowledge, skills, or hard work.

If you believe you are somehow superior to those around you (even if you wouldn't admit it to anyone), you may want to skip ahead to the next chapter. You can still discover the basics of excellence in managing, improving processes, planning, and other elements of your company in this book. You must accept that they will be more difficult to implement in a command-and-control culture because these basics of excellence rely on cooperation, a shared vision, widespread involvement, trust, respect, and mutual support—all of which grow better in the fertile fields of servant-leadership.

The modern "father" of servant-leadership is Robert Greenleaf, whose 1970 essay on the topic stated, "The business exists to provide meaningful work for the person as it exists to provide a product or service to the customer." Such sentiment contradicts the popular belief that a business exists to make money for its owners. I think a business exists to serve *all* who can benefit from it—customers, employees, and owners alike—but the needs of the owners currently obscure those of other stakeholders. The imbalance threatens the long-term survival of a company and the short-term health of its employees, as we'll discuss in a moment.

To counter this imbalance, we need to return to the basics of leadership by examining our beliefs, biases, and dreams for our companies. One of the best ways to do that is to answer a few basic questions:

➤ What is the purpose of my company?
➤ What kind of company would I like to create?
➤ What would be the benefits of creating this new company?
➤ What roles would leaders in the new company take?

➤ What roles would nonleaders take?

➤ How are these roles different from current roles?

➤ How do I feel about changing those roles?

➤ What would need to happen to transform my organization?

At some point, all thinking about leadership, management, and business success returns to these questions. An organization, like a person, must wrestle with the fundamental issues of "Who am I?" and "Why am I here?" and "What do I want?" The answers shape the culture of the organization. Of course, you can always choose not to think about these things, but a business unexamined, like a life unexamined, tends to suffer from its unconscious decisions.

Robert Vanourek has asked and answered these questions. Jack Stack, CEO of Springfield Remanufacturing Corporation (SRC) and author of *The Great Game of Business,* has answered these questions, citing four reasons his company plays the game:

1. We want to live up to our end of the employment bargain.
2. We want to do away with jobs, to give people a chance to create something.
3. We want to get rid of the employee mentality.
4. We want to create and distribute wealth.

I could work for Mr. Stack, too. SRC's reasons align with my vision of an ideal company where each employee is valued, challenged, respected, and rewarded. No jobs. No leaders and subordinates. No profits to shareholders while employees get stiffed. I like that.

The reason leaders need to ponder these issues is that leaders build organizations. Peter Senge wrote, "It is not possible to talk of a new type of institution without talking about a new type of leadership. Above all else, leaders build organizations. So, any shift in the predominant character of institutions like business will be inseparable from a shift in the predominant theory and practice of leadership."

Before we can let go of command-and-control leadership, we need to be clear about what we are leaving behind. The model permeates our society, businesses, governments, schools, and homes.

We're like Linus with his favorite blanket: We're not about to relax our grip long enough to have it pried from our fingers until we believe there's something better to hold on to.

■ AN OUTDATED LEADERSHIP MODEL

We'll start by looking at how this particular security blanket got into our hands in the first place. The command-and-control leadership model has been popular for nearly a century. It exists because of several developments, including:

1. *The growth of companies from small, local, informal, and flexible groups into regional, national, and global conglomerates.* As they grew, leaders implemented controls to standardize behaviors and outcomes.

2. *The professionalism of management.* Growth spawned a separate managerial class formed to carry out the leaders' wishes.

3. *The institution of scientific management.* In the early 1900s, an engineer named Frederick Taylor proposed breaking a person's work into categories, developing experts in those categories, then having the experts focus only on those categories. His proposition helped create the assembly line worker. It also established organizations as machines and the people in them as machine parts.

4. *The need for interchangeable employees.* Employees became interchangeable parts of a larger machine organized to make large quantities of the same product.

5. *The rise of the adversarial union.* Workers responded to the rigid controls of their leaders by banding together. Controls became institutionalized through union-management agreements.

6. *The assumption that capital was a company's most critical resource.* Leaders focused on building capital to the detriment of all other issues, including customer and employee satisfaction, environmental concerns, and quality.

7. *Organizational inertia.* "When left to run a natural course," writes James O'Toole, "all organizations become more impor-

tant than the individuals in them. They become hierarchical, bureaucratic, rule-dominated, and change-resistant. That is the course of inertia. And the individuals who lead organizations become uncaring, cautious, overly conservative, and obsessed with retaining their own power" (O'Toole 1995).

These developments produced a patriarchal contract that dominates the corporate landscape. The contract is based on several assumptions that have evolved during a hundred years of command-and-control leadership (Figure 2-1). *The assumptions are wrong.* Acting on them harms companies, leaders, managers, other employees, customers, suppliers, and shareholders by

➤ Putting money first

➤ Establishing an adversarial class system

➤ Treating employees as commodities

➤ Promoting change through crises.

➤ People care only about their own interests and must therefore be controlled.

➤ People cannot and will not act responsibly.

➤ Leaders are superior to followers and are the dominant members of the group.

➤ Leadership is the exercise of power.

➤ Managers make decisions and produce results; workers are paid to do their jobs, not think.

➤ Leaders and managers get results through manipulation, coercion, and fear; it's "us" vs. "them."

➤ The military model of line authority is the best way to ensure that everyone in the company follows the leader's direction.

➤ The company's primary and overriding purpose is to make money.

Figure 2-1. The Assumptions of Command-and-Control Leadership

➤ Putting Money First

It's hard to escape the notion that a business exists to make money. *Fortune* has stated that the most basic measure of business success is "how much you increase the value of the capital you use" (Paré 1995). Thumbs up if the financial indicators are rising (and at the rate experts think they should rise); thumbs down if they're lagging or fail to meet expectations.

Such a myopic, Scroogish definition of success reduces our best efforts to tallies on a balance sheet. Who wants to do their best when the measure of their work is how well they increase profits, and when they do not benefit from the increase? Who can feel fulfilled in their work when everything is reduced to dollars and cents? As Tom Chappell, CEO of Tom's of Maine, said, "In my darkest days, I was working for aims that were too narrow for me. I was working for market share, sales growth, and profits. It was a sense of emptiness" (Dumaine 1994).

No self-help guru worth his own consulting business would ever counsel that putting money first was the path to a happy and meaningful life. Yet somehow, when we group people together into a company, we expect them to deny what is personal and sacred to them.

Peter Senge describes how pollster Daniel Yankelovich identified "a basic shift in attitude in the workplace from an 'instrumental' to a 'sacred' view of work. The instrumental view implies that we work in order to earn the income to do what we really want when we are not working." According to Yankelovich, "People or objects are sacred in the sociological sense when, apart from what instrumental use they serve, they are valued for themselves" (Senge 1990).

Command-and-control leadership takes an instrumental view of work. The business exists to make money. People work to make money. Leaders evaluate options and make decisions based on money, a simple measurement that takes the human factor out of the equation. Downsizing would neither be popular nor prevalent without this money-first mentality.

Leaders who put money first severely limit the potential of their organizations. First, they see work as instrumental while many of those doing the work see it as sacred. More and more people want and expect to be valued for themselves, not for the contributions they make to the bottom line. Leaders who ignore the sacred view of work alienate workers, damage morale, and sow mistrust and disloyalty.

Second, putting money first means that meeting budgets and other financial goals is more important than serving customers. As Jack Welch, CEO of General Electric, said, "Making a budget is an exercise in minimization. You're always trying to get the lowest out of people, because everyone is negotiating to get a lower number" (Loeb 1995). Getting the lowest out of people is a recipe for unhappy customers.

Third, leaders who put money first often end up with worse financial results than companies focused on serving their customers. According to a study conducted by William Copulsky of Baruch College, "most companies that place shareholder value first usually do not do as well for their shareholders as those companies that dedicate their existence to the best interest of their customers." Copulsky says this occurs because the companies use short-term strategies to boost stock price, use creative accounting to show higher earnings, and lose business by cutting costs (Robert 1993).

Harvard Business School Professor Nitin Nohria has been tracking strategic moves by the 100 largest public companies since 1978. Between 1978 and 1993, each company announced, on average, fifteen layoffs in fifteen years. Each layoff averaged 2,000 people. Each company announced an average of fifty acquisitions or divestitures. *Fast Company,* which reported these results in its premier issue in 1995, asks: "If you had $100 to invest in 1978, would you have done better buying shares in these companies or buying conservative mutual funds? Answer: Only 8 of the 100 companies outperformed mutual funds. When you consider the opportunity cost of capital, only 30 companies created any positive value. The median value added per company was *negative $5 million."*

None of this is meant to imply that money is not important to companies or to the people who work for them. Companies must be profitable to serve their customers and satisfy their owners and shareholders, just as individuals must be profitable to earn a living. It's just that money can't be the top priority. When it is, we devalue our worth both as a business and as a leader. And we end up making less than we would if our top priority were service.

➤ Establishing an Adversarial Class System

If you've seen an organization chart, you've seen the typical business class system. The chief executive officer is in a class by himself (and here the male pronoun applies almost exclusively). The rest of the senior executives fill out the company's aristocracy. Managers make up the middle class, and everybody else is the underclass. A few unique groups cross the boundaries (e.g., commissioned salespeople who may earn enough to be aristocracy, but will never be mistaken for *real* royalty), but most slide nicely into the appropriate slots.

The whole arrangement smacks of the seignorial—lords of the manor living comfortably off the work of their peasants. I realize that's a little extreme, but it's also more than a little true. Anyone who's worked in a command-and-control environment (which is just about everyone) knows that you treat executives differently than you treat nonexecutives. They get the best parking spaces. They get the biggest offices. They get the largest expense accounts. They get the greatest bonuses and stock options, not to mention the highest salaries. They get to make the decisions. They get to pass judgment. They get . . . well, you get the picture.

They also get adversaries, the most formidable of which is their own workforce. As soon as you divide people into classes, all sorts of negatives set in: control, greed, resentment, fear, mistrust, disrespect. Imagine trying to create a boundaryless, flexible, fast, customer-driven, high-quality organization with people who feel such animosity. You cannot divide and unite at the same time.

The alternative to the adversarial class system is a system that has been rigorously tested for more than 200 years: democracy. In his book *Leading Change,* James O'Toole talks about Yale's Robert Dahl, an authority on political democracy, who "predicts that the next stage of social development in the West will be the democratization of workplaces." Such talk triggers images of an entire company having to vote before it can act, but that's not what O'Toole means. It "is not about voting; it is about the democratic value of *inclusion.*"

Command-and-control leadership creates a class system that necessarily *excludes* large groups of employees. Servant-leadership thrives on inclusion. One breeds fear and mistrust while the other builds trust, and trust is the oil that keeps an organization from grinding itself into little pieces. Leadership surveys show that trust is the single most important factor on which followers evaluate a leader, and on which leaders evaluate followers. "Trust comes out of the experience of pursuing what is true," writes Peter Block in his book *Stewardship.* "What is true lies within each of us. Stewardship is founded on the belief that others have the knowledge and the answers within themselves." Autocratic leadership adheres to the belief that only the leaders have the knowledge and the answers.

➤ Treating Employees as Commodities

One of the benefits of command-and-control leadership is the luxury of treating employees as commodities. Decisions about people are much easier when people are a line item on the budget, right above equipment and right below facilities. This may seem harsh until you look at the obvious signs of this attitude:

- ➤ Downsizing
- ➤ Disrespect
- ➤ Fear
- ➤ Hypocrisy
- ➤ Income disparity
- ➤ Mistrust

Let's begin with corporate America's infatuation with downsizing: 2.5 million layoffs from March 1991, when the economic *recovery* began, to the end of 1995. The message: People are expendable.

The description may seem harsh until you watch America's most admired CEOs in action. You almost can't get through an article about one of them without sensing their arrogant attitude about the other employees in their company. Here are just two recent examples:

➤ The leader of one Fortune 500 company shouts "Air ball!" when another executive proposes an idea he thinks is weak.

➤ The CEO of a bank graces the cover of a national business magazine, resplendent in hunting clothes and bearing a rifle, because he's astute at gobbling up other banks. "When he takes over a bank," the magazine reports, "his lieutenants descend on the town in one of the company's 11 jets, and almost before you can say 'disintermediation,' they've booted out the local management, ripped down the signs, fired workers, and seamlessly absorbed the hapless victims."

These childish, bullying, macho displays are demeaning and destructive. I can't understand how anyone can applaud it, nor why anyone would want to emulate it. The message these CEOs give is clear: I am superior to you.

Command-and-control leadership also lends itself to hypocrisy. According to the *Washington Post,* a national study of executives conducted by Towers Perrin, a management consulting firm, revealed that 98 percent thought improving employee performance would significantly improve their company's productivity. Nearly three-quarters of the executives claimed employees were their company's most important asset. Yet when these same executives ranked their business priorities, investing in people ranked fifth on a six-item list, well behind customer satisfaction, financial performance, and competition. The message: People are commodities.

And the commodities don't get the spoils. The average CEO now earns about fifty-three times as much as a factory worker, up from about forty-two times in 1980. According to Labor Department statistics, wages rose at the slowest pace on record during 1995—and probably the slowest pace since World War II. The median household income actually declined from 1979 to 1994, including a drop since 1991 when the economic recovery began and corporate profitability increased. The message: People deserve much less than their leaders.

All of these messages are not lost on people. They do not trust their employers; one survey found that only 38 percent of workers trusted their employers to keep promises (*Do Managers Care about Their Workers?* 1995). They fear any number of consequences, from being ridiculed by their bosses to losing their jobs. They struggle not to become mindless commodities. In a study of 30,000 U.S. workers, 47 percent said they either dislike or are ambivalent about the company they work for. Many rebel by skipping work: Unscheduled absenteeism jumped 14 percent from 1992 to 1995, with more than half of those absences taken to deal with family matters, relax, or attend to personal needs. Hardest hit? Companies with 100 to 249 employees. People get the message.

Treating employees as commodities is a characteristic of command-and-control leadership. Yet despite the arrogance and ignorance of leaders and the apathy of followers, command-and-control leadership works. It just doesn't work very well. If organizations are machines, control works, but organizations are not machines.

When we continue to think of them as machines, when we continue to treat people as machine parts, we suffer from paradigm paralysis. The world has changed and we can't see it. *Industry Week* observed that filters have become our expectations and our preferences, and those expectations and preferences encourage us to see and hear what it is we expect and want to see and hear. Acting on the real facts is a painful process. It's also invigorating and joyous and extremely rewarding, as the people at Wainwright Industries discovered.

■ A SINCERE TRUST AND BELIEF IN PEOPLE

From 1984 to 1990, Wainwright Industries ran like a well-oiled machine. Sales grew from $4 million to $20 million. Customer satisfaction soared. But Mike Simms knew something was wrong.

Mike manages Wainwright's St. Peters, Missouri, plant. Wainwright manufactures stamped and machined parts, primarily for the auto industry. Mike almost quit in 1989 to start his own company and show Wainwright he had a better way. He wasn't happy. The other managers and coworkers weren't happy. So he thought about quitting.

He was still thinking about it in January 1991, when he found himself sitting with seven other Wainwright leaders listening to an IBM Rochester vice president talk about how they won the Baldrige Award. Mike didn't want to be there. His mind wandered until he heard the speaker emphasize how IBM Rochester thrived because it had a sincere trust and belief in people. Mike wrote the phrase on a napkin: "Sincere trust and belief in people." Below it he wrote, "What is it?" He passed it to the woman sitting next to him. She wrote, "I don't know. Do we have it at Wainwright?" The napkin made its way around the Wainwright table as each leader, including CEO Don Wainwright, read it. "Wainwright Industries changed that morning," Mike remembers.

It changed because the company's leaders were ready for change. They realized that all the tools and techniques they had implemented during the '80s had created a more profitable company, but they had not made it a better place to work. Everyone suffered. Leaders set themselves up as the experts, funneling all information to their desks and making all the decisions. Rapid growth, greater customer demands, and the need to understand

and implement new tools and techniques had worn them out. The rest of Wainwright's workforce checked their brains at the door; management told them what to do and how to do it, and railed at them when they failed.

In April 1991, after taking a few months to plan Wainwright's transformation, leadership shut down the plant for an all-employee meeting. Don Wainwright told the group he needed to own up to something. "I failed you," he said. "I thought the best way to provide job security was to let the owners and managers who had all the information make all the decisions, but we can't grow and provide security if we continue like this. We failed. It's up to you to do your own job. We sincerely trust and believe in you. We'll provide the training and support you need to do your job."

Naturally, people were cynical. It's one thing to hear you're trusted and believed but quite another to actually *be* trusted and believed. Training started. Responsibilities shifted. Leaders provided support. Employees became associates, vital members of Team Wainwright. Within months, a "sincere trust and belief in people" became one of the company's core values. And Team Wainwright took off:

➤ On-time delivery for the stamping division rose from 76 percent in 1992 to 99 percent in 1994. The delivery performance of machined products improved from 59 percent in 1991 to 99.7 percent in 1994.

➤ Training as a percent of payroll now equals 7 percent, nearly twice that of Motorola, which is considered a benchmark for training excellence.

➤ At a time when most American companies average one suggestion per employee per year, Wainwright averages 1.25 *implemented* suggestions per associate *per week.*

➤ Safety improved dramatically, with Workers' Compensation claims dropping from $100,000 in 1991 to zero in 1994. The number of recordable accidents fell from sixty-six to twelve.

➤ Sales jumped from $20 million in 1990 to $28 million in 1995.

➤ Gross profit as a percent of sales rose from 8.73 percent in 1991 to 14.15 percent in 1994.

➤ Internal customer satisfaction rose from 79 percent in 1992 to 95 percent in 1994.

➤ The external customer satisfaction index rose from 84 percent in 1992 to 98 percent in 1995.

➤ The quality of its management system achieved world-class status when Wainwright Industries won the Malcolm Baldrige National Quality Award in 1994.

The ultimate lesson, says Mike Simms, is that "we choose to play the game accepting it for what it is. We took all the tools and techniques and tried to change our people. That's why we failed. People don't change; they adapt. Now we give them what they need to make this a better world. Our commitment to training came out of that. We train to help people become better people, not to change them."

"Picture the most negative person in your company," Mike continues. "Once you've got that face, I'll take you to Wainwright and show him to you. He's now one of our most positive people, a man of influence who helps guide tours of our plant. I asked him why he changed. 'I never changed,' he told me. 'The leaders finally understood that college degrees don't tell them how to run my machine.'"

■ THE ARGUMENT FOR SERVANT-LEADERSHIP

Wainwright Industries exemplifies the kind of institution Robert Vanourek described at the beginning of this chapter. By acting on "a sincere trust and belief in people," it transformed a command-and-control organization into one of shared vision, responsibilities, and rewards. Revenues are up. Profits are up. Quality is better. Customer satisfaction is higher. Associates and leaders are happier.

Each of these alone is a persuasive argument for the merits of servant-leadership. Taken together, they provide compelling evidence of a better way to lead an organization. A new way. A new leadership model free of the flaws inherent in the old command-and-control model.

Unlike the command-and-control model, servant-leadership supports the basics of business excellence:

➤ *It encourages managers to lead the change effort by giving them the information and authority to make decisions, the freedom to take action, and the safety to make mistakes.* You cannot create a flexible, boundaryless organization if you narrowly define the management position and limit managers' responsibilities.

➤ *It contributes to a shared vision that embodies the personal visions of every employee.* You cannot impose the leader's vision on employees without making it some dead thing gathering dust on reception area walls.

➤ *It engages employees in the work of achieving the organization's goals.* You cannot involve employees in transforming your company if leaders assume they know best what employees should be doing and how they should do it.

➤ *It orients the company to the requirements of its customers.* You cannot become customer-driven if the only measures leaders value are financial.

➤ *It designs and implements an organizational structure that serves the changing needs of the company.* You cannot become fast and flexible using a rigid organizational design that is hierarchical and top–down.

➤ *It fosters process thinking, providing support for the people who work and improve the company's core processes.* You cannot think in terms of processes at the same time that you impose control through permanent structures.

➤ *It distributes information to the people who can use it to assess and improve performance.* You cannot take full advantage of information gathered for use only by senior leaders.

➤ *It involves employees, customers, and suppliers in the planning process, drawing on their knowledge of the business to create plans that every employee can own and help achieve.* You cannot create a meaningful, workable plan without involving those who must act on it.

➤ *It nurtures learning, recognizing that a learning organization is not possible unless people practice it at every level.* You cannot enculturate learning without a sincere trust and belief in people.

Servant-leadership affirms the person as central to the business, then acts on that affirmation by giving each person in the organization the opportunity and responsibility to act in the company's best interests. "It is an upside-down sort of place," Charles

Handy writes, "with much of the power residing at the organization's edge. In this culture, imposed authority no longer works. Instead, authority must be earned from those over whom it is exercised. This organization is held together by shared beliefs and values, by people who are committed to each other and to common goals—a rather tenuous method of control" (Chawla and Renesch 1995).

Tenuous, but with enormous potential for growth, success, and prosperity. An autocratic organization is limited by the capabilities of a few leaders. When those leaders promote the self-sufficiency of everyone in the organization, the company dramatically expands its capabilities. Imagine a company in which:

➤ Every employee knows who his or her customers are, what their requirements are, and how he or she is doing in meeting those requirements.

➤ Self-directed employees form teams as needed to improve processes, solve problems, and explore opportunities.

➤ Employees help create the company's strategic plan, understand what actions are necessary to achieve it, and assume responsibility for their pieces of those actions.

➤ Information flows freely, information about financial measures and quality measures and customer satisfaction measures, and people use that information daily to monitor progress and initiate improvements.

➤ Learning is an attribute of the culture, each employee intent on acquiring knowledge and sharing that knowledge with the organization.

This sounds idealistic because it is. Even the most empowered organizations suffer employees who don't want to think, make decisions, or take responsibility. Problems escape solutions. Information never gets in the right hands. Learning occurs in spurts. This is real life, after all. Yet even if the ideal lives only in our imaginations, it becomes a template for the organization we wish to create, a vision that compels us to choose a new form of leadership.

Enlightened leaders choose servant-leadership because it aligns with and supports the vision and goals of their organizations. That doesn't make it an easy choice. As Peter Block writes,

"Stewardship depends on a willingness to be accountable for results without using control or caretaking as the means to reach them. This demands a choice for service with partnership and empowerment as the basic governance strategies" (Block 1993).

■ TAKING RESPONSIBILITY, MAKING DECISIONS

When you ask Larry Welliver what made him the leader he is today, he begins with his experiences as a teenager working for his father. "My father had a small business, a part of which was to produce soldering irons. I did everything related to making those soldering irons, and I didn't want one of them coming back because of something I did." At a young age he learned the value of quality, the importance of customer satisfaction, and the need to take responsibility. He applied those lessons to his job as an engineer at Honeywell's Solid State Electronics Center (SSEC). In 1986 he was put in charge of the division's Total Quality Management process. Two years later, he was leading the organization.

SSEC's 545 employees develop and produce integrated circuits and solid-state sensors for control products for aerospace and military markets and for other Honeywell divisions. In 1991 and 1993 SSEC was a finalist for the Malcolm Baldrige National Quality Award; it won the Minnesota Quality Award in 1993. It is world-class at delighting customers; in recent one-on-one interviews with twenty major customers, seventeen said SSEC exceeded their requirements. In the early 1980s, twenty-five competitors vied for business; now only two remain. Amazingly, SSEC gets 98 percent of the business it bids.

It is also world-class at innovation. Forty-two percent of its sales come from new products introduced in the past three years. 3M Company, a benchmark for product innovation, strives for 30 percent of sales from new products introduced in the past four years. I'll discuss how SSEC promotes innovation in Chapter 5 and how it satisfies customers in Chapter 6.

One contributing factor to both is the quality of its leadership. Larry Welliver used to run a very hierarchical organization. But he didn't run it for long. "My own belief was that there was no reason others in the organization couldn't make more decisions," he says. So he changed the reporting structure and eliminated levels of management, dismantling the hierarchy in favor of a flatter, more horizontal organization. He authorized formal training to help employees feel empowered and take responsibility. That training program, which continues to be refined and expanded, is now called "Creating Value for the Future" and includes courses on SSEC's vision, creativity, its Quality Star (which defines the points of value creation), and each point on the star: Customer Value, People Value, Economic Value, Supplier Value, and Community Value.

Another key factor in the evolution to a flatter organization has been communication. Larry holds meetings with all SSEC employees (100 at a time) three times a year. He has regular staff luncheons to talk about the business. Once a month he invites work groups or a cross section of employees to "Ask Larry" sessions. No subject is off-limits. "It gives me a sense of what's on people's minds," Larry says.

He believes strongly in the need for constant communication. "If you don't do it directly, it can get very garbled. And you can't just tell people once or twice." That's tell as in "inform," not as in "order."

"The easiest thing in the world is for me to sit here and tell people what to do," Larry says. "Now I'm more of a support person." Being a support person is more difficult than being a boss. As Larry remembers, the hardest thing about the transition from hierarchical to horizontal was people's resistance to making decisions. They kept trying to toss the ball back into his court, and he kept telling them he didn't want it. Once they discovered that their decisions would not be second-guessed and that a poor decision wouldn't cost them their jobs, they accepted their new responsibilities with dramatic results. "It's incredible what they can do," says Larry—and SSEC's results agree.

Larry Welliver is Peter Block's idea of a steward. He is "accountable for results without using control or caretaking as the means to reach them." His "basic governance strategies" are partnership and empowerment. Although he is a confident and articulate leader, he exudes none of the arrogance that separates so many successful leaders from their followers. He and his fellow employees walk the same path toward a shared vision of SSEC's future. His role is to support them.

Robert Greenleaf, who wrote about such stewardship nearly three decades ago, said that the most productive organization is the one where "there is the largest amount of voluntary action; people do the right things, things that optimize total effectiveness, at the right times—because they understand what ought to be done, they believe these are the right things to do, and they take the necessary actions without being instructed."

He could have been describing Honeywell's Solid State Electronics Center.

■ SWITCHING TO SERVANT-LEADERSHIP

You cannot achieve Greenleaf's vision of a productive organization for any length of time using command-and-control leadership. By its nature, it channels key decisions up through the organization to those leaders with the authority to make them. It shields people from the information they require to understand what ought to be done. It confuses them about what is the right thing to do. It discourages them from taking initiative. And it prevents the kind of voluntary action needed to delight customers, reengineer processes, and improve results.

This isn't to say that you can't be productive without servant-leadership, or that your organization cannot improve. It's like driving to the big game in second gear: You will arrive at the stadium eventually, but by the time you get there, the game will be over and everyone will have gone home. To shift your organization into a higher gear, you will need a leadership model that unleashes all the horsepower under the hood.

■ EIGHT-STEP LEADERSHIP CHANGE PROCESS

To change leadership models, consider this eight-step process:

1. Question your current leadership model.
2. Study new models.
3. Choose to change the way you lead.
4. Create a shared vision.
5. Organize to balance authority and responsibility.
6. Work to eliminate fear and mistrust.

7. Engage all employees in taking responsibility and making decisions.

8. Practice being a servant-leader.

As you can see, several of the steps are also basics of business excellence; vision, organization, and empowerment are discussed in detail in later chapters. You cannot separate leadership from the rest of the system, which is why any changes in your leadership model will affect and be affected by activities in other areas of the system. The good news is that positive changes in your leadership model will trigger positive changes throughout the organization. The bad news is that positive changes in your leadership model will also expose flaws in the rest of the organization. It's like putting a new carpet in the living room: You suddenly realize that your furniture is getting old and the walls need painting. You will need to be aware of the impact of changing leadership models, just as you will need to be ready to take advantage of the opportunities it creates.

➤ Step 1: Question Your Current Leadership Model

As important as I think it is to dump the command-and-control mentality, you can't change models based on my recommendation. *You* must believe the change is absolutely necessary for your organization's success. Before that can happen, you need to ask whether your current leadership model is serving your needs.

If you are the leader of your organization and you're not used to discussing these issues with your staff, take some time to answer the questions below as honestly and objectively as possible. If your answers suggest that a change might be in order, or if you are a leader who is comfortable discussing these issues with your staff, devote part of a staff meeting to soliciting answers to the same questions from your leadership team.

If you are not the leader of your organization, answer the questions carefully, identifying specific areas where you believe a new leadership model would benefit the organization. For example, if you think the hierarchy is preventing people from taking responsibility for meeting customer requirements, quantify weaknesses in customer satisfaction using survey data, complaint levels, sales data, or other measures of customer satisfaction. Do this for every area where you think autocratic leadership is hurting the company, then present your findings to the appropriate leader with a request that the leader perform the same evaluation.

This is not an easy course to take. One of the most common questions at any quality conference is "How do I get my boss to buy into these changes if he doesn't think there's any reason to change?" Wainwright's Mike Simms understands. "It cost us four years waiting for our leaders to change. It just doesn't happen that way in the real world. The manager in the middle has to drive change while the top leadership supports and pushes it. If all the middle managers go to the top and say 'We've got a better way,' what's the leader going to say?"

Whatever position you hold in your company, you can begin to identify a better way by using these questions to assess your current leadership model:

➤ How successful is our company? How do we measure success? Are we using the right measures?

➤ How well are we meeting our customers' requirements? How do we know that?

➤ How does our performance compare to that of our competitors? Have we made objective comparisons lately or do we just believe we are superior?

➤ How will our business change in the next five years? Are we as an organization and individually as employees prepared to take advantage of these changes? Are we leading change in our industry or reacting to it?

➤ How would I characterize our current decision-making process? Does it serve the organization's needs?

➤ Do we have a sincere trust and belief in people? What evidence supports my answer? Is such trust and belief valuable to our organization?

➤ Do I enjoy working here? Do I feel valued and recognized for my contributions? Do I feel like an important member of a unified team? Are my feelings shared by most employees? How do I know?

The trick to answering these questions is to set aside your assumptions and base your responses on objective information. Only then can you get a true picture of your current leadership model.

➤ Step 2: Study New Models

Another way to assess the effectiveness of your current leadership model is to compare it to other models. You can do this through benchmarking and reading.

Benchmarking is the process of learning how to become the best in a particular area. For the area of leadership, you can begin the benchmarking process by identifying those leaders and organizations you would like to learn from. You can find such companies through books such as this one, professional organizations, trade organizations and publications, industry experts, business magazines, local business organizations, customers, suppliers, and state and national quality award programs.

Once you've identified a few companies to benchmark, initiate contact with those organizations to arrange a benchmarking visit or discussion. A visit has the benefit of bringing the leadership model to life; you see it in action and can ask follow-up questions about how it works. However, if time or money is tight, a telephone conference can uncover the key elements of the company's leadership model.

Before talking to your peers at the company you're benchmarking, prepare a list of subjects you wish to discuss and questions you would like answered. Send the list to your contact person so that he or she can prepare for the discussion. Reassure the contact person that you will not abuse any information that is shared. You may want to adopt a benchmarking code of conduct and communicate it to your potential benchmarking partner. The Strategic Planning Institute's Council on Benchmarking created the following code of conduct:

1. Keep it legal.
2. Be willing to provide the same information that you request.
3. Respect confidentiality.
4. Keep information internal for your use only.
5. Initiate contact through benchmarking contacts.
6. Don't refer without permission.
7. Be prepared at initial contact.
8. Have a basic knowledge of benchmarking and follow the process.

9. Determine what to benchmark and complete a rigorous self-assessment.

After your benchmarking visits/discussions, compare the leadership models you learned about to your existing model. Identify gaps and opportunities for improvement and use this information to assess your current model and the value of embracing a new leadership model.

You can also learn about new leadership models in a number of business books currently on the market. I haven't read all the books on management and leadership, but of those I have read, I highly recommend:

➤ *Stewardship* by Peter Block
➤ *Leading Change* by James O'Toole
➤ *The Fifth Discipline* by Peter Senge
➤ *Reflections on Leadership* edited by Larry Spears
➤ *Open-Book Management* by John Case

➤ Step 3: Choose to Change the Way You Lead

In *Leading Change,* O'Toole writes: "To be effective, leaders must change their attitude about followers forever and under all conditions." Don Wainwright made such a change. "In our hierarchical society, people have a tendency to trust and believe in leadership positions," Don says, "but leaders don't trust and believe in associates (Wainwright's term for employees). That's where the change has to come, and it has to come from within each leader." The place to start, according to O'Toole, is with a "personal acknowledgment that no other form of leadership can be both moral and effective."

If you are a leader in your organization, you are in a position to choose the form of leadership you will use. As Peter Senge writes, "Whether it is an organization of three or three thousand matters not. Only through choice does an individual come to be the steward of a larger vision" (Senge 1990).

If you've taken the first two steps in this process, you now have a better understanding of your current leadership model, of the "larger vision" you wish to embrace, and of the alternatives available to you. The next step is to decide which leadership model is best for you, your fellow employees, your organization, owners/shareholders, customers, and suppliers.

If you choose some form of servant-leadership, make sure you consider the ramifications of such a decision. You will need to learn and develop new leadership skills. You will need to push authority to those in the best positions to exercise it. You will need to train and coach employees in taking responsibility. You will need to look at every aspect of your organization to begin aligning it with the new, horizontal structure. And you will need to be patient, trusting that servant-leadership is better than the old way and that the results will eventually bear this out.

According to Honeywell's Larry Welliver, it took five years for SSEC's new leadership model to become enculturated. If he had panicked during that period, countermanding the decisions of others or ridiculing their work or demanding attention to his agenda, the new way of leading would have disappeared like yesterday's management fad, leaving a more cynical and disillusioned work force and a widening gap between goals and performance.

For many leaders, the choice to lead differently becomes a leap of faith, like the first time you try parachuting: You must have complete faith that the parachute will open or you will not jump, but you won't know for sure until you *do* jump. If you've read about servant-leadership or met leaders who are practicing it, you know the parachute will open. Now you must *believe* it. And then you must jump.

➤ Step 4: Create a Shared Vision

The next chapter describes how to create a shared vision. For the leader, creating a shared vision means expressing his or her own vision for the company, then encouraging other employees to do the same. As Senge writes in *Reflections on Leadership*, "Building shared vision is not about people surrendering their individual visions. It is about deepening each person's unique sense of vision and establishing harmony among the diverse visions so that we can move forward together."

A shared vision flows from the new servant-leadership model. It invites participation and ownership. It is inclusionary. It speaks to the value of all employees by embodying their diverse visions for the company. In the process, it makes the dispersion of power and authority possible by giving employees a shared vision they can use to guide their decisions.

➤ Step 5: Organize to Balance Authority and Responsibility

In the hierarchical organization, authority and responsibility reside at the top with authoritarian leaders. When you choose servant-leadership, the hierarchy becomes a cocoon you must shed for the organization to be able to spread its wings and fly. Chapter 6 examines the limitations of the hierarchical design and current thinking about new ways of organizing.

The purpose of the organization, like the purpose of servant-leaders, is to support the efforts of all employees to achieve the company's goals. "What you're after is congruence among strategic direction, organizational design, staff capabilities, and the processes you use to ensure that people are working together to meet the company's goals," says Paul Allaire, Xerox chairman and CEO (Garvin 1995). Servant-leadership, a shared vision, and a flexible, horizontal organization make such alignment possible.

➤ Step 6: Work to Eliminate Fear and Mistrust

Command-and-control leadership breeds fear and mistrust, which is one reason it does not support an empowered workforce. People cannot take responsibility and make decisions if they fear the consequences of taking initiative or if they mistrust the motives of their leaders.

To determine the level of fear in your organization, compare a typical employee to the chart below. If your organization tends to fall in the left column, eliminating fear should be a top priority.

Fearful Employee

➤ Blames others for problems and/or makes excuses

➤ Takes credit for achievements

Trusting Employee

➤ Accepts responsibility

➤ Shares credit

➤ Restricts and protects information	➤ Shares information with those who need it
➤ Works alone whenever possible	➤ Collaborates with others whenever possible
➤ Believes it's "us" vs. "them"	➤ Believes "we" are in this together
➤ Gets sidetracked by differences of opinion	➤ Sees common perceptions in "big picture" issues
➤ Dislikes diversity	➤ Values each other's backgrounds and experience
➤ Keeps opinions to self	➤ Openly voices concerns, criticisms, conflicts, and ideas
➤ Complains about the company, coworkers, the job	➤ Speaks positively about his/her work, the organization, and the future

This chart is adapted from a list in an excellent book on the subject called *Driving Fear Out of the Workplace,* by Kathleen Ryan and Daniel Oestreich. The authors offer seven strategies for replacing fear and mistrust with energy and innovation:

1. *Acknowledge the presence of fear.* Just talking about it in small groups and staff meetings is a start.

2. *Pay attention to interpersonal conduct.* Identify abrasive or abusive conduct and develop a shared picture of positive relations.

3. *Value criticism: Reward the messenger.* Promote a mindset that problems are prized possessions because they suggest opportunities for improvement.

4. *Reduce ambiguous behavior.* Reduce the amount of incomplete, inaccurate, or confusing communications.

5. *Discuss the undiscussables.* Uncover the issues people aren't talking about and find ways to discuss them.

6. *Collaborate on decisions.* Practice involving more people in making decisions.

7. *Challenge worst-case thinking.* Help free people from the traps of their negative assumptions.

➤ Step 7: Engage All Employees in Taking Responsibility and Making Decisions

It's time to pull the ripcord and find out if the parachute opens. "Service-based governance strategies mean the redistribution of power, privilege, purpose, and wealth," writes Peter Block in *Stewardship*. The autocratic governance strategy must go.

Chapter 4 examines ways to engage employees. From a leader's perspective, engaging employees means letting go of the trappings of power, privilege, purpose, and wealth that set you apart and above those you now wish to serve.

Nelson Mandela could have claimed such trappings when he was elected president of South Africa. He had grown old in his country's prisons. He had suffered the abuse of apartheid. He was only recently free. Yet when asked what he had learned from his years of struggle, Mandela said, "People respond to how you treat them. If you treat them with respect, and ignore the negatives, you get a positive reaction." When he spoke to his followers after winning the election, Mandela said, "I am your servant" (O'Toole 1995).

That's a good way to launch servant-leadership, as Don Wainwright learned when he assembled all of his associates and told them his new job was to support their efforts. The transition to servant-leadership begins with such an attitude by the servant-leaders, then proceeds through specific actions that spread power, privilege, purpose, and wealth among all employees:

1. *Replace control with commitment to a shared vision.* If you've completed Step 4 of this leadership change process, you now have a vision employees can use to guide their actions and decisions.

2. *Let those who do the work manage the work.* Find out who has the information and skills to make a decision. Involve them in making it. Involve those who must implement the decision in making it. Then provide training and coaching to help them overcome their fears and anxiety, and support what they decide.

3. *Provide information to those who need it.* Key information tends to flow to the top of an organization. You want it to flow to those employees who can use it to make informed decisions. This includes financial information. Both Wainwright and Honeywell SSEC train employees to understand

financial data, then share financial information on a regular basis.

4. *Look beyond the numbers.* Take a balanced-scorecard approach to assessing performance. The classic balanced scorecard has four areas of measurement: financial, customer, internal operations, and learning/innovation. Your areas may differ depending on what's important to your organization. When you ask about measurements in all areas with equal passion, you signal a change from being driven by the bottom line to becoming a customer-driven company. We'll look more closely at this balanced-scorecard approach in Chapter 8.

5. *Help employees grow.* Servant-leadership is about treating each employee as valuable for himself or herself, not just for the work they do. "You can't just trust and believe in people," says Wainwright's Mike Simms, "you've got to support them. If you're not there to support them, you're not a good leader." That support can take many forms, from providing training to recognizing progress to removing obstacles. Quality guru W. Edwards Deming suggests asking a simple question: "What gets in the way of your doing your job?" Deming then advises leaders to sit back and listen before acting (Latzko and Saunders 1995).

6. *Redistribute wealth.* The theory behind open-book management, which is a strategy for engaging employees, is that a company of owners will outperform a company of employees. Ownership comes from knowing the company's financial situation and how you personally help move the numbers in the right direction, and from having a stake in those numbers. As John Case writes in *Open-Book Management,* "A noticeable portion of everybody's pay should come in the form of profit sharing or stock distribution." Wainwright has a profit-sharing plan that doles out an equal amount to every employee. Honeywell SSEC has a two-tiered profit-sharing approach designed by an employee team, plus a 401k plan that makes 80 percent of its employees stakeholders in Honeywell.

7. *Recognize the value of every employee.* According to Jack Stack, the ultimate higher law of *The Great Game of Business* is: "When you appeal to the highest level of thinking, you get the highest level of performance." You cannot appeal to

the best in people unless you first recognize and believe in their value.

➤ Step 8: Practice Being a Servant-Leader

Servant-leadership is about putting people first. Doing so requires a belief that people have an intrinsic value beyond their contributions to the company. It also demands the exercise of a different set of qualities, the characteristics of a servant-leader that distinguish him or her from an autocratic leader, such as:

➤ Integrity

➤ Courage

➤ Listening

➤ Empathy

➤ Healing

➤ Awareness

➤ Sense of humor

➤ Curiosity

➤ Respect

➤ Persuasion

➤ Conceptualization

➤ Stewardship

➤ Commitment to the growth of people

➤ Comfort with ambiguity

➤ Community building

Nobody becomes a servant-leader overnight. Servant-leadership is something you grow into by choosing it, by having the courage to work through relationships instead of by command, by coaching instead of dictating, by serving instead of directing.

But you will not grow alone. Unlike the autocratic leader who admits it's "lonely at the top," the servant-leader thrives on connections. Servant-leaders work *through* people. They encourage, support, inspire, and transform. To paraphrase Max Dupree, chairman and CEO of Herman Miller Inc., they begin by defining reality and end by saying thank you. In between, they serve.

It is a noble calling, acclaimed by Lao-tzu 2,600 years ago, defined by Robert Greenleaf twenty-six years ago, and embraced by leaders across the country today. Valuing people. Helping them to be their best. Uniting diverse goals and visions into a single shared vision. It is the first basic of business excellence.

Experts on leadership like to equate the role of the leader to that of the conductor of an orchestra. Esa-Pekka Salonen, the principal conductor of the Los Angeles Philharmonic, offers an unusual and compelling vision of the role of the servant-leader: "The main thing is to motivate—to try to release the energies and passion in different individuals in order to make them feel free, to create the illusion that they are actually doing what they are doing out of their own desires and not being led by somebody. That is when the best results happen. In the best possible case, the illusion of freedom becomes true. They are free" (Bowles 1995).

■ STRATEGIES FOR IMPROVEMENT

➤ Jump Start

➤ Examine your attitudes and beliefs about leadership by answering the questions presented earlier in this chapter. Ask if these attitudes and beliefs produce the kinds of leaders your organization needs to compete and grow.

➤ Assess your leadership's attitudes about employees. One way to do this is to review the assumptions of command-and-control leadership in this chapter to determine to what degree leaders agree or disagree with the statements. Another way is to ask employees through focus groups, meetings, and surveys.

➤ Ask if your organization has a sincere trust and belief in people. Then ask if such trust and belief is necessary for the organization to achieve its goals. The final step is to identify what a sincere trust and belief in people would look like in your organization, then list the qualities of leadership necessary to produce it.

➤ Tune Up

➤ Weigh the benefits of servant-leadership with the typical resistance it encounters. Spend some time as a senior leadership team discussing the pros and cons in the context of how the organization must change to succeed.

➤ Implement the eight-step process for changing leadership models.

➤ Determine the level of fear in your organization, then work to eliminate it using the seven strategies for replacing fear and mistrust with energy and innovation, outlined in this chapter.

➤ Pull Away

➤ Align your leadership model with your management system. In the course of transforming an organization, it's easy for the components of that system to get into a rut that isn't necessarily in synch with the vision for the system. Establish a process for regular evaluation and improvement of your organization's leadership system and your leaders' skills.

➤ Improve your leadership skills by benchmarking successful servant-leaders. Many of the books on leadership that are identified in the Bibliography identify respected servant-leaders. You may learn of others through new books, business magazines, or industry communication. Just keep in mind that not every featured leader is a servant-leader.

Chapter 3

Focus through Shared Vision

If I were going to use sports analogies in this book, now would be the time. Choose any team sport and you can find one team that beat the odds because its members shared a common vision. Athletes pulling in different directions began to pull together and focus on a single goal. The Cinderella team won the title.

But there's a better field than the field of competition, and that's the field of vision. And the best place to look for the field of vision isn't in the world of sports, but in the world of science. I admit I'm much more comfortable talking sports than science, but I think science offers a unique theory about why a shared vision is so important.

In the new science of quantum theory, the word *field* describes actions that exist but cannot be observed through our five senses except by their effects, actions that are connected by an unseen and nonmaterial force. Gravity and magnetism are fields. They occupy space and become known to us through their effects. The same can be said for vision.

According to quantum theory, space is never empty. Likewise, the space in an organization is not empty. It can be filled with consistent messages or with contradicting messages, but it is not empty. As Margaret Wheatley writes in *Leadership and the New Science,* "If we have not bothered to create a field of vision that is coherent and sincere, people will encounter other fields, the ones we have created unintentionally or casually."

A coherent, sincere vision acts as a collective conscience for the organization. When my words and actions support the vision, it feels right. When they don't, it feels wrong. And just to make sure we're clear about which actions support and which don't, we measure those areas we know promote our vision. In this way, a shared vision does for the horizontal organization what policies and procedures do for the hierarchical one: Everybody works on the same page, it's just that the page is now a field of vision and not a five-pound rule book. As Stephen Covey, author of *The Seven Habits of Highly Effective People,* says, "Everything is created twice: first in the mind, then in the physical world." Creating an image of the ideal company in every employee's mind is the purpose of a shared vision.

One example of a company acting on a shared vision is Levi Strauss & Co. CEO Robert Haas believes that "Values provide a common language for aligning a company's leadership and its people." The alignment is critical because, in Haas's words, "It's the ideas of a business that are controlling, not some manager with authority" (Morin 1995). When the vision, values, and ideas of a business reflect the personal vision, values, and ideas of its employees, the alignment produces an effective field of vision. The collective conscience of the organization, like the conscience of each individual, serves as an omnipresent counsel on the morality of actions and behaviors.

Not many companies enjoy a coherent, sincere vision. Instead, employees confront a daily dose of conflicting messages: We are committed to our customers, but you'd better perform financially; we value our people, but we're not about to share profits, provide training, or worry about employee satisfaction; we're proud of our quality, just don't ask us to prove it; we trust you to do the right thing, and we'll tell you exactly what's right for all situations.

"As employees bump up against contradicting fields," Wheatley writes, "their behavior mirrors those contradictions. We end up with what is common to many organizations, a jumble of behaviors and people going off in different directions, with no clear or identifiable pattern." If that sounds like your company, you need to make "the vision thing" a top priority.

In this chapter we'll address two ways of thinking about the future: *shared vision* and *strategic thinking*. I decided to wrap strategic thinking with vision because strategic thinking expands a company's shared vision. It looks more specifically at what an organization wants to become. Like a shared vision, strategic thinking helps employees make decisions that move the company in the right direction. Chapter 8 focuses on *strategic planning*, which is concerned with *how* the company will get there.

■ LEADING WITH A SHARED VISION

When Wainwright Industries decided to operate on a "sincere trust and belief in people," it quickly realized that it did not have a vision its associates could embrace. The company decided to hold a two-day, off-site meeting of about fifty managers and associates to begin the process of creating a mission statement.

"I came into that meeting with about five pages of the most beautiful prose you've ever seen," remembers co-owner Don Wainwright. "They told me that wasn't anything like what we are, and my pages ended up in the trash."

Don shared his vision for the company. The managers and associates shared their visions. The off-site meeting concluded with nothing decided, but with a much better understanding of how people felt about the purpose and mission of the company.

Two months of debate followed, with associates submitting their ideas for the mission of Wainwright Industries. When the final mission statement was chosen, it reflected the personal visions of Wainwright's associates: *Continuous Commitment to Our Customers' Future*. It was suggested by a man who had been with the company for forty years.

To lead with a shared vision, leaders must recognize that the vision may not appear exactly as they would choose. Don Wainwright thought hard about his vision for the company. He invested considerable time in putting it on paper. He exposed himself to the judgment of his managers and associates by offering it for consideration. And he accepted their opinion that his vision, while contributing to the discussion, was not the company's vision.

Autocratic leaders have trouble with this process. They believe that creating the vision is their job. They expect their vision to be accepted without modification. They are surprised when anyone questions it. What they end up with is a vision that looks good and sounds inspiring, but that no one in the company shares. The leader's vision fails to keep employees from continuing to pursue their own interests, and that prevents the company from moving as one into the future.

Shared vision is a basic of business excellence because it focuses everyone in the company on a mutually beneficial, morally superior quest. Effective leaders value a shared vision because it:

➤ Connects everyone in the organization
➤ Simplifies the operation
➤ Aligns all activities
➤ Focuses actions for a more effective transformation

A shared vision connects everyone in the organization to a larger purpose. Just as a personal vision reflects something we care deeply about, a shared vision reflects a common caring. People contribute to and embrace a shared vision because they want to feel connected to something larger than themselves. As George Bernard Shaw said, "This is the true joy in life, the being used for a purpose recognized by yourself as a mighty one."

A shared vision simplifies the operation of an organization. Organizations consist of people who are both customers and suppliers, who hold differing views on what's important and how it should be done, who carry their own personal knowledge and experience and agendas to every task, and whose natural tendency is to congregate with like-minded employees and exclude others. These diverse worlds keep leaders from knowing much for certain about their organizations, and that uncertainty spawns complexity. A shared vision cuts through this complexity by creating, as James O'Toole describes it, "a collective view that followers recognize as morally superior to their own narrower interests even while encompassing them" (O'Toole 1995).

A shared vision aligns the activities of every member. Each individual in an organization faces constant choices. As the organization becomes flatter and employees more empowered, the choices multiply. A shared vision shapes their choices by expecting the individual to align them with the organization's vision. If it serves the greater good as defined by the shared vision, it is a good choice. If it undermines the vision, it's a bad choice.

A shared vision focuses all activities for a unified transformation. One reason companies fail to transform their organizations through reengineering, TQM, teams, benchmarking, or any other change strategy is because they lack a shared vision to guide the transformation. As John Kotter wrote, "Without a sensible vision, a transformation effort can easily dissolve into a list of confusing and incompatible projects that can take the organization in the wrong direction or nowhere at all" (Kotter 1995).

A shared vision is the reason an organization exists. It illuminates a path through the maze of uncertainty, confusion, and complexity that lies ahead, connecting each person to the larger purpose while simplifying, aligning, and focusing their choices.

Spearheading the effort to define and articulate such a shared vision is one of the first and greatest responsibilities of senior leadership.

■ CREATING A SHARED VISION

I should take a moment here to define mission, vision, and values. As I see it, mission is purpose, vision is direction, and values bring mission and vision to the daily work level. Not every organization needs all three. Some lump mission and vision together, while others use additional terms (e.g., principles, objectives, strategies). You will need to decide what is required to realize the benefits of a shared vision. For the purposes of this chapter, we will focus on the creation of a shared vision. At the end of this section you will find the shared visions that guide many of the companies featured in this book.

The visioning process consists of seven steps that often stretch over a period of months:

1. Gather ideas and information.
2. Develop first draft.
3. Debate first draft.
4. Rewrite.
5. Test the vision.
6. Finalize the vision.
7. Implement the vision.

Gather Ideas and Information

The only way to create a shared vision is to involve the people who will share it in its creation. A shared vision cannot come from on high. You can involve people through small focus groups of five to seven employees or larger meetings of 50–100 employees. Later in the process you will want to give everyone in the company (and perhaps even selected customers and suppliers) the chance to offer their suggestions. In addition to gaining valuable input, widespread involvement helps prepare the entire organization to embrace the final vision.

The responsibility for organizing the meetings and soliciting feedback rests with senior leadership. Leaders may choose to form a vision team to handle this responsibility, but the team should include leaders, and the leaders should fully participate in the information-gathering sessions.

The purpose of these initial meetings is to get ideas on the table. Participants may have thought about their vision for the company, but most are probably clueless about what an effective vision statement contains. Begin the meetings by discussing the criteria of a great vision:

> ➤ *It is intrinsic.*   Rather than focusing on achievement relative to competitors, a great vision statement speaks to the larger purpose embodied in the organization's products and services.

> ➤ *It is shared.*   A great vision reflects the desires of all stakeholders: customers, employees, suppliers, owners/shareholders, and the community.

> ➤ *It reflects the organization's culture and values.*   You cannot borrow someone else's vision. It must capture the unique nature of your organization.

> ➤ *It sets bold and imaginative goals.*   The challenge unites employees in a common cause while describing how the organization must act to meet its goals.

> ➤ *It guides decision making.*   The common cause represents a desired end that will guide the decisions of employees throughout the organization.

> ➤ *It can be changed.*   No vision statement is timeless. You want to create the best vision for your organization today, understanding that you will need to revisit the vision as circumstances change.

You may want to show examples of other companies' vision statements to help participants see what good ones look like, although you have to be careful they don't adopt another company's statement for their own.

As with any brainstorming process, you want to encourage participants to contribute by withholding your judgment of their ideas. You may want to ask the following questions to stimulate the group's thinking:

➤ What is my personal vision as it relates to my work?

➤ What kind of company would I like this to be?

➤ What would our company be like if it were truly customer-driven?

➤ What would this company look like if it supported each employee's growth and development?

➤ What would it be like if everyone sincerely trusted and believed in each other?

➤ How would we know we were successful?

➤ What absolutely must occur for our company to thrive?

Write down every idea, without regard to relevance, appropriateness, or wisdom. When the group has answered the questions or run out of things to say, invite the participants to look for patterns and common themes in their ideas. Through this distillation process, they begin to recognize the truths that will be at the foundation of their shared vision.

Develop First Draft

The leaders and/or vision team organize the most important ideas identified by the employee groups into a vision statement. At this point, resist the urge to edit the statement down to one or two pithy sentences. It's more important to include all of the truths proposed by the groups. You will use this first draft to begin a broader discussion of the company's shared vision among all employees, a discussion that will mold the statement into a vision everyone can share.

Debate First Draft

Distribute the first draft to all employees with a request that people read it, think about it, and improve it. You may want to arrange several ways for employees to contribute, such as:

➤ By electronic mail, suggestion system, phone message, or internal mail

➤ Through discussions at department, team, or work group meetings, with leaders of these groups submitting ideas to the organization's leadership or vision team

➤ By posting the vision statement throughout the facility and inviting employees to write their changes right on it

To help employees provide constructive suggestions, include the criteria of a great vision statement that are listed above.

Rewrite

The leaders and/or vision team use the suggestions to refine the organization's vision. The vision should meet the criteria in a concise, understandable format, with the understanding that you can expand on the vision by developing values, principles, objectives, or strategies that help you chart a more detailed course.

You may also want to communicate the process used to refine the vision. An article in the company newsletter or a memorandum can publicize many of the employees' suggestions, letting them know that all ideas were considered. Repeating the criteria and explaining how they were used to arrive at a vision can clarify the reasoning behind your decisions. You can also use this written communication to ask employees to comment on the new and improved vision statement.

Test the Vision

Ask employees if the new vision effectively captures their personal visions for the organization. Pilot the vision, encouraging departments, work groups, or teams to use the vision to guide their decisions, then getting their feedback on how well the vision works. You may also want to invite key customers and suppliers to comment on it.

Finalize the Vision

The leaders and/or vision team make the last improvements to this version of the vision and publish it in its final form.

Implement the Vision

Implementing the vision goes beyond communication, although communication is a critical first step. Implementation means using the vision to align personal values with the organization's values and individual and group decisions with the vision's direction. It begins with communication.

■ COMMUNICATING THE SHARED VISION

"In a field view of organizations," Margaret Wheatley writes, "clarity about values or vision is important, but it's only half the task. Creating the field through the dissemination of those ideas is essential. The field must reach all corners of the organization, involve everyone, and be available everywhere. Vision statements move off the walls and into the corridors, seeking out every employee, every recess of the organization" (Wheatley 1992).

Marlow Industries' vision defines the company's fundamental purpose in seven areas. Ray Marlow makes it a point to review each of the areas at monthly employee meetings. Honeywell Solid State Electronics Center (SSEC) and Custom Research Inc. (CRI) both use a star symbol to communicate their visions and values.

SSEC calls it the "Quality Star," with each point representing a different value—customer, economic (shareholder), community, people (employee), and supplier—and all points linked by its "innovation value." It communicates its quality values through training, laminated pocket cards, newsletters, bulletin boards, management meetings, displays, communication meetings, and myriad informal ways.

The points on CRI's star represent results, requirements, relationships, processes, and people. At the center of the star is CRI's goal: *Surprising and Delighting Our Client Partners*. The star and the values it represents are prominently displayed throughout the company's offices, are reinforced in initial orientation, training, and company meetings, and appear on such things as Post-It notes and computer mouse pads.

Marlow, SSEC, and CRI make sure their shared visions reach every corner of their organizations. They practice four rules for communicating a shared vision:

➤ *Repeat* it often, using every opportunity to bring the vision to people's attention.

➤ *Clarify* what it means to you by expanding on one or more elements of the vision.

➤ *Discuss* it during meetings, asking others what it means to them, questioning whether decisions advance or weaken the vision.

➤ *Praise* and publicize those who put the vision into action.

■ ALIGNING PERSONAL VISIONS WITH SHARED VISION

Christopher Bartlett and Sumantra Ghoshal describe this process as converting "the contractual employees of an economic entity into committed members of a purposeful organization" (Bartlett and Ghoshal 1994). The commitment begins with employee involvement in creating a shared vision. It deepens as leaders and managers communicate the vision, as employees encounter it in newsletters, on bulletin boards, and during training, and as work groups, teams, and departments are recognized for acting in support of the vision. As Wheatley says, "All employees, in any part of the company, who bumped against that field would be influenced by it."

In an article in *Fortune* magazine, Jerre Stead, CEO of what was then AT&T Global Information Solutions, advised leaders to go beyond preaching the vision to managing it. "Measure your followers by their concrete progress toward realizing the vision, and insist that they do the same." GIS did this by linking all objectives to the organization's key results, which are customer or shareholder satisfaction and profitable growth. The key results support the division's vision (Stewart 1994). We'll talk more about aligning through measurement in Chapter 7.

An example of the power of such alignment comes from the Nature Conservancy. In an interview in *Harvard Business Review,* John Sawhill, who heads the organization, said, "People in this organization are deeply committed to its mission. They care about it; they think about it all the time. Fundamentally, it's what drives them. There is something about a nonprofit's mission that motivates people by closely aligning personal values with professional values." Sawhill sees a lesson here for profit-making organizations, and a benefit. "When mission comes first, people are more open to change: They accept changes that would probably cause a lot of anxiety if they weren't committed to the larger purpose" (Howard, Magretta, and Sawhill, 1995).

A shared vision is the servant-leader's most treasured tool, the only force with the power to connect everyone in the organization, focus all activities on a single goal, create a flatter and more flexible organization in which each person makes decisions that support the vision, and facilitate change. As Wheatley writes, "What leaders are called upon to do in a chaotic world is to shape their organizations through concepts, not through elaborate rules or structures." A shared vision is the collective conscience that sees an organization through the chaos.

■ THE SHARED VISIONS OF EXCELLENT ORGANIZATIONS

The shared visions of these six organizations provide a good cross-section of the different types and structures being used. As you will notice, they do not inspire awe in the reader, although they do inspire the people in the companies/divisions because they capture what those organizations are about. Typically, the clearer an organization is about its purpose in life and the more involved employees were in defining that purpose, the better the vision.

➤ Honeywell Solid State Electronics Center

SSEC acts on a set of values that have been in place since 1981. The division updated its values in 1994. The values are reinforced by SSEC's Quality Star (see above) and its goal of delighting customers.

What We Value

> ➤ **Integrity** and the highest ethical standards

> ➤ **Mutual respect** and trust in our working relationships

> ➤ **Communication** that is open, honest, consistent and two-way

➤ **Diversity** of people, cultures and ideas and acceptance of individual differences on teams

➤ **Innovation** and encouragement to challenge the status quo with creativity and new ideas

➤ **Continuous improvement,** development and learning in all we do

➤ **Teamwork** and meeting our commitments to one another

➤ **Performance** with recognition for results

➤ Marlow Industries

Marlow Industries defines its purpose through a corporate vision, its moral values through a code of conduct, and its direction through strategic goals.

Corporate Vision

➤ Provide thermoelectric products and services that will meet or exceed the **customers'** requirements, without exception

➤ Provide an environment that encourages our **employees** to achieve a high degree of productivity through job satisfaction

➤ Grow in revenues and net worth for the **shareholders** at a controlled rate demonstrating financial stability

➤ Maintain **market leadership** in the thermoelectric industry

➤ Remain the **technical leader** in thermoelectric cooling through continually advancing the state-of-the-art

➤ Maintain the highest **Code of Conduct** in all affairs

➤ Remain a dynamic corporation that is an asset to the **community**

➤ Custom Research Inc.

CRI's goal of "Surprising and Delighting Our Client Partners" is supported by principles that guide how CRI views its business, works with clients, and treats its staff. CRI has eight values that describe the environment of the company:

➤ Integrity
➤ Quality

➤ Profit
➤ Growth
➤ Professionalism
➤ Teamwork
➤ Innovation
➤ Recognition

➤ Wainwright Industries

Wainwright's mission statement is "Continuous Commitment to Our Customers' Future." The values supporting its mission are:

➤ Customer-driven quality
➤ Leadership
➤ Continuous improvement
➤ Full participation
➤ Fast response
➤ Environmental responsibility
➤ Design quality and prevention
➤ Long range outlook
➤ Management by fact
➤ Partnership development
➤ Public responsibility
➤ Stewardship

➤ Lyondell Petrochemical

Values for Excellence

"Our goal is to be the best in every business in which we participate while providing consistent high quality products and services that meet and fully satisfy our customers' requirements and needs. We will produce these products and services at the lowest cost while maximizing value for our shareholders.

"We will accomplish our goal through:

➤ Empowerment of all Lyondell employees
➤ Partner relationships with our customers and suppliers

➤ Innovation

➤ Integrity

➤ Continued improvement of our safety, health, and environmental performance

➤ Total quality management

➤ High equal opportunity standards

"We will succeed because maximizing every Lyondell employee's potential and clearly identifying our values will bring out the best in our resources—both people and processes."

➤ Granite Rock Company

Granite Rock Company's mission is to supply high quality goods and services to the construction industry with facilities that are within a 100-mile radius of Watsonville, California, at prices that are competitive, provide profits for reinvestment and growth, provide shareholders with a fair return on their investment, and provide opportunities for individual employee growth and development.

The company believes the following about the organization and its people:

1. The people in the organization are achievement oriented, unsatisfied with "things the way they are" when improvements are possible, and strive to increase their own skill and knowledge level to improve their ability to contribute.

2. The organization depends on having objectives and leadership that generate enthusiasm, confidence and a "can do" attitude in all areas of the corporation.

3. The organization shall conduct its affairs with uncompromising honesty and integrity. People at all levels of the organization are expected to adhere to the highest standards of business ethics.

4. We operate the company in an atmosphere of trust and belief in the individual's ability to do the best job possible. We do not operate the company in a "directive, order-giving style," but rather provide a set of corporate objectives from which business unit and individual objectives can be devel-

oped. After that each person is expected to desire the freedom and accompanying responsibility of implementing his/her individual objectives in ways he/she determines best.

Granite Rock then identifies corporate objectives for profit, customer satisfaction and service, financial performance and growth, management, community commitment, product quality assurance, people, production efficiency, and safety.

■ STRATEGIC THINKING

Strategic thinking shouldn't be confused with strategic planning. Strategic planning focuses on how the organization will achieve its vision. It is primarily an analysis of information to determine short- and long-term goals for the future and the development of plans to achieve those goals.

Strategic thinking explores who you are as an organization and who you want to be ten years down the road. It is primarily a synthesis of information to produce a profile of what an organization wants to become. Strategic thinking expands on the thinking that went into creating a shared vision. It reflects on the nature of the organization, its central challenges, the nature of the industry, the present and future requirements of customers, possible changes in technology, societal trends, governmental forces, economic forces, environmental forces, and other areas of influence. It helps leaders and other employees understand what is truly essential to the organization's survival and prosperity in a changing world.

Strategic thinking helps leaders step outside the box of unconscious, unquestioned assumptions that keeps them from anticipating threats to their survival or opportunities for prosperity. As Peter Schwartz writes in *The Art of the Long View,* "Each of us responds, not to the world, but to our image of the world." Strategic thinking helps us set aside the image and look at the world from a new perspective.

One of the best tools for developing this new perspective is the *scenario.* According to Schwartz, a scenario is "a tool for ordering one's perceptions about alternative future environments in which one's decisions might be played out." Scenarios are the "what if's" of strategic thinking:

➤ What if your business stays the same but your company gets better?

➤ What if your business changes fundamentally, but your company still gets better?

➤ What if everything goes to hell?

Scenarios are stories that contain your answers to those questions. You can then use those stories to recognize and adapt to changes in your business. "In the real world, you don't know ahead of time which scenario will take place," Schwartz writes. "But you prepare for all three, and then train yourself to look for one or two small details so that you can recognize the full play before you're called upon to act." None of the scenarios will unfold exactly as you see it. The goal of strategic thinking and scenario writing is not to predict the future, but to anticipate it. In the process of pondering the future, you will gain a clearer picture of your company's current strengths and areas for improvement, discover opportunities you had not considered, and add layers of depth to your strategic plans.

■ WRITING SCENARIOS

Scenario writing is most effective when done in teams. The many forces and uncertainties that will affect your organization's future cannot be identified by one person. You may want to form several teams with the same mission. In *Whole System Architecture,* Lawrence Miller recommends ten groups of ten people who understand your business, asserting that the common elements in their scenarios "will be as reliable as any predictions you can get anywhere."

As with the creation of a shared vision, scenario writing will benefit from broad and diverse participation. You may want to extend an open invitation to any employee who feels he or she has something to contribute to the process. Knowledge of an industry and of the forces shaping it is often richest among those employees who interact with customers, suppliers, new technologies, competitors, and regulatory agencies.

There are seven steps to thinking strategically by writing scenarios:

1. Assess the current situation.
2. Identify key uncertainties and driving forces.
3. Rank by importance.
4. Develop tentative scenarios.
5. Explore the implications of each scenario.
6. Identify critical issues for immediate attention.
7. Develop strategic responses for future possibilities.

Assess the Current Situation

Before your can think about the future, you need a clear and accurate picture of the present. The best instrument for performing this assessment is the criteria used for the Malcolm Baldrige National Quality Award. The criteria cover every element of a management system, including:

➤ *Leadership:* how senior executives are personally involved in leading the organization's customer focus and quality improvement; how a shared vision is developed and communicated.

➤ *Information and analysis:* how the organization decides what information to collect and use; how information and data are analyzed; how the organization uses benchmarking to improve.

➤ *Strategic planning:* how the organization conducts planning; what its short- and long-term plans are.

➤ *Human resources:* how the organization builds high performance work systems; how training is promoted; how employee satisfaction is improved.

➤ *Process management:* how products and services are designed to meet customer requirements; how processes are improved; how supplier products/services are improved.

➤ *Results:* how effective the organization's approaches have been.

➤ *Customer focus and satisfaction:* how the organization determines customer requirements and satisfaction; how it manages customer relationships; how well it satisfies customers.

I outlined a process for using the criteria to assess your management system in my first book, *The Baldrige Quality System* (George 1992). I strongly encourage you to send for a free copy of the current criteria and to involve senior leadership in the assessment process.

To satisfy your immediate needs for a "snapshot" of your current situation, I've streamlined the Baldrige assessment into an organizational analysis presented in Appendix A. The analysis includes guidelines for using your findings for scenario writing, identifying strengths and areas for improvement, and developing action plans.

Whichever form of assessment you choose, you will need to base it on the highest quality information. The assessment is only as accurate, and therefore as useful, as the accuracy of the information upon which it is based.

Identify Key Uncertainties and Driving Forces

It's crystal ball time. As a team, you want to root out every possible issue, trend, movement, innovation, action, and development that could influence your organization in the future.

For our purposes, a *key uncertainty* is the potential for an unexpected change in an important area. For a company that makes parts for use in an automobile, an unexpected change might be a shortage of oil, the availability of a new metal, or the public perception that a car should never cost more than $20,000.

A *driving force* is a force that influences the outcome of events. The same auto parts maker might identify a driving force as OPEC, innovations in metallurgy, or interest rates.

To prepare for the first brainstorming meeting on key uncertainties and driving forces, each team member should consider how each of the following could affect your business in the future:

➤ New technologies
➤ New or changing customer requirements
➤ Global forces
➤ Changes in public perceptions
➤ Current or potential environmental issues
➤ Regulatory issues

➤ Competitive developments (i.e., innovations, alliances, strategies)

➤ Economic issues

You can find information about these issues from a variety of sources, including industry conferences and publications, business magazines, books, association memberships, personal networks, television, and radio. Schwartz gets his ideas from unconventional thinkers, sources of surprise (such as books on nonbusiness subjects), magazines, music, fringe movements, and his travels. The more people you involve in this early brainstorming process, the more information from different sources that will be available.

When the team gathers, encourage participants to share their ideas on each of the subjects listed above. Do not judge, dismiss, label, or prioritize. Understand that the filters that help you make sense of the world around you also inhibit your ability to see other realities or imagine other futures.

Rank by Importance

As a team, sort through the lists created in the previous step to identify which driving forces and uncertainties would have the greatest impact on your organization. Select the top two or three.

Develop Tentative Scenarios

Using the assessment from step one, the top two or three driving forces and key uncertainties from steps two and three, and other factors the team feels are relevant to any scenario for the future, create written scenarios in narrative form around the answers to these three questions:

➤ What if our business stays the same but our organization gets better?

➤ What if our business changes fundamentally, but our organization still gets better?

➤ What if everything goes to hell?

You may want to rephrase these questions or explore different questions as you attempt to anticipate the likely directions your industry and organization may go. The goal is to end up with approximately three very different scenarios built on the same driving forces and key uncertainties, influenced by factors such as technology, economic, political, and social drivers; competitors' strengths and weaknesses, behaviors, and strategies; internal strengths and weaknesses, behaviors, and constraints, and human resource and technical capabilities.

Schwartz identifies three common plots in the scenarios being written today (in bold) and other, spicier plots he finds illuminating:

> ➤ **Winners and losers,** characterized by conflict, covert alliances, and conspiracies.
>
> ➤ **Challenge and response,** characterized by step-by-step successes, learning, and compromise.
>
> ➤ **Evolution,** characterized by slower change and resistance to sudden challenges.
>
> ➤ *Revolution,* characterized by sudden, unpredictable change.
>
> ➤ *Cycles,* characterized by repeating cycles of feast and famine.
>
> ➤ *Infinite possibility,* characterized by the perception that the world will expand and improve forever.
>
> ➤ *The lone ranger,* characterized by a belief that *our* way is the only way to succeed.
>
> ➤ *My generation,* characterized by the influence of a particular generation.

Whatever plots your team chooses, keep the focus on the external forces and uncertainties that, if they occur, will strongly affect your organization. Do not rank the scenarios or try to pick which one you think is most likely to take place. The purpose of strategic thinking is not to predict the future, but to anticipate it.

Explore the Implications

For each scenario, discuss as a team what it means for the future of your organization. Debate the positive and negative implications. Consider how it affects the critical issues or decisions your company currently faces. Walk through the chronology of each scenario, pausing at points along the way to think about the condition of your organization at that point and the issues you may be facing.

As you explore the implications of each scenario, identify any indicators or signposts that will warn you that the future is unfolding according to a particular scenario. The indicators could be changes in public perceptions, technology, the competitive environment, global markets, or any area with the power to redirect your organization and/or your industry. Naming signposts is the real value of thoughtful, fact-based scenarios: They can give you the lead time you need to succeed in a changing world, no matter how dramatically or unexpectedly it changes.

Identify Critical Issues for Immediate Attention

It is possible your scenarios will reveal critical issues facing your organization right now. These issues and the information supporting them should be fed into your strategic planning process, which can prioritize them, develop action plans and goals, and assign resources. For a complete discussion of the strategic planning process, see Chapter 8.

Develop Strategic Responses for Future Possibilities

Based on the scenarios and their implications, senior leadership can list the possibilities the organization may face and develop strategies that respond to them. The strategies will surely need to be revised and expanded if they are needed, but developing them early allows the organization to act quickly when an indicator or signpost is encountered.

Strategies for the future tend to focus on serving customers in three areas:

➤ The benefits of new and/or improved products or services that customers may require or want in the future

➤ Core competencies your organization will need in order to deliver those benefits

➤ Changes in relationships with customers that allow them to receive the benefits

In the process of developing strategic responses, you may recognize the opportunity to build a key advantage or capability that will give your organization the edge in most or all of the scenarios you have written.

■ FOUR SCENARIOS FROM A QUALITY PERSPECTIVE

In 1995, the American Society for Quality Control (ASQC) decided to use scenario planning to look at where quality is heading. An eighteen-person team met over a period of six months to develop four scenarios of the year 2010.

The team identified nine key forces it believes will drive change:

> ➤ Changing values, such as environmentalism, drug use, wealth distribution, ethnic nationalism, and employee/employer loyalty
> ➤ Globalization, including the growth of world-spanning organizations, the influence of China and India, and the expansion of liberal democracy
> ➤ Changing makeup of the workforce, including increased immigration and age shifts
> ➤ Information revolution
> ➤ Velocity of change
> ➤ Increased customer focus
> ➤ Leadership
> ➤ Quality in new areas
> ➤ Change in quality practices

The team then developed four scenarios describing possible outcomes for the year 2010. Each of the four is summarized below, written as if they have already occurred, with a focus on the impact on quality professionals (American Society for Quality Control 1996).

> **Global Reality,** the first scenario, is an extension of current issues and opportunities, and was thought to be the most likely prospect:
>
> The years between 1996 and 2010 were prosperous, not only in North America but also around the world, espe-

cially among the developed countries. The most obvious changes were the new technologies, products, and services spawned by the information revolution. Understanding and influencing systems behavior in social, business, and process areas has become critical. Information technology continues to drive great change for all, and mass customization is the rule. Despite rapid growth, the gulf between the "haves" and the "have nots" has widened, for both individuals and nations. By 2010, quality has become ubiquitous in manufacturing and widely deployed in multiple service areas and government. The great accomplishment of the quality field was the development of new concepts, methods, and tools for demassified quality control, or the "customization of quality" that emphasizes service. Quality experts helped to design production systems that automated many quality control functions. In essence, they have nearly put themselves out of business.

Hard Times, the second scenario, presents a gloomier forecast:

Due to a failure of leadership to identify convergent, synergistic opportunities, society in 2010 is in a state of near-collapse. The poor, functionally illiterate, unemployed, immigrant, and minority population, confined to drug-plagued inner cities, confronts an affluent upper class. The well-educated, multiskilled professionals and managers with high incomes live in barricaded communities with extensive security or hide away in remote areas. Economic growth is sluggish, and politicians argue endlessly about why. Deforestation has brought about the spread of deserts and soil erosion. The collapse of fisheries, conflicts over limited water supplies, and other environmental problems are undermining the economies of many developing countries. Ethnic nationalism breeds countless bloody conflicts, ranging from local tribal battles to large-scale, regional warfare. Quality practice has diminished as the need for survival now dominates most thinking and action. Where it does exist, it is often for appearances sake, but lacks real substance. In the worst case, it is deployed in criminal organizations where quality professionals now use quality to "do things better" while failing to "do the right thing."

Mixed Bag combines many positive advances globally, but predicts an economic downturn in North America:

In the fast-paced global marketplace of 2010, virtually every market is open to increased competition, made possible by error-free products and services. Global restructuring has changed living standards. In nations that were emerging in 1996, new factories and homes are now appearing daily, attesting to these countries' success in delivering high quality at lower costs than their North America competitors. The result is that most American workers spend fewer hours on the job, and some capable individuals have been laid off and unable to find work. In an effort to address the needs of its people, the United States has once again created escalating national debt. Quality pervades society, and has become a driver in the public sector, education, and health care. In the field of quality itself, "deep niche" specialists remain, and in fact, prosper. However, the overall number of quality specialists has declined, as the number of knowledgeable generalists has grown.

Designer Nation is the world where everything comes together:

The country emerged from a difficult restructuring with a sense of pride and accomplishment. Trust has been restored in the government, as reforms have eliminated many abuses. Achieving society-wide consensus on national issues has led to improved public policy. The center of power now resides in communities rather than the state or federal government, resulting in reduced costs. Enlightened tax reform has resulted in a distribution of wealth that is less painful, as well as more effective and efficient. The economy is strong; quality-driven processes throughout society have dramatically increased the production of wealth. Families now need only one wage-earner. The size of the work force has decreased to 100 million, and some 70 million additional people are now comfortably able to participate in not-for-profit or avocational activities with little or no pay. Health care and education systems have become much more effective in delivering upon their promises, and access to both is now inexpensive and open to all. As medical problems have been successfully resolved, the senior generation enjoys longer life expectancy—with the emphasis on "enjoys." Cities are now safer, pleasanter places to live and work, and the land is green and abundant. The quality sciences have become universal, and are now the accepted approach for dealing with change. Quality now plays a significant role in strategy development, and the profession both provides and applies new tools in this effort. At the unit operations level of both public and private organizations, knowledge of quality is widespread. It is used daily by virtually everyone.

■ LINKING VISION AND STRATEGIES

Strategic thinking and a shared vision provide clarity in a complex world. The vision gives everyone a destination without telling them exactly how to get there. Leading by shared vision means trusting employees (who are empowered, trained, rewarded, and recognized, as we'll discuss in the next chapter) to use the vision to guide their decisions. It makes flatter, faster, more flexible organizations possible by connecting the actions of every employee to a unifying vision without restricting those actions by voluminous rules and tight controls.

Strategic thinking keeps the vision alive by compelling the organization to look outside itself. It frames the vision in the context of what customers will want in the future, how competitors will respond, and how other forces will influence the organization. The shared vision is the destination; strategic thinking produces more than one route to get there. Both vision and strategies are necessary to help the organization master change.

■ STRATEGIES FOR IMPROVEMENT

➤ Jump Start

➤ If you don't have a shared vision, create one. Follow the seven steps in this chapter to involve people in developing the vision.

➤ Revisit the vision. If you have a vision everyone ignores, what good is it? Revisiting the vision is an opportunity to energize the organization, to promote participation, and to unite everyone in a common quest. Follow the seven steps.

➤ Live the vision. Take it off the walls and translate it into daily actions, weekly reviews, monthly measures, and annual goals. Evaluate what you do by asking whether or not it contributes to the vision. Invite those who report to you to do the same. Cascade this process throughout the organization.

➤ Begin to think about the context of your vision: what your customers may require in five or ten years; how your competitors will change; what other forces will influence your company. Gather information from industry and trade publications, business magazines, and other sources to initiate this strategic thinking.

➤ Tune Up

➤ Push the shared vision to every corner of the organization. Repeat it often at every opportunity. Clarify what it means to you, either all of it or elements of it. Discuss it at meetings, training sessions, workshops, conferences, lunches, and any other time groups of employees are gathered. Praise those who live the vision, publicly and often.

➤ Write scenarios that anticipate the major changes that may occur in your industry. Follow the seven-step process described in this chapter.

➤ Explore the implications of your scenarios. What critical issues do they raise for your organization right now? How will you know when your industry is traveling along the path defined by a particular scenario? What can you do to put your organization in the strongest position no matter which scenario is played out?

➤ Pull Away

➤ Align plans and performance with the shared vision. Excellent companies identify goals and objectives that move the company closer to achieving its vision. They then align the activities of all divisions, departments, teams, and individuals with the goals and objectives, thus aligning them with the vision.

➤ Develop and implement key indicators of performance on the shared vision. An effective vision can be translated into goals and objectives and into measures of performance. Identify those measures and short- and long-term goals for each. Review them at every senior management meeting. Have divisions, departments, teams, and individuals identify measures of their performance that support the organization's measures. For more on this process, see Chapter 7.

➤ Develop strategies that respond to the possibilities generated by scenario writing. As your industry changes, you will pull away from the competition if you are first to anticipate and take advantage of the changes.

Engage Employees

It's important for each person to have as much responsibility as they want and can handle. Every type of responsibility, including profit responsibility, should be placed as far down the organization as possible. Everyone working with clients has the authority to speak for CRI and commit the company's resources to getting the client's projects done.

Engaging employees is about respect, trust, and responsibility. In organizations where employees are engaged in achieving a shared vision, people treat each other with respect, no matter what positions they hold. They trust each other to do what needs to be done without being ordered, supervised, or threatened. People take responsibility for handling what's in front of them, for making improvements every day, for learning and growing. Because of respect, trust, and responsibility, people are free to act according to their shared vision for the organization. As Ira Chaleff writes in *The Courageous Follower,* they "trust themselves, and are trusted by the organization, to be interpreters of the organization's values when applying a rule to a specific circumstance."

Without respect, trust, and responsibility, you cannot engage employees in any long-term effort to make your organization stronger, more flexible, more customer-focused, or more profitable. Without respect, trust, and responsibility, an organization is a sweatshop in which employees endure work in order to support their "real" lives outside of work. Intel's David Marsing, who manages the largest microprocessor fabrication plant in the world, puts it this way: "As far as I'm concerned, having to change your life when you arrive at work each morning is tantamount to slavery" (Malone 1995).

Yet changing your life is exactly what many companies expect. People who are trusted and respected members of their families and communities outside of work, who are responsible for raising children, choosing political leaders, obeying laws, and supporting social and religious organizations, are treated as slaves at work. They are expected to do their jobs without question. They are not trusted to complete tasks without supervision. They are ridiculed, abused, and threatened. They are given minimal responsibility, then told exactly how to carry out that responsibility.

Not that the chains of slavery are always so overt. For many companies, mistrust and disrespect permeate their cultures to such a degree that they *are* the culture. Here's one example from Brian Joiner's book, *Fourth Generation Management*. A company had a bereavement policy that stipulated exactly how much time an employee could miss work for a death in the immediate family. It defined immediate family. It specified when the time could be taken. It set the limit at three days. Not surprisingly, the average amount of bereavement time taken by the company's employees was 2.98 days.

The company changed its policy to one sentence: "If you need time off due to the death of a close relative or friend, please notify your supervisor." The bereavement time taken dropped to 1.57 days. As Joiner concludes, " 'Close the loophole' thinking, always defining more and more limits, is inherently flawed and will only drain your organization's energy. Trust and working toward the ideal is far better."

Custom Research Inc. trusts its employees, and it puts that trust in writing. The paragraph at the beginning of this chapter is one of the company's principles, written in 1977. It engages every employee in working toward the company's ideal, which is to surprise and delight its clients.

And it does this quite well. CRI is a marketing research company of about 100 full-time and 125 part-time employees. All but eight of its full-time people and all of its part-time people work directly on clients' projects, leaving only eight employees in support departments such as Human Resources and Accounting.

Every full-time CRI employee is on one of two teams: an account team, which has full responsibility for clients' research projects, or a support department team, which has full responsibility for improving quality and performance in its department. The company's organization chart reflects the company's focus: clients at the top, served by eight account teams, which are served by the Steering Committee, support departments, and part-time employees.

The employees take their responsibilities very seriously. A 1993 survey asked employees if they cared about doing a good job. Ninety-nine percent of full-time employees and 94 percent of part-time employees responded favorably.

The value of their commitment can be seen in the satisfaction of their clients. CRI sits down with each client before a project begins and defines the client's expectations for that project. After the project is completed, CRI asks the client to rate its satisfaction. In 1995, nearly 100 percent of its projects met or exceeded the clients' expectations—and 67 percent were in the "exceeded expectations" category.

The value of its employees' commitment can also be seen in CRI's productivity and profitability: Revenue per full-time employee is nearly 40 percent greater than its closest competitor, and the company's operating profit is twice the industry average.

Other elements contribute to its success, including strong leadership and well-managed processes, but CRI excels because of its people. They are fully engaged in surprising and delighting clients.

In contrast, many organizations foster an environment that promotes disengagement by creating fear among employees. Fear is a natural response to the kinds of crushing behavior rampant in most organizations. It is a cancer that saps commitment, kills motivation, ruins confidence, and inhibits imagination. You may recognize the presence of fear in these typical reactions of employees:

➤ I just had my credibility questioned.

➤ I wasn't asked to help make an important decision.

➤ I was criticized in front of my peers.

➤ I don't get the information I need to do my job.

➤ I wasn't given a plum assignment.

➤ I disagreed, and it has hurt our relationship.

➤ I'm stuck in a dead-end job.

➤ I don't get the recognition I deserve.

➤ I know I'm going to get fired.

You may also notice fear in the negative attitudes of employees:

➤ I have no intention of doing any more than I'm told.

➤ I never admit to making a mistake and I hide them when-ever possible.

➤ I don't care if we're over budget or late.

➤ I don't take risks.

➤ I have no idea what I should work on first.

Fear is the biggest obstacle to engaging employees. It stops an organization from building trust and respect. It discourages employees from taking responsibility. It subverts all attempts to transform an organization from an autocratic, hierarchical, product-focused business to a democratic, horizontal, customer-focused organization. Driving fear out of the workplace is the first step to engaging employees in the transformation. Chapter 2 iden-tifies seven strategies you can use to reduce fear in your organi-zation.

Another obstacle to engaging employees is the anxiety and frustration caused by asking fewer employees to achieve ever higher goals. The popular rush to downsize rarely slows long enough to look at how work is getting done and how it could be done more efficiently. Instead, companies lay people off, then assign their work to the employees who remain. According to one study, 40 percent of the major U.S. companies with layoffs in 1994 increased employees' hours or their overtime after employees were laid off (New survey tracks layoffs 1995). Another survey of more than 900 downsized U.S. companies found that 74 percent of the companies' leaders thought that morale, trust, and productivity had suffered. A third survey found that 71 percent of the companies involved in downsizing did so to increase productivity, but only 22 percent of those companies thought that goal had been achieved (Downsizing 1995).

Downsizing may be a quick fix for disappointing profits, but the aftermath erodes efficiency and sabotages any attempt to engage employees in transforming the organization. Fearful of losing their jobs, employees exhibit a siege mentality, avoiding risks, withholding ideas, and staying within the narrowest definition of their jobs. No company can become flexible, fast, high quality, and customer focused when its people are preoccupied with holding onto their jobs.

At the same time that companies are downsizing—or threatening to downsize—they are asking people to meet significantly higher goals. "Most organizations don't have a clue about how to manage stretch goals," says Steve Kerr, chief learning officer at General Electric. "It's popular today for companies to ask their people to double sales or increase speed to market threefold. But then they don't provide their people with the knowledge, tools, and means to meet such ambitious goals" (Stretch goals 1995).

To meet these goals, Kerr says, "people use the only resource that's not constrained, which is their personal time. I think that's immoral. People are under tremendous stress." Stress blocks change. It prevents employees from being proactive, innovative, motivated, and responsible. Combined with the fear of losing their jobs and the everyday fears caused by mistrust and disrespect, the anxiety caused by unrealistic goals creates an oppressive workplace. A sweatshop. A place that requires you to change your life at the door in order to survive. And that is wrong.

■ WHAT IS A HIGH-PERFORMANCE EMPLOYEE?

Before you can begin to develop a culture of trust, respect, and responsibility, you need a clear picture of what a high-performance employee would look like *in your organization.* Few companies take the time to think about the attributes of the ideal employee, the knowledge needed, the behaviors required, the attitudes valued. Instead, an organization hires new people based on narrow job definitions, trains for specific skills, and passes along attitudes through on-the-job encounters. They end up with a fractured culture, frequent turnover, average productivity or worse, and an inability to sustain long-term, positive change.

The value of high-performance employees has been quantified in a study by the *Journal of Applied Psychology.* The study compared the productivity of the top 1 percent of all performers in a range of organizations with average performers and the bottom 1 percent performers in the same organizations. If you have any doubts about the value of developing high-performance employees, consider the survey's results:

➤ In low-complexity jobs, top performers were 50 percent more productive than average performers and 300 percent more productive than low performers.

➤ In medium-complexity jobs, top performers were 85 percent more productive than average performers and 1,200 percent more productive than low performers.

➤ In high-complexity jobs, top performers were 125 percent more productive than average performers and immeasurably better than low performers (Grant and Schlesinger 1995).

High-performance employees enjoy autonomy and self-expression. They are self-motivated and self-directed, assuming responsibility and authority eagerly. They devise and implement solutions, then make improvements until they get it right. They own their work and the results they produce. They feel satisfied with their jobs, and that satisfaction has a positive impact on other employees and on customers.

A study by Bain & Company of trucking clients found that the truckers could increase profits by 50 percent if they cut driver turnover in half. The study found a direct link between employee retention and the retention and acquisition of customers. In the car service business, it discovered that outlets with the highest employee retention also had the best customer retention. How important is customer retention? According to Bain & Company, a 5 percent increase in customer retention rates can increase profits by 25 to 80 percent.

The creation of a high-performance organization relies on high-performance employees, and the development of high-performance employees begins with a precise definition of that employee for your organization. To develop this definition, consider the following questions:

➤ For each of our short- and long-term goals and plans, what employee skills and behaviors are or will be required to achieve them?

➤ For each of our core processes, what employee skills and behaviors are or will be required to deliver customer value through them?

➤ To become the kind of organization we must be to compete and prosper, what employee skills and behaviors are or will be required?

➤ To complement and support these skills and behaviors, what attitudes among our employees would we value?

Before you try to answer these questions, you may want to review the planning process in Chapter 8 and the management of core processes in Chapter 6. The chapters help you explore where your organization is today and how you can improve tomorrow. In the course of this exploration, you will learn more about the qualities your workforce will need to possess.

As you answer the questions, list the skills, behaviors, and attitudes you will want in a high-performance employee. The list should also reflect your organization's culture. For example, CRI's eight values, which were developed by the Steering Committee and a task force of sixteen employees, defines the behaviors of all employees: integrity, quality, profit, growth, professionalism, teamwork, innovation, and recognition. Honeywell Solid State Electronics values integrity, mutual respect, communication, diversity, innovation, continuous improvement, teamwork, and performance.

Your list will suggest what you need to do to engage employees in creating a high-performance organization. No two lists will be identical, but most lists will share similar attributes, as CRI's and Honeywell SSEC's lists do. To compete today and into the future, companies must be flatter, more flexible, and more customer focused. This requires employees who feel empowered to make decisions and take responsibility for them, who work well in teams, who are eager to learn, and who are compensated, rewarded, and recognized for their contributions. The rest of this chapter describes how you can develop an organization of high-performance employees.

■ RELEASING POWER THROUGH EMPOWERMENT

Nordstrom department stores are famous for their customer service. Employees seem to have no limits on what they can do to help you, perhaps because the store's employee handbook is one page long. It has one rule: "Use your own good judgment in all situations." How many organizations have cultures that can support such freedom? Does yours?

This single rule illustrates the nature of empowerment. It has never been about increasing the power of employees. Empowerment means releasing the power employees already have, the power inherent in their knowledge, skills, and experience, the power that enables them to use their own good judgment.

In an empowered organization, each employee knows what his or her roles and responsibilities are. Each employee has subsidiarity, which means they have power because they are closest to the action. Employees are given—and assume—responsibility for activities and decisions in their areas. They know the essential core of their jobs and the limits of their discretion. They are willing to initiate action without being told to do so. They acquire the knowledge and information they need to do their jobs, when they need them. They are rewarded and recognized for their contributions. They are active participants in every activity that is essential to the organization's success, including planning, process management, information analysis, quality improvement, customer service and satisfaction, and operational performance.

Such empowerment is rare, suggesting that any organization able to engage employees in a shared vision significantly improves its competitive position. According to a study of 279 of the U.S.'s 1,000 largest manufacturing and service companies by the University of Southern California School of Business Administration's Center for Effective Organizations, 37 percent of employees do not participate in any employee involvement activities. Only 10 percent of employees are engaged in the approaches to participatory management described in this book. Comparisons between companies that share power (40–60 percent employee involvement) and those that don't (20 percent or less involved) found that the companies with more employee involvement consistently outperformed the companies with less employee involvement on a range of measures (Report finds that managers 1995).

Organizations that empower employees perform better than those that don't. Engaging employees is a basic of business excellence.

Companies like Lyondell, CRI, and others featured in this book engage employees individually and collectively. Employees act on the same rule that guides Nordstrom's employees, to use their own good judgment in all situations. Individually, each employee understands that he or she possesses the personal power to take responsibility, serve, challenge, and lead. Their power exists apart from their leaders; each acts independently toward a shared vision.

In his book *The Courageous Follower,* Ira Chaleff lists the sources of an employee's power:

➤ The power of purpose

➤ The power of knowledge

➤ The power of personal history

➤ The power of faith in yourself

➤ The power of relationships

➤ The power to speak the truth

➤ The power to set a standard that influences others

➤ The power to choose how to react in a situation

➤ The power to follow or not to follow

Not everyone feels powerful, especially in situations where they've never had much authority or responsibility. And not everyone wants to be empowered. Empowerment is not as simple as throwing a switch. Employees need to understand the limits of their authority, the nature of their responsibilities, and the criteria by which their performance will be measured. They need to be reminded of the power that resides within them, the power inherent in each item on the list above. They need time to accept and grow into their new roles. And they need to be motivated to exercise the power within them.

You can begin to develop an empowered workforce with the following steps:

1. *Embrace empowerment as a key business strategy.*   Lyondell Petrochemical states that it will accomplish its goal through "empowerment of all Lyondell employees." CEO Bob Gower is quick to point out that the company achieves low cost, high flexibility, and operational excellence through empowerment. "You can only have empowerment if the top person makes the decision to have it," he says. And you can only empower people if you sincerely trust and believe in their ability to act responsibly.

2. *Drive out fear.*   Work on reducing fear through the strategies described in Chapter 2.

3. *Teach managers and supervisors how to encourage participation.*   Lyondell teaches all managers and supervisors how to involve employees during a two-day course, "Managing the Lyondell Way."

4. *Teach employees how to take responsibility.*   "It's not a natural instinct for people," Bob Gower observes, "so we have to train them in how to accept responsibility."

5. *Make needed information easily accessible.*   In 1954, Peter Drucker wrote in *The Practice of Management* that an employee needs enough information to "control, measure, and guide his own performance." More recently, Christopher Bartlett and Sumantra Ghoshal wrote that executives "now realize that they must ensure that all employees have access to information as a vital organizational resource" (Bartlett and Ghoshal 1995). Chapter 7 looks at how to get information in the hands of employees who need it.

6. *Communicate and support.*   As trust grows, empowerment grows. You build trust through constant and consistent communication about the value of empowerment and support of those who act empowered. Talk about taking responsibility at every meeting. Cite examples within your organization. Describe what empowerment means to you and to the organization. Ask what is keeping people from accepting responsibility and act to remove the obstacles.

7. *Align compensation, rewards, and recognition.*   Although the concept isn't difficult, the execution often falters because of traditional thinking about who gets paid for what. The concept is: Pay, reward, and recognize employees who assume responsibility for their jobs, processes, team activities, decisions, and results. Traditionally, nonexecutives are paid for performing a list of tasks, not for their total contribution to the organization. Empowered employees quickly become cynical when they are expected to take on more responsibility without being compensated for it. As you develop a plan for engaging employees, review your compensation, reward, and recognition programs to make sure they support empowerment.

■ ENGAGING EMPLOYEES THROUGH TEAMS

You cannot talk about high-performance companies without talking about high-performance teams. In a 1994 industry report by *Training* magazine, 44 percent of the 2,300 companies responding to the survey said they were making the transition to a team-based structure. And 69 percent are giving their employees team-building training.

Companies such as Custom Research Inc. and Lyondell Petrochemical function through teams. The team is their basic unit of performance. They engage employees in the work of their companies by empowering them individually and collectively, in teams. They turn to teams because the demands for faster, better, and cheaper exceed the abilities of any one person and the capabilities of larger organizational groups.

According to the gurus of teaming, Jon Katzenbach and Douglas Smith, a team is a small number of people (2–20) with complementary skills who are committed to a common purpose, specific performance goals, and a common approach for which they hold themselves mutually accountable. The small number of people makes a team more flexible than a department or other large group. The common purpose and specific goals make it more productive than work groups. The complementary skills bring a significant force to bear on a single issue or process. As a result, companies that function through teams move faster and deliver higher quality at a competitive price (Katzenbach and Smith 1993). They realize the benefits of teams:

➤ *Flexibility.* Teams can be quickly assembled, deployed, refocused, and disbanded.

➤ *Productivity.* Teams are committed to delivering tangible performance results.

➤ *Speed.* Teams reduce the time it takes to get things done.

➤ *Complexity.* Teams improve an organization's ability to solve complex problems.

➤ *Customer focus.* Teams focus the organization's resources on meeting customers' needs.

➤ *Creativity.* Teams increase the organization's creative capacity.

➤ *Organization learning.* Team members are more easily able to develop new skills, learn other disciplines, and understand how to work with all kinds of people.

➤ *Single point of contact.* Teams provide one point of contact for customers and one source of information about a project or program.

A lot of companies say they have teams when what they really have are work groups. A work group reflects the hierarchical structure of the organization: strong leader, individual accountability, individual work products, and a focus on discussing, deciding, and delegating. By contrast, teams have shared leadership roles, individual and mutual accountability, collective work products, and a focus on discussing, deciding, and doing the work together. Work groups are not inherently bad, just as teams are not always good.

High-performance companies use different types of teams for different purposes. Empowered individuals pull together ad hoc teams as needed to solve urgent, onetime problems. Formal, longer-term teams tend to come in two flavors: cross-functional and self-directed.

A cross-functional team consists of individuals from different functional groups who bring to the team knowledge and skills that no single individual possesses. Cross-functional teams are formed to address a particular process, issue, or problem and are disbanded when their work is completed.

A self-directed team is an intact group of employees responsible for an entire work process or self-contained segment of a process. They are responsible not only for getting their work done but also for managing themselves. Although recent media coverage makes self-directed teams seem very new, the concept has been around since the 1920s. Ten years ago, Toyota already had 5,800 self-directed teams in place.

Companies form cross-functional teams to solve problems that cut across functional boundaries, to improve processes, to design products and services, to serve specific clients or markets, and to address other opportunities that will benefit from the pooling of diverse knowledge and experience. Cross-functional teams may exist for as long as it takes to solve a complex problem, which is rarely less than a few months, or for a period of years. CRI's account teams have been in place for several years, although team membership may change annually. Lyondell Petrochemical has three types of cross-functional teams: quality breakthrough teams, which resolve quality opportunities or problems; quality improvement teams, which direct and implement process improvements; and business teams, which help run the business.

Some companies certify their cross-functional teams to make sure they work on problems or processes that contribute to the organization's goals. The certification process requires the proposed team to submit a document identifying the name of the team, its members, the team leader, the issue the team will address, how the issue promotes one or more of the organization's strategic goals, possible measures of the team's progress and success, a tentative timeline for completion, and a team champion, which is an executive or manager one level higher than the team members who is responsible for the team's results. In many cases, the certified teams must periodically report on their progress to the organization's executive leadership.

Companies form self-directed work teams to hand over nearly all responsibility to those doing the work. As the authors of *Self-Directed Work Teams* describe them, "Work teams plan, set priorities, organize, coordinate with others, measure, and take corrective action—all once considered the exclusive province of supervisors and managers. They solve problems, schedule and assign work, and in many cases handle personnel issues like absenteeism or even team member selection and evaluation. To make sure this happens smoothly, each team member receives extensive training in the administrative, interpersonal, and technical skills required to maintain a self-managing group" (Orsburn, Moran, Musselwhite, and Zenger 1990).

While self-directed teams sound ideal, especially for organizations that want to get rid of layers of management, they don't work for every organization. First, *they cannot coexist with fear and mistrust.* If senior leaders are not personally committed to the idea of self-direction, don't bother with self-directed teams. If employees do not trust management, don't bother. If people hesitate to take risks, don't bother. If information is hoarded and not shared, don't bother. If you're not going to give team members the time, resources, and training to make their team work, don't bother. You must have a culture of empowerment in place—or at least an honest commitment to it—for a self-directed team to thrive.

Second, *self-directed teams won't work if employees hate the concept.* Team members must be willing to learn and practice human resources skills such as hiring, disciplining, recognizing, and evaluating other team members. "We've found that nonmanagers don't want to be self-directed outside their own jobs," says Mike Simms, plant manager for Wainwright Industries. "They do not want to get involved in making HR decisions about their peers in public. So we don't believe in self-directed work teams." Wainwright *does* believe in fully supported cross-functional teams, of which it has many.

Third, *self-directed teams fail when managers interfere with their operation*. Managers who are used to making critical decisions, controlling their work group's agenda, judging performance, and ordering people to act may resist their new roles as coaches, facilitators, teachers, and support people. Just as team members must be willing to accept broader responsibilities and trained in how to do that, managers must be willing to accept different responsibilities and must be trained to carry them out. And all must be supported during the transition to their new roles.

■ THE TRANSITION TO TEAMS

As with any major change in how you run your business, the transition to teams requires four key elements:

> ➤ *A supportive corporate culture* allows the team to focus on its goals without worrying about power struggles and other political problems. You can begin to develop a supportive culture by following the steps presented in the previous section. While you may also want to dismantle a hierarchical management structure (see Chapter 2), experts are split on whether hierarchy helps or hurts teams. What is more certain is that a culture focused on strong performance standards tends to produce more effective teams.

> ➤ *Training* prepares executives, managers, supervisors, and other employees for the new roles and skills that a team-based organization demands. Books such as *The Team Handbook* by Peter Scholtes provide exercises in team building, quality tools, process improvement, and productive meetings.

> ➤ *Patience* gives teams the time they need to hit their stride. Teams typically go through four stages: forming, storming, norming, and performing. Impatient expectations prevent teams from evolving to their most productive stage.

➤ *A pilot team* helps the organization learn from an actual team what works and what doesn't. "We tested the concept by pulling together one team," says Diane Kokal, executive vice president of CRI. "We tracked the team's productivity and profitability throughout the pilot, then interviewed participants when it was completed. For most people it wasn't a major change in their jobs, but it was a change in roles. We laid out the process of what had to be done on pieces of paper and assigned them to team members."

CRI made the transition from functional departments to teams all at once. "Given the choice, our employees wouldn't have done it," says Jeff Pope, a founder and partner at CRI. "We took them way out of their comfort zone, but we provided crosstraining and the support of leadership."

While the actual transition was quick, the preparation for it was not. "We spent a year working with a consultant to plan for the change," says CRI founder and partner Judy Corson. "At that time there weren't a lot of companies doing teams." Employees participated in planning for the transition, including identifying the roles for team members. The transition went smoothly, and CRI has continued to improve its team approach since making the switch in the late 1980s.

Such complete reliance on teams is not for everyone. As Katzenbach and Smith remind us in *The Wisdom of Teams,* "The primary role of top management is to lead the organization toward performance, not to create teams." The transition stage allows you to discover the approach to teaming that promises the greatest impact on performance.

■ BUILDING SUCCESSFUL TEAMS

Most companies that wish to broaden the use of teams begin with cross-functional teams because the organization has problems or opportunities beyond the scope of a single functional area or department. You can use the following steps to build a successful cross-functional team:

1. Establish goals and authority.
2. Select team members.

3. Express leadership and management support.
4. Define roles and individual goals.
5. Provide training.
6. Communicate rules, procedures, and responsibilities.
7. Focus on the first meetings.
8. Follow the scientific approach.
9. Promote participation.
10. Resolve conflicts immediately.
11. Provide information.
12. Seek and applaud early successes.
13. Allow time to practice.
14. Challenge the team.
15. Recognize and reward team members.

Establish Goals and Authority

The goals may be the end result of the team's work, such as task completion, problem resolution, or process improvement, or they may be ongoing improvement goals in quality, productivity, delivery, profitability, or cost. Cross-functional teams tend to have end result goals while self-directed teams have ongoing goals. In either case, urgent and measurable interim goals should be established that make it possible for the team to see more immediate results for its efforts.

Select Team Members

The choice should be based on knowledge, skills, experience, and potential, not on personalities. Cross-functional teams need representatives of every function that has or may have an impact on the issue before the team. Self-directed teams typically include all members of an existing work group, although some companies form cross-functional, self-directed account teams to focus on a particular customer or market.

Express Leadership and Management Support

Leaders must constantly communicate the value of teams to the organization in speeches, meetings, internal publications, memos, conversations, discussions, and other forms of communication. Leaders need to publicly applaud team successes, make it a point to tell stories about teamwork and team accomplishments, and set an example of effective team behavior in their leadership team. Leaders and managers must provide tangible resources to teams (i.e., budget, work space, equipment), encourage risk taking, and remove obstacles that limit the team's effectiveness. Leaders and managers must also give the team the authority to act consistently with its responsibilities.

Define Roles and Individual Goals

Team members need to understand what their roles will be in addition to active participation, which is everyone's role. For example, the role of the manufacturing representative on a product development team might be to voice concerns about the manufacturability of the potential product, to explain manufacturing processes and equipment, and to project how long production might take.

In addition to understanding their roles, each team member needs complementary personal goals. In 1994, Disney, General Motors, Kellogg's, Kodak, and the American Society for Quality Control (ASQC) sponsored an archetype study of teams in the United States. Archetypes are the underlying structures or patterns of a culture that exist in people's unconscious and that determine how they perceive their world and react to it. The study found that employees want to know how being on a team will benefit them personally. According to ASQC's *Journal of Record*, "For a team to succeed, it must recognize and promote the achievement of each individual. If there are no personal benefits to being on a team, individual motivation is sapped" (Making perfect harmony 1995). Motivation begins with individual goals that complement the team and organization goals and builds with recognition and rewards that honor individual contributions as well as team success. Katzenbach and Smith concur: "Real teams always find ways for each individual to contribute and thereby gain distinction."

Provide Training

Team members need to be trained in both social/relationship skills and problem-solving/task skills. The social/relationship skills include team building, team dynamics, and conflict resolution. The problem-solving/task skills include process improvement and problem-solving tools. The most effective training is provided when the team will actually need it and is customized to meet the team's specific needs.

Communicate Rules, Procedures, and Responsibilities

One of the team's first tasks will be to set clear rules for attendance, confidentiality, the analytic approach the team will take, the results the team will focus on, the process the team will follow to resolve conflicts, and the responsibilities of each participant. The team will need to agree on the procedures that will guide team activity and on the methods of communication to be used for raising issues, expressing concerns, assigning and reporting progress on action steps, and communicating the team's progress to the organization's leaders and other employees.

Focus on the First Meetings

You may want to bring in a facilitator to help launch the team in the right direction. In addition to determining roles, goals, training, rules, procedures, and responsibilities, the first meetings will establish the dynamics of the group. The more team members are committed to the team's goals and to each other, the better the team will perform. Building this commitment is one of the most important objectives of the team's first meetings.

Follow the Scientific Approach

The scientific approach is a systematic way for teams to learn about processes. As Brian Joiner writes in *Fourth Generation Management*, "It means agreeing to make decisions based on data rather than hunches, to look for root causes of problems rather than react to superficial symptoms, to seek permanent solutions rather than rely on quick fixes." The problem-solving tools of the scientific approach include flowcharting, Pareto charts, cause-and-effect diagrams, operational definitions, stratification, time plots, control charts, checksheets, and scatter diagrams. We'll look more closely at the scientific approach and these tools in Chapter 7.

Promote Participation

It seems like every team has a few people who tend to dominate the action and a few who tend to sit back and observe. However, each member of the team was selected for his or her unique perspective, knowledge, and experience. The team leader and/or facilitator will need to encourage everyone to participate for the team to perform to its capabilities.

Resolve Conflicts Immediately

Ignoring conflicts will not cause them to go away. The value of conflict resolution training is that it acknowledges the natural tendency of conflicts to arise anytime people work together, and it provides a process for discussing and resolving the conflicts so that the group can move forward.

Provide Information

At the beginning, the team requires any information that can help it understand the nature of its process or the scope of its problem. It also needs information it can use to establish baselines that will allow it to measure its performance. Typical information includes indicators of quality, scheduling, cost, and customer satisfaction. As the team addresses the process or issue, it will need timely and easy access to information and data that clarifies the process/ issue, portrays the potential of improvements (benchmarks and competitive comparisons), and suggests the impact of possible improvements or solutions on customers and on organizational goals. We'll discuss information and measurement in more detail in Chapter 8.

Seek and Applaud Early Successes

Formal teams typically spend long periods of time working on their processes or issues. Interim goals help break the challenge into bite-sized chunks that give team members a sense of progress, urgency, and accomplishment. One of the team's first tasks is to set milestone goals along the path to the team's primary objective. The milestone goals may include completion of essential training, working knowledge of the existing process/issue, completion of benchmarking, development of a better process or resolution of the issue, completion of a pilot to test the new process/solution, and roll-out to all relevant areas of the organization. In addition to identifying its short-term goals, the team decides how it will celebrate each accomplishment. Senior leaders applaud early successes by congratulating the team, talking about the team during meetings and speeches, and writing about the team in newsletters, memos, and E-mail.

Allow Time to Practice

No athletic team would think of jumping into a competitive event without practicing first, yet we expect business teams to know what they're doing without ever having the chance to practice. People need to learn how to work together. They need the repetition of reacting to similar situations to discover what works and what doesn't. They need to gain confidence in their abilities as individuals and as a team, which is hard to come by when the team's success hangs on every action and decision.

Practice can take many forms: brainstorming solutions to a similar, fictional problem; mapping a different, simple process; or applying training in team dynamics to a "safe" issue. Team leaders and facilitators should schedule practice sessions at those points where team members will be asked to use new skills. The practice sessions need not take much time, but they should not end until the team is satisfied it has mastered the required skills and is confident it can apply them to the real process/issue.

Challenge the Team

Although interim goals and ongoing practice and recognition help keep the team on task, teams still reach plateaus that slow progress and demoralize team members. Senior leaders, team leaders, facilitators, and team members can push the team past those plateaus by challenging it with fresh information:

➤ A competitor who's doing particularly well at the very process/issue before the team.

➤ World-class performance by another organization in a similar process/issue.

➤ Data from within the organization that relate to the team's process/issue, but that contradict the team's data.

➤ Reasonable projections of the future that challenge assumptions made by the team.

➤ Insight into the process/issue from customers of or suppliers to the process/issue.

Recognize and Reward Team Members

The difference between recognition and rewards is that recognition is an activity or action and is usually not monetary (e.g., awards, special events, personal thank-yous, team parties) while rewards are monetary (e.g., bonuses, cash awards, trips, and merchandise). Both contribute greatly to team members' satisfaction with the work they do in their team. Honeywell Solid State Electronics Center provides both recognition and rewards to project teams through a plaque and $500 reward, and to empowered cross-functional teams through its Total Quality First Team Award. In 1994, nearly 18 percent of its employees were on teams that applied for the award; all were recognized and the top three teams also received cash awards. SSEC also uses cross-functional teams to evaluate and improve its approaches to recognition and rewards. We'll talk more about this subject later in this chapter.

■ EMPOWERING EMPLOYEES THROUGH TRAINING

According to the American Society for Training and Development, 0.5 percent of all U.S. companies account for 90 percent of the $30 billion spent on training annually. It seems you either believe in the value of training and invest in it, or you don't. If you're one of those who don't, consider the lessons of those who do.

Motorola estimates that for every dollar it spends on training it gets back $30 in productivity gains. Many companies can rationalize investing in technology and equipment to boost productivity but lack the insight to see the connection between increasing training and productivity. The National Center on the Educational Quality of the Workforce reported that a 10 percent increase in workforce education level raised total factor productivity by 150 percent more than a 10 percent increase in the value of capital equipment (How a Little Company Won Big 1995).

A study of auto plants worldwide concurs. Wharton Professor John Paul MacDuffie, commenting on the study, said, "We've found that the companies that fail in their efforts to increase flexibility do so not because they haven't bought the right hardware but because they either don't understand the importance of worker training or are hampered in their efforts to institute it" (Product variety 1994).

Motorola understands the importance of training. Yet when you look at investment per employee, smaller organizations commit even more to educating their people. Custom Research Inc. provided 138 hours of training per employee in 1995 (100 hours is considered world-class). Honeywell SSEC spends approximately $2,000 on training per employee per year. Wainwright Industries invests 5.8 percent of its payroll in training (5 percent is considered world-class).

The value of such extensive training is quantifiable. To analyze the impact of training on profitability, CRI correlated employee development with productivity, client satisfaction, and the growth of key clients. The correlations show a solid relationship between CRI's five key business drivers. When a multiple regression is done, these variables explain 75 percent of the variation in CRI's profit—strong evidence that they are, in fact, "key drivers" for CRI.

➤ Creating an Effective Training Program

The first step in creating an effective training program is to make learning an attribute of your culture. Honeywell SSEC, Wainwright, and CRI believe that knowledge breeds success. They agree with Christopher Bartlett and Sumantra Ghoshal, who wrote, "In a fast-changing, competitive, global environment, the ability to exploit knowledge is what gives companies their competitive advantage" (Bartlett and Ghoshal 1995). You exploit knowledge by giving everyone at every level the ability to process information, devise solutions, make decisions, and act creatively and positively according to the organization's vision and goals. We'll look at creating a learning organization in Chapter 9.

The second step is to determine the knowledge and skills employees need. This can be done by human resources or by a cross-functional team facilitated by human resources. The determination is based on an evaluation of the following:

➤ *The organization's strategic plan.* What knowledge and skills will be necessary to implement the plan? What will be needed to improve customer satisfaction?

➤ *The organization's short- and long-term goals.* What is necessary to improve performance (e.g., flexibility, job certification, crosstraining, human resources skills, etc.)?

➤ *Employees' needs.* What knowledge and skills do employees say they want and need? What do line managers perceive as the most important training needs?

➤ *Competence assessment.* What is the current level of knowledge and skills?

By studying the organization's plan, goals, and employee needs, you can develop a matrix of knowledge and skills that all employees will need and that segments of the employee population will need. For example, Honeywell SSEC forms a cross-functional team led by Human Resources to select core training based on the strategic plan and other sources of information. Part of the core training for all employees is the Quality Star Series, with modules focused on customers, people, economics, suppliers, and the community.

A competence audit helps you fix a starting point for your training. Companies that conduct such an audit are often surprised to find significant weaknesses in basic reading and math skills. A 1993 National Adult Literacy Survey reported that 90 million Americans have serious literacy problems—problems that are often hidden from view. For example, when Motorola conducted a competence audit in preparation for converting a plant from radio technology to cellular technology, it discovered that only 40 percent of the facility's employees passed a simple math test. Further testing revealed that 60 percent of those who failed couldn't read the questions. Motorola responded by establishing a standard based on seventh grade math and reading skills, then providing the training to help employees achieve the standard.

The competence audit should check basic knowledge and skills for all employees and specific knowledge and skills for segments of employees. Employees on the manufacturing line require different skills than employees in customer service (although they may not be *that* different as we strive to increase flexibility). When combined with an evaluation of the organization's plan, goals, and employee needs, the audit helps you create a training plan for all employees and for key employee groups (departments, teams, work groups, etc.).

The third step in creating an effective training program is to prioritize the training based on the organization's greatest needs. No organization can afford the time and expense of providing all of the training all at once, nor would it if it could. People need time to absorb what they have learned and to apply it in their jobs. A comprehensive training plan identifies the needs by group and the objectives of each training program and includes a chronology of when each program will be offered.

The fourth step is to deliver most training just-in-time. In the rush to train, many companies have heaped new knowledge on employees who have no opportunity to actually apply it in their jobs. While some training, such as understanding processes and customer requirements, is relevant at any time, other training has little value unless it's going to be used right away. For example, training in team building doesn't mean much to employees who aren't on teams and won't be on teams in the near future. Just-in-time training means the training is provided just in time for the employee to put it to use.

The fifth step in creating an effective training program is to involve both managers and employees in the continuous improvement of each individual's knowledge and skills. Training should be part of every employee's performance review with his or her manager. The discussion should focus on what knowledge and skills the employee needs to serve both the employee's and the organization's near- and longer-term requirements. An individual training plan should come out of the discussion. Employee and manager should then work together to identify training opportunities that align with the plan and to follow up any training with hands-on application of the new knowledge and skills.

The sixth step is to establish a process to evaluate and improve the training program. This is typically a human resources responsibility carried out annually near the end of the strategic planning process. In addition, human resources tracks training involvement (by number of employees taking courses) and effectiveness (by participant survey upon completion of the course and by tying training to business results and tracking performance before and after the course) and uses that information to improve subsequent training.

■ MANAGING PERFORMANCE

W. Edwards Deming hated performance ratings. "In practice," Deming said, "annual ratings are a disease, annihilating long-term planning, demolishing teamwork, nourishing rivalry and politics, leaving people bitter, crushed, bruised, battered, desolate, despondent, unfit for work for weeks after receipt of rating, unable to comprehend why they are inferior . . . sending companies down the tubes" (Latzko and Saunders 1995). Performance appraisals that rank or rate employees or that place them in groups based on their perceived performance demotivate employees for three reasons:

1. *The appraisal assumes that the employee's performance can be judged separately from the system in which he or she works.* Yet Deming, Joseph Juran, and other management experts agree that the system is responsible for at least 85 percent of the results of that system. How can you evaluate the perceived performance of one employee when the results of that performance are so entwined with the performance of the system?

2. *The managers making the appraisals vary in their perceptions of performance.* One manager ranks high. Another ranks low. One expects exceptional performance. Another expects doing your job. How can you rate performance when there's so much variation among the raters?

3. *Performance appraisals oppose cooperation.* If an organization seeks to improve cooperation, pitting one employee against another by ranking their performance is not the way to get it. Why cooperate with someone who may improve his or her performance as a result, thus pushing him/her past you in the ranking or rating and raising his/her compensation at your expense?

A popular alternative to performance appraisals is performance management, which focuses more on employees and their managers working together to set goals, give feedback, review performance to goals, and recognize and reward progress. Compensation is often separated from the performance management process and is based solely on providing wages competitive with industry, regional, and local standards.

The performance management process typically involves formal semiannual meetings between manager and employee and frequent informal discussions. To create an effective performance management process, consider the following steps:

➤ *Involve employees in developing and improving the process.* You may want to form a cross-functional team to tailor a performance management process to your organization.

➤ *Establish clear expectations.* According to a 1994 study of performance management programs, "clear expectations and feedback matter more to employees than the amount or type of compensation they receive" (Performance management 1995). When expectations are vague, employees worry about whether or not the expectations are being met. Clear expectations are more likely to produce better results.

➤ *Link each employee's performance plan with the organization's strategic plan and measurement system.* At CRI, all account teams and departments develop their own goals to align with the company's goals. Every employee then develops individual goals that support his or her team/department goals, thus linking individual goals with the company's goals. We'll discuss alignment through planning in more detail in Chapter 8.

The measures of individual performance should align with the measures of organizational performance. The most common areas of measurement are quality, scheduling, cost, and customer satisfaction. We'll focus on the alignment of measures in Chapter 7.

➤ *Provide ongoing feedback, coaching, and recognition.* Studies have shown that most people prefer immediate feedback and recognition for the job they are doing rather than waiting for a formal review. However, most managers are not prepared by training and experience to offer such support. One element of your performance management implementation process may be training managers and supervisors (and all employees, for that matter, since providing feedback and recognition is also a team activity) in how to provide ongoing feedback, coaching, and recognition.

➤ *For formal reviews, use input from managers, peers, and customers.* This is called a 360-degree review because the employee receives input on his or her performance from every angle. The team developing the performance management process may want to create a simple form that solicits this kind of feedback.

➤ *Make each employee responsible for his or her performance plan.* Engaging employees is about respect, trust, and responsibility. Making the employee's performance the employee's responsibility—and not the manager's responsibility—helps turn followers into leaders.

➤ Rewarding for the Organization's Performance

More companies have gotten into trouble trying to pay for performance than have benefited from the exercise. At the same time, a few companies have found ways to pass along some of the profits generated by improved performance to their employees. Their bonus or profit-sharing plans succeed because:

1. *They are clear about why they are offering bonuses or profit sharing.* If the plan is some cynical form of manipulation, it will only promote cynicism. The best plans genuinely wish to share the riches with those who helped earn them.

2. *They set a few key, attainable goals.* The goals reflect what's most important to the organization. If all key goals are met, the bonuses are paid. If not, no bonuses.

3. *They involve as many people as possible in setting the goals.* As with all new initiatives, the best way to get buy-in is to involve those who will be affected by the new initiative in designing it.

4. *They communicate the plan and performance clearly.* People are not motivated by a plan they don't understand and hear little about. Performance to the plan must be tracked and displayed where every employee can see it.

5. *They train employees to understand the financial side of their business.* It's called open-book management. John Case wrote a book about it, *Open-Book Management,* in which he said, "Once people come to understand that they're in business to make money—and that it's the financials that indicate how well they're doing—they need no motivation other than a stake in success." We'll look more closely at open-book management in Chapter 7.

6. *They make the amount of the bonus or profit sharing meaningful.* In response to his own question about how much employees should receive, Case writes, "The short answer is, all your company can afford."

7. *They make few distinctions in how much people get.* Wainwright Industries used to divide the amount for profit sharing according to how much its employees earned. "That continued to feed individual recognition," says plant manager Mike Simms, "so we changed it to make profit sharing equal for all employees." This is a critical point: A lot of well-intentioned companies have demotivated their employees by trying to reward one group more than another. Being clear about why you're offering bonuses or profit sharing (the first point in this list) can help you avoid this land mine.

8. *They revisit the goals every year.* The more employees understand the organization's competitive and financial situation, the easier they will accept raising the bar when it becomes necessary.

From an ethical standpoint, bonuses and profit sharing reward the very people who made the bonuses and profit sharing possible in the first place. They give people a financial stake in the organization's performance, helping to turn a company of employees into a company of owners. And a company of owners will outperform a company of employees any day.

➤ Recognizing Performance

While a reward program can just as easily offend as inspire, a recognition program rarely is seen as negative. When it is, it's usually because the recognition is designed to manipulate rather than motivate, a natural mistake for the command-and-control organization.

Recognition falls into one of three categories:

➤ *Formal recognition* includes such things as annual awards and award celebrations at the company/division level. The criteria for receiving the recognition are well defined. Winners are announced in company publications.

➤ *Informal recognition* tends to be given at the department or work unit level. Managers typically decide the nature of the recognition, which may include parties, outings, or gifts.

➤ *Day-to-day recognition* occurs when one employee recognizes the performance of another employee. It may be done verbally or in writing, by leaders, managers, subordinates, and/or peers.

For most companies, recognition programs mean formal recognition. As they become more horizontal, companies seek ways to improve work unit performance, encouraging managers to find the best forms of recognition for their unique circumstances. Day-to-day recognition further supports the flatter, faster organization by encouraging people to recognize the contributions of their peers, and to feel valued by the recognition they receive. A short note saying, "Way to go." A moment of praise at a team meeting. A pat on the back. A simple thank-you.

It's no surprise that day-to-day recognition is most valued by employees. We all want regular, positive feedback on our performance. Annual awards are nice. A celebratory pizza party is fun. But nothing makes you feel as good as personal recognition by someone who knows exactly what you have done and what it means.

To design an effective employee recognition system, consider these guidelines:

1. Separate recognition from compensation. One has nothing to do with the other.

2. Make everyone a winner. The purpose of recognition is to build on success, not to punish failure. Every employee contributes to the success of the organization. An effective recognition system makes it possible for every employee's contributions to be recognized.

3. Involve employees in the design. If you're new to the cross-functional team idea, here's a good place to start. Assign the task of evaluating and improving your recognition system (or designing one if none exists) to a cross-functional team. Be clear about your expectations for the team and the recognition system (including financial, quality, and time concerns), then turn the team loose.

4. Encourage personal recognition. Not many people are skilled at spontaneously recognizing the contributions of their coworkers. Lead by example, dashing off quick notes as you catch an employee doing something well. Better yet, make it a point to recognize the contribution as it occurs, in front of the employee's peers.

5. Make recognition fun. Throw a party. Hand out tickets to a movie/play/sporting event. Give a balloon bouquet. Bring in a cake. Create a traveling trophy. You don't need any group's guidance or approval to initiate personal recognition.

■ ENGAGED EMPLOYEES AND THE FLAT, FAST, FLEXIBLE ORGANIZATION

Engaging employees is about respect, trust, and responsibility, which can be created by developing teamwork, providing training, and managing, rewarding, and recognizing performance. These actions make it possible for an organization to be flatter because you don't need bosses telling people what to do, then making sure they do it. They make it possible for an organization to be faster because you don't have levels of bureaucracy slowing down important decisions and actions. They make it possible for an organization to be more flexible because its people are more flexible: crosstrained, motivated, proactive, and focused on a shared vision.

In the process, they also make the workplace interesting, challenging, and fun. Leaders who can think of nothing other than the bottom line are not likely to value such an environment. But then, as the Southern California study quoted earlier in this chapter showed, companies that engage employees consistently outperform those that don't. It's time for leaders to recognize that the best way to improve the bottom line is to engage all employees in the process.

■ STRATEGIES FOR IMPROVEMENT

➤ Jump Start

➤ Define what a high performance employees is for your organization. Involve leaders, managers, and high-performance employees in identifying the skills, behaviors, and attitudes that are important to your organization. For guidance, see the questions earlier in this chapter. Once you know what is needed, develop a training plan that addresses the areas of greatest need.

➤ Make empowerment and learning key business strategies. Take them out of the wouldn't-they-be-nice category and make them we've-gotta-have-them-to-survive. Then spend some time as a leadership team thinking about what the strategies mean to the design and operation of the organization.

➤ Drive out fear. Use the strategies described in Chapter 2 to create an environment that encourages participation.

➤ Train for participation. Teach managers and supervisors how to encourage it and employees how to do it.

➤ Begin using cross-functional teams for critical cross-functional issues. Train team members for their new roles. Set aggressive performance standards. Then let them perform and support their decisions and actions. For more on the process, see the steps to building successful teams earlier in this chapter.

➤ Tune Up

➤ Make empowered employees heroes within the organization. Talk about them at every opportunity. Write about them in the in-house newsletter. Use their examples to talk about what empowerment means to you and to the organization. Encourage all employees to take responsibility. Offer your help—and that of all leaders—in removing any obstacles that keep them from accepting responsibility.

➤ Align compensation, rewards, and recognition with the added responsibilities you are asking employees to take. Walk the talk.

➤ Move toward becoming a team-based organization, keeping in mind that the goal is to improve performance, not to create teams. Look for opportunities to involve employees in cross-functional teams. Explore the feasibility of self-directed teams where appropriate and pilot the concept in one or two areas. Modify compensation, rewards, and recognition to show that team participation and results are important.

➤ Develop a profit-sharing plan as another way for employees to own their work. People become even more vested in their work when they enjoy some of the profits of that work.

➤ Develop a recognition program that supports the organization's goals.

➤ Pull Away

➤ Help every employee feel responsible for the organization's success. This means communicating all critical information, including financial information, to all employees. It means providing training at world-class levels (100 hours per employee per year is a good standard). It means establishing compensation and rewards commensurate with responsibilities. It means thanking and applauding and praising all the time.

➤ Make all training meaningful to the jobs at hand. Involve each employee in developing his or her training plan. Involve all managers and supervisors in reviewing these plans, in helping the employees carry them out, and in applying what they learn to their jobs.

➤ Establish processes to evaluate and improve human resources planning, empowerment, training, compensation, performance management, and recognition. Involve employees in this, if possible through cross-functional teams.

Know Your Customers

Once there was an organization that decided it wanted to delight its customers. Since it wasn't sure exactly what that meant, the organization set about finding out. Its leaders met with the customers' leaders. It created a database for each customer and asked everyone in the company to add to the database when they learned something about a customer and to use the database when they wanted to understand the customer. It began annual Executive Review Boards to talk about key issues with strategic customers. It held conferences with customer employees from various functions and levels in their organization. It trained employees to recognize unarticulated needs, which are needs even the customer has trouble naming. It conducted surveys and interviews, asked questions, and listened.

Its hard work paid off. Customer satisfaction jumped from 76 percent in 1990 to 92 percent in 1995. It now gets 98 percent of the business on which it bids. It has never lost a customer because of poor performance. All of which suggest delighted customers.

One story confirms it. It seems a major customer came to the organization to ask if it would consider supplying the customer with related products the organization did not currently produce. The customer said it would show the organization how to compete in the related field. It offered to train the organization's employees. It promised whatever assistance it could provide to help the organization succeed in this new venture. All because the customer was so delighted with the organization and it wanted to expand their relationship.

The organization, Honeywell Solid State Electronic Center, delights its customers, which is a major reason it is one of only two survivors in an industry where twenty-five companies competed just twelve years ago. It continues to use the strategies listed above to know its customers. Although the knowledge is easier to acquire because SSEC has thirty to forty customers, a small customer base does not guarantee that you will know your customers. Understanding customer requirements requires a conscious, ongoing effort on many fronts to acquire information about customer needs and expectations, aggregate and analyze the information, identify key requirements, and validate those requirements by asking customers to review them.

Few companies perform this process well. Worse yet, they *assume* they know what their customers require without having any factual basis for their assumptions. Even worse, everything they do as a company is geared toward meeting these specious requirements. It's like investing all your resources in building a world-class station wagon when what your primary market really wants is a minivan. You may still sell a few station wagons, but you will struggle to satisfy your customers and you will never delight them.

And delighting customers is critical to your long-term success. Next to the assumption that you know what your customers require, the assumption that satisfied customers are loyal customers is the greatest threat to a company's future. The reason is that only total satisfaction (delight) secures customer loyalty. For example, Xerox has found that "its totally satisfied customers were six times more likely to repurchase Xerox products over the next eighteen months than its satisfied customers" (Jones and Sasser 1995). Their study of customer satisfaction revealed that, "except in a few rare instances, complete customer satisfaction is the key to securing customer loyalty and generating superior long-term financial performance." As they concluded, "any drop from total satisfaction results in a major drop in loyalty."

You cannot achieve total satisfaction without a companywide customer focus, a rock-solid understanding of your customers' requirements, and a commitment to building strong customer relationships. This chapter explores each of these areas, but the concept of total customer satisfaction touches every chapter in this book in fairly obvious ways. An organization that is truly customer-driven has leaders who relate to key customers regularly, a vision directed toward customer satisfaction, employees trained and empowered to meet and exceed customer requirements, an organizational design best suited to serving customer needs, processes that add value to customers, timely and accurate information about customer requirements and satisfaction, and a strategic plan for delighting and retaining major customers and adding new ones.

It is a systems approach to total customer satisfaction that begins with a shift in thinking.

■ INTERNALIZING THE CUSTOMER'S VIEW

In the course of conducting day-to-day business, it is easy to become internally focused. Are we delivering our products on time? How can we improve our services? What does the newest technology mean for our business? How can we reengineer our processes to make them easier to manage? How can we jump ahead of our competitors? What problems need our immediate attention?

These are important questions. Unfortunately, they may not be the best questions. By focusing on how well our management system is meeting internal needs and expectations, we lose sight of the external needs of customers. You may argue that addressing all of these questions will help you serve customers' needs, and you would be correct. But it is an inside-out approach to serving those needs, not outside-in. It looks at the organization through the eyes of the producer, not the eyes of the customer. The different perception changes emphasis and priorities. Leaders act to improve quality, shorten cycle time, reduce waste, and empower employees because they assume that the actions will improve customer satisfaction. Yet the only way to *know* such actions will improve customer satisfaction is to know exactly what customers require, then to organize, plan, work, and improve with those requirements constantly in mind.

In her book *World Class: Thriving Locally in the Global Economy*, Rosabeth Moss Kanter encourages companies to "move from thinking like producers to thinking like customers." According to Kanter:

> ➤ Producers think they are making products. Customers think they are buying services.

➤ Producers want to maximize return on the resources they own. Customers care about whether resources are applied for their benefit, not who owns them.

➤ Producers worry about visible mistakes. Customers are lost because of invisible mistakes.

➤ Producers think their technologies create products. Customers think their needs create products.

➤ Producers organize for internal managerial convenience. Customers want their convenience to come first.

Another way to think like a customer is to look at everything you do as providing a service to your customers. Most companies think of themselves as manufacturers or service companies. In their book *Return on Quality,* authors Roland Rust, Anthony Zahorik, and Timothy Keiningham "see the primary purpose of every business and, in fact, every organization as performing a service for customers. The service always centers upon meeting customer needs. Thus, a mission of management is to identify and fulfill customer needs." If you are in the business of serving customers (and not in the business of manufacturing products), their needs become paramount and understanding their requirements becomes an ongoing priority.

This shift in thinking is necessary because being customer focused is the surest way to acquire and retain customers. In an increasingly competitive marketplace, being good at what you do is no longer enough. You must be good at what the customer wants. That means creating value that cannot be matched by your competitors by following a process that begins with commitment:

1. Commit your organization to being customer focused.

2. Use every available method to learn the requirements of individual, key customers.

3. Pull the information from these sources together for aggregation and analysis.

4. Identify specific requirements for key customer groups.

5. Verify the requirements with internal experts and key customers.

6. Prioritize the requirements with input from key customers.

7. Identify the unique value your organization can provide to serve any or all of the key requirements.

8. Develop strategies to be good in all areas and great in a few that the customer values.

9. Align internal processes and measures with customer requirements.

10. Internalize the customer focus by making sure all employees know what key customer groups require and how the organization creates value in meeting those requirements.

■ DETERMINING CUSTOMER REQUIREMENTS

Creating value for customers is an organizational effort. To the customer, it means a more innovative and better quality product or service delivered faster at a competitive price. To the producer, it means focusing the entire organization on creating this value for the customer.

Such an effort depends on a clear, accurate, and complete understanding of customer requirements. Before such knowledge can be acquired, an organization must identify the target customers for the products and services most important to its business. It must then identify the key customers for each product/service and find out what product/service characteristics are most important to those customers.

There are several ways to do this, including:

➤ *Interviewing key customers—new, current, and defecting.* Once you've identified who the contact people are at the key customers (contact people may be top executives, those who buy the product/service, those who use the product/service, etc.), sit down with them face-to-face and ask them what they think are the most important characteristics of your product/service. Listen. Ask how you rate on those characteristics and how you compare to your competitors. Listen. Take notes. Confirm that you are hearing what they are telling you. Senior executives at Custom Research Inc. do this with every new client, confirming the key points in their conversations by letter.

➤ *Conducting focus groups.* The benefit of focus groups is the discussion that occurs naturally as customers with similar requirements debate the value of your products/services. The focus groups typically consist of six to ten people who have similar positions at their companies. The groups can be facilitated internally or by an outside party if you feel the participants would contribute more freely in a more neutral environment.

➤ *Surveying customers.* One way to systematically gather customer information is to survey all customers in a particular customer group on a regular basis. Many companies do this through an annual customer satisfaction survey. To learn about customer requirements, the survey needs to include statements that ask how well you are recognizing and responding to the requirements.

➤ *Soliciting feedback on recent transactions.* This can be done by phone, personal contact, bounceback cards included with the product, mail, or fax. Solectron requests feedback from its customers weekly by fax, then uses the responses to assess performance and improvement and initiate corrective action. The request can be structured to solicit information about changes in customer requirements.

➤ *Encouraging comments, suggestions, and complaints.* The easier you make it for customers to contact people who will listen and respond to their concerns, the better your chances of gathering valuable information. This often involves training front-line employees to listen and respond, then to communicate what they hear and learn within the organization. Customer-focused organizations establish formal complaint management systems that promote rapid correction of the problem, trigger a review of the process on which the complaint focused, and provide for communication of the complaint and its resolution to all appropriate parts of the organization.

➤ *Establishing customer advisory groups.* Ask eight to ten representatives of your key customers to serve on a customer advisory board. Have them meet quarterly or semiannually to discuss your organization's strategies, potential products/services, industry trends, and changes in their requirements. Use the group to verify that you understand their key requirements for your products and services.

➤ *Involving key customers in strategic planning, product/service design, reengineering, and other internal processes.* Bringing key customer representatives into your organization is one way to make sure the voice of the customer is heard. Another way is to invite key customer representatives to speak at internal meetings, such as senior executive and department staff meetings and process improvement team meetings. If you are an important supplier to these customers, they will welcome the chance to tell you what is important to them.

➤ *Studying customers under normal conditions.* The best way to learn what customers require is to observe them using your products or services or your competitors' products/services, or in situations that require a product or service you could provide. This may be the only way to discover the customer's unarticulated need for products and services that either don't exist or aren't being used for this purpose. Products such as fax machines and cellular phones and services such as express package delivery and 24-hour cable news responded to unarticulated needs. Customers were not able to express these needs and, therefore, to define their requirements for innovative products and services. In fact, most customers initially resist new ways of doing things because they cannot think outside the box. The company that can do such thinking for them can tap into a demand no competitor is addressing.

"It's our job to help customers articulate their expectations," says Marlow Industries' Chris Witzke, "because quite often you can totally meet their specifications and not give them what they want. We need to help the customer be more successful."

Honeywell SSEC trains its employees to identify unarticulated needs. In addition, it gathers information about customer requirements through semiannual customer surveys and through executive review board meetings two or three times each year, during which senior executives at SSEC and the customer meet face-to-face.

The more methods you use to understand and keep current with your customers' requirements, the more accurate your knowledge of those requirements will be. In addition to gathering such information, however, you must also know what to do with it once you have it. The methods described above bring customer information into the organization at several different points. If you don't have a process in place for reporting this information internally, comparing it, analyzing it, and checking it with internal experts and key customers, you will be left with a perception of what your customers require without actually knowing it.

■ DETERMINING WHAT CUSTOMERS VALUE

Once you know what your customers require, you can segment them into groups according to like requirements, then prioritize the requirements according to what the customer group values most.

As the marketplace becomes increasingly competitive, companies can gain and maintain an advantage only by providing value to their customers. The value may mean lower prices, faster delivery, higher quality, greater innovation, or a better total solution. The value you choose to provide will depend on your knowledge of customers' requirements and your organization's core competencies.

As defined by Gary Hamel and C. K. Prahalad in *Competing for the Future,* "a core competence is a bundle of skills and technologies that enables a company to provide a particular benefit to customers. To be considered a core competence, a skill must meet three tests: customer value, competitor differentiation, and extendability. A core competence," they conclude, "is a source of competitive advantage in that it is competitively unique and makes a contribution to customer value or cost."

A core competence may be a particular technology, an area of expertise, a method of delivery, a relationship with customers, or any other skill that meets the three tests. Matching your core competencies with your customers' key requirements helps you create value for your customers, differentiate your organization from the competition, and align all internal processes and resources with value creation.

Understanding customer requirements and value creation can also help you outperform your competitors by customizing your products and services. The concept, called mass customization, focuses on identifying and serving niche markets, which are fragments of mass markets distinguished by a large number of common requirements. Television sets serve a mass market. Televisions for home entertainment centers serve a niche market.

Companies use mass customization to gain an edge with a profitable segment of a broader market. They design custom products and services to more closely match the requirements of a smaller group of customers, which allows the companies to build customer loyalty and, hopefully, charge premium prices.

■ COMMUNICATING CUSTOMER REQUIREMENTS THROUGHOUT THE ORGANIZATION

Once you have identified customer requirements, the next step is to internalize them. An organization cannot be customer driven if only senior executives, sales and marketing people, or the customer service department know what customers require. Customer driven means anyone in the company can tell you who your key customers are and what they require. Only then can you feel confident that everyone is focused on creating value for the customer.

To achieve this level of understanding, consider the following approaches:

➤ *Communicate the key requirements of key customer groups at every opportunity, including staff meetings, team meetings, internal publications, speeches, and videotapes.* When a customer compliments your company, make a point to cite the specific requirements on which your organization excelled. Make customer focus a cultural characteristic.

➤ *Invite customers to speak to employees at any and all levels.* Most customers will jump at the chance to talk to an important supplier. With this in mind, ask them to describe their business, list the keys to their success, and explain how your organization can help them be more successful.

➤ *Visit customers.* Pull together a small group representing a cross section of functions and levels for a field trip to a customer's site. Observe how your organization's products/ services are used. Talk to the people who use them. Learn how your products/services fit into the customer's grand scheme.

➤ *Collect customer data.* The people who work a process are in the best position to improve. They are also in the best position to translate customer requirements, suggestions, and complaints into process improvements. Customer data collected at the company level should be communicated quickly to those who need it. Employees should also be encouraged to seek customer data that directly relates to their internal quality, delivery, and cost data, both to verify their performance and to make sure they are measuring the right things.

➤ *Organize cross-functional teams or task forces.* As processes are aligned to serve customer requirements, representatives of the different functions involved in a process can form a team to look at how value is added throughout the process and how it can be improved. By involving customers in the process improvement, team members validate their understanding of customer requirements and better understand what improvement will have the greatest impact on customer satisfaction.

The goals of these approaches are to have all employees understand: (1) who your key customers and customer groups are; (2) the key requirements of each group; (3) how the organization's products/services serve these requirements; and (4) how the employee's work adds value for the customer.

To assess the effectiveness of your approaches, consider the following questions posed by Brian Joiner in his book *Fourth Generation Management:*

➤ If I were to act in the best interests of our customers, what would my decision be?

➤ What can I do personally to better understand our customers' needs?

➤ What can I do to help my employees put a customer focus into action?

➤ What are the systems by which we achieve a customer focus? What of those are most in need of attention?

If it seems like we're going overboard on the customer focus idea, it's probably because you've gotten used to thinking like a producer or you're worried about the bottom line. When companies are small, staying close to customers is easy. You spend a great deal of effort just trying to find customers, and a great deal more trying to keep them happy. As companies become bureaucracies, the focus shifts away from the customer to the products or services being produced. You think like a producer, not like a customer.

When you're small, you know that more happy customers means more money. When you're big, the impact of more happy customers isn't as easy to measure. The link between customer satisfaction and profitability is harder to see. You worry that spending more to delight customers cuts into profits. After all, shareholders want you to sell less for more and customers want to buy more for less. The two perspectives are opposed, and in this age of the bottom line, the shareholders' viewpoint rules.

Among the correlations Custom Research Inc. performs, one is the number of clients who tell CRI it exceeded their expectations compared to operating profits. The correlation is extremely strong. You can safely say that, as CRI exceeded the expectations of more of its clients, it made more money. Or, as B. Joseph Pine II wrote in *Mass Customization,* "a company that better satisfies its customers' individual wants and needs will have greater sales. With higher profits as well as a better understanding of customer requirements, the company can provide even more variety and customization."

That's the bottom line value of delighting your customers.

■ DELIGHTING CUSTOMERS

Internalizing customer requirements is the trigger that sets into motion all of the processes that exist to meet and exceed those requirements. Measuring customer satisfaction is the end result, the hits or misses on the target, that tells you how well you did. When you measure customer satisfaction with your performance on their requirements, you close the loop on your management system. Requirements dictate processes and levels of performance. Satisfaction measures the effectiveness of those processes.

CRI clarifies the specific requirements of a client before every project. It then measures satisfaction with its performance to those requirements when the project is completed. The company uses a five-point scale (which is considered one of the least-biased scales) to ask whether it met or exceeded expectations for each area the client had identified. The client's responses are communicated immediately to senior management and to the client's account team. Client satisfaction for the company and by team is tracked, graphed, and reported throughout the company every quarter. The trends show that nearly all projects meet expectations and two-thirds exceed them, a percent that has grown steadily for several years.

CRI calls this "surprising and delighting our clients," which is the company's goal. Its focus on total client satisfaction confirms the findings of Thomas Jones and W. Earl Sasser Jr. that delighting customers is the key to superior long-term financial performance (Jones and Sasser 1995). In fact, Jones and Sasser's three steps to improving customer satisfaction reflect the process CRI follows:

1. Make the measurement of customer satisfaction and loyalty a priority following a process that is unbiased, consistent, broadly applied, and able to capture information on individual customers.
2. Track your performance by plotting individual customer responses.
3. Using the individual responses and the broader trends, determine the most appropriate strategies for raising customer satisfaction.

To raise customer satisfaction, you must know not only what customers' requirements are, but also how they feel about those requirements. Some requirements are nonnegotiable; if you don't provide them, the customer is dissatisfied. When you buy a new television set, you expect the color to be accurate, the buttons and knobs to work properly, and the set to be cable ready.

Other requirements are expected; if you don't provide them, the customer will be disappointed but may not be dissatisfied. You expect to get a remote control with your television set that is easy to use and to be able to adjust color and contrast with little difficulty. If the remote is particularly intuitive and/or powerful, you feel increasingly satisfied with your purchase.

A few requirements are really wishes, as in "I wish I could afford the more expensive set with all its features." When you "surprise and delight" customers by addressing their wishes (including their unarticulated needs), you exceed their expectations and build loyalty. If your new TV has high-quality stereo sound, you feel delighted with the television-watching experience even if you knew stereo sound was part of the package.

In *Return on Quality*, authors Rust, Zahorik, and Keiningham describe these three categories as:

1. Basic attributes assumed to be present in any product/service.

2. Articulated attributes that customers generally mention as desirable or determinant in their choice of a product/service.

3. Exciting attributes that would delight and surprise customers if they were present.

Jones and Sasser group the requirements into four elements that affect customer satisfaction:

➤ The basic elements of the product or service that customers expect all competitors to deliver.

➤ Basic support services such as customer assistance or order tracking that make the product or service incrementally more effective and easier to use.

➤ A recovery process for counteracting bad experiences.

➤ Extraordinary services that so excel in meeting customers' personal preferences, in appealing to their values, or in solving their particular problems that they make the product or service seem customized.

Whichever method of categorizing you prefer, the reason for grouping your customers' requirements is to help you set priorities and interpret customer feedback. It does no good to attempt to delight your customers if you are not meeting their nonnegotiable requirements. You must excel at the basics before you can attend to the extras.

Grouping requirements also helps you interpret what customers are telling you. If they are complaining about issues related to basic requirements, you need to act immediately to satisfy those customers and to prevent similar problems from recurring. If they are complaining about "nice to have" requirements, you still need to respond to gain their satisfaction, but you may or may not decide to pursue time-consuming or expensive remedies. If they aren't complaining at all, you cannot assume they are completely satisfied unless you ask them. You may have satisfied their basic requirements but done nothing to delight them, in which case they won't complain, nor will they feel any compelling reason to buy from you again. And as we discussed earlier in this chapter, repeat business is a lot likelier when customers are totally satisfied.

■ STRENGTHENING CUSTOMER RELATIONSHIPS

As you identify customer requirements, you will discover that some of them are not about the product or service but about your relationship with the customer. Listening to customers, caring about their problems, responding quickly, showing courtesy, and being knowledgeable about their situation or business are all relationship requirements.

You can uncover these requirements through the same methods you use to find out the requirements for your products/services. You must be careful not to discount these relationship requirements or assume they are less important than the product/service requirements. How you rank them will depend on what your customers tell you and on the nature of your business.

Relationship requirements tend to fall into five categories:

➤ Tangibles such as the appearance of personnel and facilities

➤ Reliability, or responding to customers dependably and accurately

➤ Responsiveness, or providing timely and helpful service

➤ Competence, or possessing the skills and expertise to respond knowledgeably

➤ Empathy, or caring about the customer's concerns

Your list depends on what your customers value. For example, if you manufacture television sets, customers don't care about the appearance of your personnel and facilities but want to know that, when they call with a question about their new television set, the employee who helps them has the skills and expertise to respond knowledgeably and cares about their concerns. On the other hand, if you sell television sets, your customers *will* care about appearance—and about competence and empathy as well.

Once you know your customers' relationship requirements, you need to identify or establish processes that meet those requirements, communicate the requirements throughout the organization, train employees in the attitudes and skills needed to work the processes, make it easy for customers to gain access to the organization, and empower people to take responsibility for responding to customer issues.

Charles Weiser, head of British Airways' customer relations department in the early 1990s, described such an approach in a recent article in *Harvard Business Review* (Weiser 1995). When he joined British Airways, he found that it took an average of twelve weeks to respond to customer correspondence. Customers who called were no luckier: 60 percent of such calls were lost every day.

After surveying customers to understand the extent of the problem, British Airways instituted four companywide objectives:

1. Install systems to collect and analyze customer data, then distribute the findings throughout the organization.
2. Involve line operations in monthly reviews with the management team to discuss customer perceptions of service quality.
3. Change the approach to customer compensation to meet customers' needs, not the company's.
4. Practice customer retention, assessing performance on the basis of customer-retention rates.

To deal with customer issues, the customer relations department developed a four-step process that was then incorporated into all human and technical systems:

1. Apologize and own the problem. Customers don't care who was at fault or to blame.
2. Do it quickly. The company's research showed that nearly half of the customers who complained defected if it took the company more than five days to respond.
3. Assure the customer that the problem is being fixed. Retention improves if customers are confident that the cause of the problem is being fixed.
4. Do it by phone. The company found that customers with complaints were delighted to have customer relations call them.

To make it easier for customers to comment and complain, the department established twelve listening posts, including return cards, customer forums, and a Fly with Me program that had department members fly with customers to share their experience firsthand.

As a result of its efforts, British Airways doubled its retention rate among those customers who complain to customer relations and increased its return on investment in the department by 200 percent.

Most studies have shown that it costs five times more to get a new customer than it does to keep one. We'll talk more about customer retention at the end of this chapter. Companies that work hard at retaining their customers know that relationship requirements play a key role in keeping customers. Customers who feel that a company cares about them as customers are more likely to remain loyal than customers who have no relationship beyond the purchase of a product or service.

One way Granite Rock builds loyalty is through the Granite Rock Short Pay Method. The back of every Granite Rock invoice states: *"If you're not satisfied with the Granite Rock service or construction services you just received, then don't pay us for it."* No justification is required. The customer marks the item he or she isn't happy with, subtracts the amount, and pays the rest. The bold guarantee provides many benefits: building trust, confidence, and loyalty among customers; communicating to employees the company's customer focus; establishing high standards for quality, speed, and cost; and providing customers with another way to express their displeasure.

"When we implemented the Granite Rock Short Pay Method, 1.6 percent of our sales were held up by legitimate customer complaints," says president and CEO Bruce Woolpert. "Those were complaints we wouldn't have gotten otherwise. We've had no one cheat us. Today, by focusing on those areas, finding out what those problems were and eliminating them, we have that down to less than one-half percent."

To develop such trusting relationships, an organization must remain focused on the customer. Employees must understand that customers belong to the entire organization, not just to one functional area. Every employee must be trained and empowered to take personal responsibility for responding to and resolving customer issues. Customer retention must become a top priority, measured by retention rates and customer satisfaction surveys and reviewed regularly by company, division, and department leadership.

■ MEASURING CUSTOMER SATISFACTION

The most common method of measuring customer satisfaction is by survey. The survey may be performed periodically (annually is most common) or conducted at the conclusion of a transaction. Marlow Industries and Custom Research measure customer satisfaction with their products and services on an ongoing basis. They conduct a formal customer satisfaction survey annually. Marlow mails its survey to key contacts within its customers' organizations. At CRI, steering committee members interview major clients about the health of the overall relationship across key performance characteristics. Every third year, Marlow hires a graduate M.B.A. class to design and conduct an independent customer satisfaction survey, then correlates the results with its own surveys to make sure the company is collecting the right data. CRI has used a similar process to validate its surveys.

The most effective customer satisfaction surveys:

➤ Ask how the company performed on the customers' key requirements

➤ Are sent to all customers or to a statistically representative sample

➤ Are free of bias and ambiguity

➤ Are easy to understand and complete

➤ Ask questions about the competition

➤ Ask about intent to repurchase

➤ Leave room for comments, suggestions, and complaints

To design an effective survey, ask about performance on the key requirements defined by the customer using a 5-point scale (1 = strong disagree; 2 = disagree; 3 = neutral; 4 = agree; 5 = strongly agree). Pilot the survey with a representative number of customers to see if the survey solicits the quantity and quality of responses you need.

When you distribute the survey, you may want to explain briefly why it is important to your company and how you plan to use it. Encourage customers to be honest and thoughtful in their responses, then segment the responses by each of the five points on the scale. The goal is to get 5s, which suggest total satisfaction and stronger loyalty. Anything less than a 5 means that an opportunity to improve satisfaction exists. While satisfied customers are desirable, only totally satisfied customers are loyal.

■ BUILDING CUSTOMER LOYALTY

Loyalty increases profits. At a basic level, a company can increase profits by reducing costs and/or increasing sales. You increase sales by getting new customers, motivating existing customers to spend more, and/or keeping existing customers for a longer time. Since it's cheaper to keep customers than to acquire them, and since sales to existing customers can be expanded by selling more and selling for a longer time period, it makes sense to make customer retention a key goal of the organization. As John Humphrey, chairman of the Forum Corporation, said, "The most successful companies are those that view customer satisfaction and retention as the critical measure of prosperity."

The strategies and approaches in this chapter all contribute to customer satisfaction and retention. First, you must know who your customers are and exactly what they require and value. You must then communicate this information throughout the organization. You must focus all efforts on the processes that serve those requirements and on the steps that add value to the final product or service. You must make it easy for customers to comment and complain. You must formalize processes that assure rapid response to comments and complaints. You must make it everyone's job to be responsible for making and keeping customers happy. You must measure customer satisfaction and retention and establish goals that compel the organization to improve in these critical areas.

But you can't stop there. No organization has the resources to exceed expectations on every customer requirement or to do whatever it takes to respond to customer complaints. You will want to focus your resources on those areas that cause customers to leave or to remain loyal, which aren't necessarily the areas with the most complaints or where satisfaction is rated worst. If you conduct satisfaction surveys, measure customer retention, and gather information from other sources listed in this chapter (i.e., focus groups, advisory boards, customer visits, and feedback on transactions), you have the data you need to analyze customer satisfaction and retention to find out what causes customers to leave or stay. By improving in these areas, you can leverage your resources to make more customers totally satisfied.

By staying close to your customers, you can also anticipate what will delight them in the future. There is a danger in focusing so much on today's customer that you become complacent about what tomorrow's customers may require. Strategic thinking (Chapter 3), benchmarking and competitive comparisons (Chapter 8), and strategic planning (Chapter 9) can help your organization prepare for and profit from a changing world.

■ STRATEGIES FOR IMPROVEMENT

➤ Jump Start

➤ Identify your primary market segments, then determine the key requirements for each. Use as many of the ideas in this chapter as possible to gain a rock-solid understanding of customer requirements. ,

➤ Measure customer satisfaction with your performance on their requirements. Ask customers how you did after the delivery of every product and service. At least once a year, use a formal survey to assess customer satisfaction. You may want to design the survey based on excellent examples from other organizations or with help from outside experts on the subject.

➤ Make it easy for customers to comment, provide feedback, and complain. Evaluate and improve the processes that encourage and allow customer input. If no processes exist, create them by forming teams that include the people who will be responding to customers. Ask customers how they prefer to contact your organization—and how they would like you to respond—then design processes that meet their requirements.

➤ Tune Up

➤ Communicate customer requirements and customer satisfaction measurements to everyone in the organization. This information is essential to making an organization customer focused. Encourage people to think in terms of who their customers are, what they require, and how they are meeting and exceeding their requirements.

➤ Align internal in-process and end-of-process measures with customer satisfaction measures. If you manage only what you measure, and you measure what's important to the customer, you will manage what's important to the customer. By aligning internal and external measures, you compel the organization to focus on customer requirements.

➤ Develop partnering relationships with your customers. As Marlow Industries believes, a customer-focused organization strives to make its customers successful. To do that you need to be partners with your customers, promoting trust, integrity, commitment, and loyalty.

➤ Pull Away

➤ Focus on customer retention. Analyze customer information and data, including information about the customers of competitors and customers won and lost, to identify why customers leave and why they remain loyal. Act on those areas that have the greatest impact on customer retention to eliminate the reasons you lose customers.

➤ Tie a portion of compensation to measures of customer satisfaction. At Custom Research, every full-time employee is rewarded for meeting company, team/department, and individual goals. Client satisfaction is a part of everyone's incentive compensation calculation.

➤ Guarantee that your products/services will satisfy your customers' requirements. As Granite Rock has shown, the benefits of a no-questions-asked, money-back guarantee far outweigh the risks.

Chapter

Organize to Optimize

We've gotten matrixed, networked, clustered, and webbed. The circle. Molecular and ecosystems. Process and team-based. Horizontal. Boundaryless. And virtual, as in a virtual ode to ODs (organizational designs). A host of Davids clamoring for attention in the very large shadow of a Goliath called Hierarchy, the organizational design we all know and abhor.

Nobody used to care much about organizational design back when it was the only game in town. If you worked for an organization, it had a president/CEO/owner who had a few vice presidents reporting to him; they in turn had managers reporting to them, and the managers had supervisors reporting to them; at the bottom were the employees who designed, produced, and delivered the organization's products and services. The OD was a pyramid. The structure was the org chart. No one gave much thought to this structure because it monopolized the OD landscape. You would no more complain about your organization being a hierarchy than you would about the grass being green or the sky blue.

But the hierarchy is showing its age. It demands, when it should ask. It controls, when it should empower. It values conformity, when it needs creativity. It plods, when it should hurry. It resists change, when it should embrace it. Desperate attempts to breathe life into the hierarchy confront a structure nearly petrified after decades of going unchallenged.

Granite Rock Company was founded in 1900. In 1986, its leaders realized that it had become too centralized in its decision making, too bureaucratic. Bruce Woolpert, president and CEO, describes a hierarchy to which we can all relate:

You couldn't order business cards or the simplest things with-
out getting one of our vice presidents' approval. We had two
vice presidents that truly enjoyed helping and getting in-
volved, so the more they helped, the more people in the com-
pany believed that these individuals wanted to make all the
decisions. And in a strange way, as the telephone messages got
thicker and thicker on these vice presidents' desks, and they
were rushing around more and more in the company, they felt
more valuable to the company. In fact, bureaucracy was start-
ing to kill us and our employees were starting to tell us this: It
takes too long to get decisions made.

The hierarchy didn't work. Granite Rock decided to turn its
organization chart upside down, putting the customers in charge
and the president at the bottom. Bruce found himself in a new role,
"trying to stabilize this triangle, to support what the customer has
asked for." Granite Rock's new customer-focused design transformed the organization, helping it earn the Baldrige Award just
six years later.

Like the leaders at Granite Rock, we awaken to the idea of organizational design like all the other dramatic changes in our business world: surprised, skeptical, and grateful. We thought a
hierarchy was our only choice. We can't believe any other organizational design could possibly work. Yet we often wished there
were a better way.

We've lived with hierarchies for so long that we've forgotten
why we have them. An organization exists to enhance the work of
the people in it. People give structure to the organization to help
it serve its customers by providing them with something of value
in return for their money, and to do so at a profit. If every organization thought about the best way to design itself to achieve its
purpose, few would choose a hierarchy.

■ REQUIEM FOR A HIERARCHY

Before we can kiss the hierarchy good-bye, we need to acknowledge
why we feel so attached to it.

One reason is that it's been with us forever. The command-and-
control mentality that drives a hierarchy has been around since
the 1870s. Peter Drucker compared the command-and-control

organization to an organism held together by its shell. The shell encased its employees with systems, policies, procedures, and rules that controlled all activity (Drucker 1995).

In the early 1900s, Frederick Taylor described how to mechanize the shell. Taylor wrote that management's role was to define, measure, and control work in order to make people as consistent, reliable, and efficient as the machines they ran. It was a brilliant idea. Companies standardized everything they could. They told their employees exactly what to do and how and when to do it. They instituted conformity and control in the mass production for mass markets. They valued consistency and efficiency above all else.

Peter Senge describes this system of management as linear, from establishing goals, to organizing to achieve the goals, to controlling how we get there. The holy trinity of Western management: plan, organize, control (Spears 1995).

Christopher Bartlett and Sumantra Ghoshal call it the strategy-structure-systems framework. Its objective, they write, is "to create a management system that could minimize the idiosyncrasies of human behavior." Minimize enough and the people, like the machines they operate, become replaceable (Bartlett and Ghoshal 1994).

Leaders liked the hierarchy idea because it matched their mental model of employees in a company. The best people became the leaders. The rest became followers. Since the followers couldn't be trusted, either because they were stupid or lazy or both, the structure of the organization required bosses in a hierarchy of intelligence and power.

The idea fit the times. The times have changed. Since we are here to bury the hierarchy, not to berate it, let's look at why the hierarchy is well past its prime.

➤ Shortcomings of the Hierarchy

It Focuses on the Wrong Thing

An organization really has two very different customers: the people who buy the product or service and the people who profit from it. Picture the pyramid. Buyer-customers are at the bottom and owner-customers are at the top. Now think about where the focus is. Which direction do career paths move? Where does the power reside? Who gets the nicest offices? How does the organization (and the business press) measure success?

Everything points to the top of the pyramid. Hierarchies exist to create value for their shareholders, not for their customers. When the interests, priorities, and time frames of buyer-customers and owner-customers conflict, the owner-customers usually win. Just look at downsizing, which makes stock prices jump and customers jumpy. What happens to quality and customer service when fewer people must pull the load?

The leaders in a hierarchy report to boards of directors that represent the interests of stockholders; it's no surprise these leaders see their organizations as profit-making enterprises. The owner-customers can fire them . . . or they can reward them with stock options, which makes the leader an owner-customer, too. This is not what is meant by being customer focused.

It's Slow, Rigid, and Dull

In *Mass Customization,* B. Joseph Pine II writes, "Organizational forms suitable for mass production are decidedly unsuitable for mass customization." The differences, according to Pine, are that "organizations suited for mass production are characterized by stilted hierarchies with deep functional separations, rigid specialized resources (both workers and technology), and the separation of thinking and doing. On the other hand, organizations suited to mass customization . . . are characterized by integrated functions within dynamic boundaries . . . flexibly specialized resources, and the integration of thinking and doing."

By their nature, hierarchies are slow to respond. They resist change. They alienate customers. They stifle employees. They obstruct fast and flexible.

It Wastes the Organization's Most Valuable Resource

At some point during this century, Frederick Taylor's ideas about scientific management—defining, measuring, and controlling the work—were applied to those doing the work. Jobs were reduced to a series of tasks to be performed. Workers were paid to conform to the company line. They were not paid to think; the separation of thinking and doing became a characteristic of the hierarchy.

The approach worked as long as a company had all the time in the world to produce a narrow range of products for customers willing to pay top dollar for them. It stopped working when global competitors and savvy companies delivered the same products faster with higher quality at lower costs. It stopped working when global markets and savvy companies created niche markets large enough to profit fast, flexible producers. It stopped working when savvy companies integrated thinking and doing, flattening the organizational structure, improving their speed and flexibility, and taking advantage of an untapped source of knowledge and experience and a company's most valuable resource—its people.

The hierarchy is no longer an effective organizational design in practice or in theory. As Margaret Wheatley writes in *Leadership and the New Science,* "Our concept of organizations is moving away from the mechanistic creations that flourished in the age of bureaucracy. We have begun to speak in earnest of more fluid, organic structures, even of boundaryless organizations. We are beginning to recognize organizations as systems."

The mechanistic view of an organization fragments everything into functions, departments, specialties, and tasks. The systems view looks at the organization as a whole, a shift in mind that Senge describes as "seeing interrelationships rather than linear cause-effect chains and seeing processes of change rather than snapshots."

This holistic perspective is essential to sustainable, long-term change. One major reason change initiatives such as reengineering, reorganizing, and total quality management fail is because the implementers focus on parts of the system while ignoring the whole. You cannot optimize one part of an organization without suboptimizing the organization. As Geary Rummler and Alan Brache write in *Improving Performance,* "An organization behaves as a system, regardless of whether it is being managed as a system."

And the system rules the day. Rummler and Brache note that, "if you put a good performer against a bad system, the system will win almost every time." Senge agrees. "Different people in the same structure tend to produce qualitatively similar results," he writes. "When there are problems, or performance fails to live up to what is intended, it is easy to find someone or something to blame. But, more often than we realize, systems cause their own crises, not external forces or individuals' mistakes" (Senge 1990).

The basics of business excellence are holistic approaches to optimizing the system. And nothing is more basic or more critical to optimizing the system than the design of the organization.

■ THE ELEMENTS OF ORGANIZATIONAL DESIGN

In April 1995, *Quality Progress* reported on a study conducted by Gemini Consulting of more than 1,450 managers and executives from twelve global corporations. The study asked each manager and executive to choose the keys to his or her company's success from a list of thirty-four different corporate capabilities. The capability receiving the most votes—identified by nearly half the respondents—was organizing around their customers' requirements. ("Being flexible to meet competitive conditions" was cited by 41 percent, pointing to another reason to look at organizational design.)

The primary elements of organizational design are the wants and needs of customers and the resources and competencies of the organization. In the previous chapter we discussed the importance of knowing who your customers are and what they require. The best organizational designs focus all business operations on meeting and exceeding these requirements. The quality of the design depends on knowledge: how well the organization knows its customers and how well it knows itself.

Knowledge of the organization grows as you practice the basics of business excellence:

➤ Articulating a shared vision compels leaders and others to think about what the organization is and what it hopes to become. (Chapter 3)

➤ Developing employees means spreading knowledge about customers and the company throughout the organization. (Chapter 4)

➤ Process thinking depends on knowledge of customers, suppliers, inputs, outputs, and processes. (Chapter 7)

➤ Managing by fact demands the identification, collection, analysis, communication, and use of key information and data, transforming intuition and assumptions into quantifiable measures. (Chapter 8)

➤ Strategic planning requires extensive knowledge of current and future customers, markets, competitors, risks, and the organization's capabilities and resources. (Chapter 9)

The chapters in this book describe the components of knowledge and learning as basics of business excellence. In this chapter, we focus on what all of this knowledge tells you about your organization and its design. What value do you bring to your customers? What are your unique capabilities and resources? What are your core competencies?

There are several ways to describe the value you bring to your customers. In *The Discipline of Market Leaders*, Michael Treacy and Fred Wiersema identify three value disciplines, "so called because each discipline produces a different kind of customer value." The three are operational excellence (low price and hassle-free service), product leadership (best product), and customer intimacy (best solution and all the support you need). According to the authors, a market leader must excel in one of these dimensions while maintaining threshold standards in the other two. Treacy advises small growing companies to "stay out of the path of the focused market leaders, choose another value discipline, and leverage their natural strengths to deliver unprecedented value to their chosen customers."

Rosabeth Moss Kanter writes in her book, *World Class*, that companies excel in one of three generic ways: as thinkers (edge comes from continuous innovation), makers (executional competence means high-value, cost-effective production), or traders (help move goods/services from one country to another). According to Kanter, world-class companies are more entrepreneurial (seeking better concepts), more learning oriented (searching for ideas and experience), and more collaborative (valuing relationships with other companies as partners).

In their book *Competing for the Future*, Gary Hamel and C. K. Prahalad preach that core competencies are the source of competitive advantage. As noted in the previous chapter, a core competence is a bundle of skills and technologies that enable you to provide value to your customers.

Whichever way you choose to look at what your organization does best, the key is to look at it from the customer's perspective. If you are best at producing high-quality products but your primary customers buy on price, you need either to carve a niche out of the market or reassess your core competencies.

Once you are clear about your customers' requirements and the value your organization provides, you can design (or redesign) the organization to leverage your capabilities. The design itself can be a source of competitive advantage if it supports the ability to customize products and services to specific customer requirements, the flexibility to anticipate and adapt to change, and the capacity to design, produce, and deliver products and services quickly. Variety, change, and speed are the criteria for evaluating an effective organizational design.

The structure of an organizational design can take many forms. In his book *The Democratic Corporation,* Russell Ackoff states that "the need to organize derives from the need to divide labor" and "there are only three ways of dividing labor, hence three types of organizational units":

➤ Functionally-defined (input) units that typically support internal customers, i.e., purchasing, finance, research and development, and human resources.

➤ Product- or service-defined (output) units that provide products and services to external customers.

➤ Market-defined units that sell the outputs of the product/service-defined units.

Based on these three types, Ackoff proposes an organizational design he calls the multidimensional organization, a hybrid structure that sees the organization—and every unit within it—as a three-dimensional cube. The three dimensions are input, output, and marketing units.

In *Designing Organizations,* Jay Galbraith, another organizational design expert, suggests five possibilities for structuring your organization that include Ackoff's three types:

➤ Functional, if your organization is small and offers a single product line

➤ Product, if you have multiple products for separate customers

➤ Market, if you have products or services unique to market segments

➤ Geographical, if closeness to the customer is critical

➤ Process, if you need to reduce cycle times

The best structure for your situation depends on your customers' requirements and the capabilities of your organization. While Galbraith discusses hybrid structures that overcome the weaknesses of one structure by combining the elements of two or more structures, he emphasizes the need for process thinking no matter what structure is chosen. "The newest organizational structure is the process structure," he writes. "The process structure is the culmination of three strategic initiatives that all focused on work flow processes and fought against the barriers of the functional organization: total quality, cycle-time reduction, and reengineering." We'll look more closely at process thinking in the next chapter.

Custom Research Inc. provides an excellent example of an organizational design that uses a process structure to be client focused. Roughly 90 percent of its employees are on account teams, each of which serves specific clients. Each account team is responsible for entire marketing research projects, start to finish, inputs to outputs: the whole process. This team-based organizational design was implemented in 1988 as a better way to meet and exceed client expectations. The focus of the change was outward, not inward. "We focus more on how things get done than on how they're organized," says partner Jeff Pope. "As long as teams are working well for clients, that's all we're concerned about. Clients are very much in the middle of our process." Like Granite Rock, CRI's organization chart (which it had to create when it first applied for the Baldrige Award; until then, no such chart existed) has the client on top to show where the energy of the organization is directed.

Hierarchical designs channel energy toward the needs of the boss, not the needs of the customer. Their functional silos inhibit process thinking. To break down these barriers, new organizational designs seek to support the core processes of the organization. The idea of the **horizontal corporation** evolved from a desire to organize along a company's core processes. The **circular organization** promotes process thinking and personal responsibility by making it possible for each member to participate in all decisions that affect him or her directly and to make and implement decisions that affect no one else. The **molecular organization,** described by Gerald Ross and Michael Kay in their book *Toppling the Pyramid,* has the boss at the center as strategic nucleus and the operating people spinning around the nucleus, putting them as close to the customer as possible. "Holding the whole atom together is a strong shared vision and a set of values, displacing traditional supervision," the authors write. The **virtual corporation** is a network of independent companies who apply their particular areas of expertise to the core processes that serve customer requirements.

Process thinking is one attribute of the new organizational designs. Another is the use of teams. As Jon Katzenbach and Douglas Smith write, "Most of the models of the organization of the future that we have heard about . . . are premised on teams surpassing individuals as the primary performance unit in the company" (Katzenbach and Smith 1993).

Teams fit well with the goals of the new organizational designs. They focus on customer requirements. They produce tangible results. They offer flexibility and speed. They promote problem solving and creativity. They facilitate organizational learning. And they organize unique sets of knowledge and skills around processes that are critical to the organization's success.

Rubbermaid offers one example of how teams have been at the heart of a new organization design (Loeb 1994). The company's CEO spends a lot of time thinking about his organization's structure, strategies, and new products (for which Rubbermaid is renowned). Reflecting on nature "got him thinking about the best way to organize people to create and market products. He came up with this idea: Construct a series of teams that replicate the management structure of the parent, like leaves on a plant. Give each team responsibility for creating, improving, and marketing a series of products." Each team consists of five people from sales, marketing, finance, manufacturing, and research and development, a structure that replicates Rubbermaid's management structure. Each team develops its own strategic and operating plans. Each team must make a profit.

The design sounds like Ackoff's multidimensional organization with input (R&D and finance), output (manufacturing), and marketing (marketing and sales). Each team is a fractal, replicating the structure of the parent organization. Margaret Wheatley believes that "the very best organizations have a fractal quality to them," a pattern that can be found at every level of the organization. "An observer of such an organization can tell what the organization's values and ways of doing business are by watching anyone," she writes in *Leadership and the New Science*. The patterns evident in the behavior of all employees are shaped by a shared vision that they understand, embrace, and act upon (see Chapter 3).

Virtual corporations are intriguing because they are built along core process lines, they make wide use of teams within and beyond the organization's boundaries (by including customer and supplier representatives on the teams), and they tend to have a fractal quality about them. The fractal quality derives from the organization's strategy for defining exactly what its core competencies are, making sure everyone in the organization shares that vision, and outsourcing functions beyond the organization's vision and scope.

For example, one of Chrysler's core competencies is assembling automobiles, yet the actual assembly is only part of the process involved in making an automobile. As a virtual corporation, Chrysler works with a network of companies, each doing what it does best, to produce automobiles. Chrysler contributes about 30 percent of the total value to the cars it makes; its subcontractors add the other 70 percent. The customer sees only Chrysler, the virtual corporation.

The benefits of such virtuality as an organizational design are:

➤ *Clearer strategic direction:* You know exactly who you are and what you do.

➤ *Access to leading practices:* By working with other organizations that excel in their particular fields, you always bring the best practices to your products/services.

➤ *Process orientation:* The interdependence of customers and suppliers forces an organization to work along process lines.

➤ *Customer focus:* "Going virtual" means knowing exactly what value you provide your customers and what you need from your virtual partners to meet all customer requirements.

Marlow Industries operates four small business teams focused on its four market segments, what Chris Witzke, the chief operating officer, calls "virtual organizations within the organization." Each team is led by a marketing person because Marlow wants to make sure the teams are customer driven. Most employees are on one of the teams, which meet weekly. Each team has a senior management mentor to help break down barriers and stretch the team's horizons. Each team operates as a business team, with pseudo P&Ls to help them track their performance to the bottom line. "The structure has been in place for five years," Chris says. "It took a while for everyone to understand how it works, and we're still finding ways they can work better."

Virtuality can also be practiced internally with shared services. Some organizations consolidate support activities into one function that serves all units. For example, at 3M the human resources activities are consolidated into one function that supports all of the company's divisions. Shared services get rid of redundancy and allow organizations to concentrate on their core competencies, providing the benefits of virtuality within the organization.

Another dimension of virtuality is strategic alliances. A strategic alliance allows your organization to leverage its core competencies by combining them with the competencies of another organization. In a way, outsourcing can be a form of strategic alliance to the degree that the partnership supports the organization's strategic direction. A strategic alliance can be formed to exploit a strength of either or both organizations in the alliance. It usually occurs when neither organization wants to buy the other's unique competence.

The virtual corporation helps an organization focus on what it does that is important to its customers. Some companies have embraced the idea as a way of cutting costs by cutting whole departments. The problem with this approach is that it is a reactive solution to a bottom line problem, not a proactive solution to a performance problem. Companies obsessed with financial results rarely see the opportunity to better match their customers' needs with their organization's capabilities. As a result, "going virtual" has the same effect as reengineering or downsizing or implementing any other management fad: It produces short-term gain before the organization returns to the dysfunctional behaviors that define its culture. Real cultural change rarely occurs without a vision for the future that everyone shares. Making more money is not enough.

■ TIME AND SPACE

Organizational design is more than theory. As you reorganize people and relationships to promote speed, flexibility, and innovation, you will need to reorganize the space in which they work. "Real time forces you to organize structures that are more reflective of how life actually works," says Carlene Ellis, Intel's vice president of organization. "And once we start reflecting life, we have to let go of those false barriers that were built in when work reflected the machine" (Helgesen 1995).

Most work spaces reflect the mechanistic, command-and-control view of their organizations. People work individually in offices or cubicles. The higher your ranking in the organization, the better your space. The only common areas are conference rooms, which are rarely used except for scheduled meetings. Noise is discouraged. Energy is low. Fun is almost nonexistent. People are machine parts, expected to do their jobs as defined by themselves.

In the new organizational designs, the walls that separate people—and ideas, conversations, and creativity—are removed. People work together as teams in shared space, with no one in the team owning better space than another. Many organizations design team work areas that have a central, open area for team meetings, brainstorming, and discussions, with individual work areas around the outside of the central hub. The areas, like the teams they support, are flexible and adaptable to changes in the team or to new teams.

The best way to design the space is to give the people who will be using it control over it. You may need to provide some options to get them started—most people need a little help thinking beyond the cubicle mentality they're used to—but they should have the freedom and support they need to experiment with their space until it meets their needs. Allowing such freedom will be easy *if* leadership has committed to engaging employees in making the organization stronger, more flexible, more customer focused, and more profitable. It will be impossible if leadership intends to maintain command and control.

Organizational design, like the other basics of business excellence in this book, is about respect, trust, and responsibility. As you consider the best design for your organization, think about how that design would support a high-trust work environment in which people behave in the following ways:

➤ Instead of blaming each other, they give credit for good work that is being done.

➤ People take responsibility rather than make excuses.

➤ Information is shared rather than restricted.

➤ People collaborate on important issues.

➤ Instead of creating "us and them" distinctions, people talk in terms of "we."

➤ People focus on the big-picture issues and do not get side-tracked by differences in details.

➤ People respect organizational structures and roles and do not use them as weapons.

➤ Rather than discrediting each other's competence, employees and managers value each others' background and experience.

➤ Concerns, criticisms, and conflicts are openly voiced.

➤ Rather than expressing cynicism, employees and managers speak positively about their work, the organization, and the future.

Imagine an organizational design that makes your organization more effective at meeting customer requirements, improves speed and flexibility, and encourages respect, trust, and responsibility. The design is a conscious choice, selected because it fits the bigger picture: the organization's vision, goals, and strategies; approaches to engaging employees; process thinking; and the organization's ability to learn and grow. As it is implemented, the organization moves from internal competition to cooperation, from confusion about tasks to clarity of purpose, from avoiding work to taking responsibility, from loneliness to camaraderie, from drudgery to joy.

All because people want a chance to contribute the talent, knowledge, and experience they possess. And the new organizational designs give them that chance.

■ STRATEGIES FOR IMPROVEMENT

➤ Jump Start

➤ Before changing your organizational design, assess its current condition. Among the ways to measure the structure, consider (1) the number of levels from the top executive to a first-level employee; (2) the ratio of first-level managers to employees (the lower the ratio, the less you trust employees to act responsibly); and (3) barriers to work flow, including who is empowered to make what decisions.

➤ Based on your organization's shared vision, commitment to engaging employees, understanding of customer requirements, and knowledge of core competencies, assess whether the current organizational design serves your needs. You may want to do some strategic thinking ("what-ifs" described in Chapter 3) about changes in your industry that will affect quality, speed, and cost, what kinds of pressure those changes would put on your current organizational design, and how other designs may be better.

➤ Get outside help. You need to know what you're doing before embarking on the radical redesign of your organization. Such knowledge may come from other companies that have taken a similar approach or from outside experts in organizational design. You can flatten the learning curve and avoid mistakes and delays by learning what works for others.

➤ Tune Up

➤ Consider the physical design of work space and facilities. Based on how you want employees to work, determine if the design supports or inhibits their efforts. Ask employees how it feels to work in their physical environment. Invite ideas on how to change the environment to help them work more productively, cooperatively, creatively, or in any other way that serves the organization.

➤ Analyze customer information—surveys, complaints, retention, etc.—to determine if the organization is meeting customer requirements. Ask key customers if they feel that the organization is focused on their needs. Compare that data and information to internal data such as employee surveys and cycle-time measures to see if the trends correlate. Use the analysis to help identify those points in the system that distract from a customer focus.

➤ Analyze customer and internal information to clarify the value you provide your customers. The thinking behind value disciplines and core competencies can help put customer requirements and company capabilities in a new light. When the value you provide as an organization is clear, you can examine the design of the organization to see if it is the best choice to deliver that value.

➤ Pull Away

➤ Continually reassess the organizational design to determine if: (1) it is the best structure to meet customer requirements; (2) it makes the organization adaptable, fast and flexible enough to respond to a changing marketplace; (3) it facilitates learning; and (4) it provides a high-trust environment in which people take responsibility for being creative, innovative, effective, and customer focused.

Chapter 7

Think Process

Most managers manage by results and outcomes. Call it the scatological approach to management: Study what comes out of the process to figure out what went into it and how it might have worked. Of course, it's after the fact. Spend the day reacting to problems, putting out fires. Figuring out who to blame. Yelling. (Monty Python alumnus, actor, and business videotape producer John Cleese, when asked about cultural differences between British and American businesspeople, said: "I have noticed over the years that in America, more so than in Europe, there is a tendency toward a certain type of manager who makes himself [or herself] feel good by shouting at his or her employees. Just awful stuff" [Lane 1996].)

So why do managers manage by results and outcomes? Because they don't know how else to manage. The problems that stampede across their desks every day demand their attention. The best way to get a problem off their desks is to blame someone and make him or her responsible for the solution. When the stampede threatens to trample them, they yell. Management by intimidation.

An alternative is to manage by process. An organization is a system. The ways in which the components of that system interact to achieve the aims of the system are processes. Whether or not you manage the system, you have a system. Whether or not you manage the processes, you have processes. "Processes are how we work," writes Thomas Davenport. "Any company that ignores its business processes or fails to improve them risks its future" (Davenport 1995).

If you don't manage your processes, you're stuck with whatever they produce. And no amount of yelling will make it better.

151

. . .

Marlow Industries has been thinking about, managing, and improving its processes since 1988. It started by focusing on the front end of its manufacturing process, reducing variability in the materials that fed production. When something failed, managers began asking what was wrong with the process, not who was to blame. They started measuring the parameters that keep their processes in control and stable, rather than the parts the process produced. They believed that stable processes would improve quality and reduce cycle time, and they were right.

Marlow achieved its goal of nearly 100 percent on-time delivery of high-quality products and has reduced cycle times and improved quality continuously ever since. Its quality and cycle-time results were good enough to help it win the Baldrige Award in 1991. But that's not the story for this chapter. The process story is what happened at Marlow *after* it achieved its goals.

"When problems exist, people are on the phones handling customer problems, everybody's reacting and putting out fires," says Chris Witzke, Marlow's chief operating officer. "Once we established stable processes, all of a sudden we had more resources available than we ever imagined. We freed up half the organization to work on improvements—and then the improvements accelerated. You free up the time and resources that allow people to work on proactive, continuous improvement." And on customer delight.

Chris remembers one of the first customers to benefit from Marlow's resource-rich position. The customer called to mention that it had experienced failures in a Marlow part in its manufacturing process. Three devices in the last year out of several thousand. No big deal, the customer said.

Chris and two other employees got on a plane the following Monday and flew to Pennsylvania to meet with the customer. They looked at the defective products, studied the manufacturing process, and identified and solved the problem. They flew back to Dallas.

"About two weeks later," Chris remembers, "I was talking to the customer and he admitted that we really surprised them by getting there so fast." Almost too fast, according to the customer, who told Chris, "We thought you were trying to cover something up."

It's not hard to imagine the competitive advantage such customer service provides. But that's not all of Marlow's process story, either.

Marlow has always focused on the high end of the market by providing high-quality products backed by extensive research and development, engineering services, and customer support. Improving quality and reducing cycle times has made Marlow even more competitive in this market. It's also helped the company cut costs. "We've gotten to the point where we can be the world's lowest cost producer in what would be considered a high overhead environment," Chris says. "Now we can compete with companies who try to do it with much leaner operations. That's opened up markets at the low end, and it's all because of process control."

If you've never thought of what you do in terms of processes, the shift in paradigms can be a little unnerving. According to process expert Thomas Davenport, a process is "a specific ordering of work activities across time and place, with a beginning, an end, and clearly identified inputs and outputs: a structure for action" (Davenport 1993).

When most people think of processes, they picture the structure for action called manufacturing. Raw materials (inputs) arrive on the floor. Employees use machines to transform the materials (process) into products (outputs).

Companies that provide services see the work process a little differently. Their structure for action begins with information, ideas, and knowledge (inputs). Employees apply their expertise to the customer need (process) to produce solutions (outputs).

All work is part of one or more processes. But not all processes are work processes. Organizations conduct business through processes such as marketing and selling, handling complaints, receiving payment, planning, and issuing financial reports. Organizations manage people through processes such as creating a shared vision, training, performance management, rewards and recognition, and audits and assessments. For process improvement to show any long-term benefits, it must address processes in all three areas of management, business, and work. As Xerox CEO Paul Allaire said in an interview with David Garvin, "Chief executives have always focused on management processes. They're the way you get things done. What's different now is that senior managers are also involved in business and work processes . . . For the first time, they are reshaping business and work processes to align them with strategy while making them more customer oriented and efficient" (Garvin 1995).

Process thinking promotes alignment. Leaders who feel like parts of their organizations are pulling in different directions can use process thinking to pull them together.

➤ *Process thinking builds a customer focus.* Process thinking begins with a rock-solid understanding of customer requirements. Each process concludes by delivering products and/or services that serve those requirements. Process thinking contributes to a customer focus by making it easier to identify and eliminate work that does not add value to customers.

➤ *Process thinking improves quality and cycle time.* Core processes cut across functional boundaries. Improving these processes means improving within the functions, but it also means improving between functions. The cross-functional nature of process thinking brings new perspectives to old ways of doing business. Cross-functional and customer focused means decisions are made based on the needs of the customer, not the needs of the function.

➤ *Process thinking reduces costs.* According to Allaire, "A process orientation allows you to take huge amounts of costs out of the system while still improving customer satisfaction. It keeps your eye on both objectives simultaneously."

➤ *Process thinking helps drive fear out of the organization.* The functional organization encourages blame. If something fails, someone must be at fault. Process thinking means blaming the process, not the person. As quality expert Joseph Juran discovered in studies of a variety of companies in the early 1950s, only 20 percent of production-level problems could be controlled by workers. The other 80 percent were problems with the system. Process thinking focuses on the system, transforming a culture of blame into a culture of cooperative problem solving.

➤ *Process thinking promotes creative, empowered employees.* As an organization gains control of its processes, it can free people to act creatively as long as their improvements respect the process and the organization's objectives. Clear objectives and well-managed processes keep people focused far better than the old command-and-control approach.

➤ *Process thinking supports strategic thinking and organizational design.* Strategic thinking and organizational design help an organization be flexible enough to anticipate and respond to major change. Process thinking helps the organization be agile enough to act quickly and decisively in new directions.

➤ *Process thinking helps optimize the entire organization.* "Viewing an organization as a collection of processes rather than as a rigid departmental structure is particularly useful," write Rust, Zahorik, and Keiningham in *Return on Quality,* "because to improve satisfaction it is necessary to optimize the organization as a whole, and processes are the relevant, logical framework for analyzing a firm's effectiveness across the entire organization."

■ WHICH PROCESSES TO THINK ABOUT

People new to process thinking often feel overwhelmed by the complexity of their organizations. Functional thinking has the great benefit of putting everyone into neat, well-labeled boxes. You want to know what someone does, you look for the department in his or her title. You want to know how something is done, you figure out which functional area is responsible. The process is hidden, indistinct from any other set of activities.

The first step in process thinking is to identify which processes to think about. Not all processes are created equal. The process that publishes an annual report is important, but it is not as important as a process that produces a product or service. The difference—the first criteria for selecting a core process—is what provides value to your customers.

➤ How to Identify Core Processes

1. Based on what your key customers tell you, what does your organization provide them that they value? (For more ideas about getting at customer needs and requirements, refer to Chapter 5.) What are the main products or services that key customers expect to buy from you? What are the processes for each? What are the steps from the input of materials and/or information to the output (product or service)? How would you name the process for internal identification?

2. Consider core processes from other perspectives. Which pro-
    cesses are essential to the organization's business? Which
    processes cost the most in terms of time and money?
    Which processes will help you compete in the future?
    Which processes transform information to make it valuable
    to your customers?

3. Rate each process using these questions: How central is the
    process to the organization's strategic plan and competitive
    success? How central is the process to attracting new cus-
    tomers and retaining existing ones? Which processes do
    key customers feel are central to their satisfaction and loy-
    alty (and don't assume you know the answer; ask them)?

The act of identifying core processes plants the seeds of process thinking. For leaders new to the notion, answering the questions can be both frustrating and enlightening. We are not used to
thinking as farmers: plan, plant, tend, harvest, sell; inputs to outputs; start to end. A few phases. Many steps. One core process.

Farmers have other core processes—different crops, machinery/
technology issues, livestock to raise, commodities to exchange—
depending on the size of their operations. Other businesses are no
different: the number of core processes varies depending on their
size and complexity. Large companies like IBM and Xerox may have
between ten and twenty core processes. Smaller organizations may
have three to five. The number doesn't matter as long as the processes you identify are critical to your business.

The list is likely to change over time, and that's normal. The
goal of this first foray into process thinking is not to create the
definitive list of core processes, but to begin recognizing the processes that serve your customers.

■ IMPROVE OR REENGINEER?

The goal of process thinking is to improve the performance of all
processes, especially those that serve customers. However, no organization new to process thinking has the resources to work on all
processes at once.

The organization may be able to focus on most of its core processes if there are few of them and the organization is committed to

improving them quickly. If resources are scarce and/or the number of core processes is too high, leaders will need to prioritize the core processes and decide which ones to address. To select which processes to study, consider:

> ➤ How central the process is to customer satisfaction and the organization's key strategies
> ➤ Whether the scope of the process is manageable (or does it need to be broken down into subprocesses?)
> ➤ How healthy the process is (which, at this early stage, will have to be determined by the perceptions of the leaders and/or process customers)

After you have identified which core processes to study, the next step is to become familiar with each process. Gather enough information about a process to help you determine whether to improve or reengineer it. Improving a process involves incremental change of an existing process. Reengineering a process involves radical change starting with a clean slate. One of the best ways to decide which course to take is to determine the condition of the current process.

You can gather this information by forming a cross-functional team consisting of representatives from key phases of the process. The team is instructed to define the current process, then analyze it for quality, speed, and cost. In most cases, team members will need to be trained in process management, including what a process is, how to map the process, how to measure its performance, and how to relate performance to the process customers' requirements.

The team will also need to understand that its purpose is not to improve the process—yet—but to recommend *how* it should be improved. The organization's leaders will use this information to evaluate the scope of the task at hand, prioritize process improvement/reengineering projects, and allocate resources.

To determine whether a process is a candidate for improvement or overhaul, consider the distinctions between process improvement and reengineering described by Thomas Davenport in *Process Innovation:*

> ➤ Incremental vs. radical change
> ➤ Starting with the existing process vs. starting with a clean slate

➤ Short vs. long time required

➤ Bottom-up vs. top-down participation

➤ Functional vs. cross-functional scope

➤ Moderate vs. high risk

The comparison doesn't mean that a cross-functional process has to be reengineered or that process improvement cannot have top-down participation. What it does mean is that reengineering costs more time and money, involves more risk, and results in more radical change. Despite that, it may be the better option if the current process is so convoluted or dysfunctional or ineffective that it cannot be saved. (We'll look at the benefits and drawbacks of reengineering later in this chapter.)

■ IMPROVING A PROCESS

Process improvement differs from reengineering in that the current process is improved, not abandoned. The goal is to improve quality and speed, reduce costs, and better satisfy the customers of the process. To achieve this goal, use the following process:

1. *Identify the key process to be improved.* By this point you should have a short list of core processes. If this is the first process to be improved, choose one that has the greatest likelihood of success. A positive experience will help the organization make a smoother transition to process thinking.

2. *Agree on the purpose of the improvement, i.e., improve quality, shorten cycle time, reduce costs, and/or serve customers better.* You may want to do everything (and indeed, serving customers better often results from improvements in the other areas), but the object is to make success possible. Accept that this process will be continually improved and it will be easier to set more achievable targets in the first phase.

3. *Select and train the process improvement team.* Odds are the process to be improved cuts across functional units. You will want representatives from these units to work together on the improvements, which suggests a cross-

functional process improvement team. See Chapter 4 for ideas on creating high-performance teams.

4. *Document the current process.* The best way to document a process is to map it: Create a flowchart that visually depicts the process from the input of materials/information to the output of products/services. Identify how long each step normally takes and the measures of quality, speed, and cost in place.

5. *Identify the links to other processes.* Most processes depend on other processes for material and/or information. By identifying these points of contact now, you can include an assessment of the quality of those links in your analysis.

6. *Analyze the current process for quality, speed, cost, and its ability to meet customer requirements.* Ask why each step is performed. Determine the gap between where the current process is and where it needs to be to serve customers and the organization's strategic plans.

7. *Identify disconnects in the process.* Look for those places where communication is poor, the process bogs down, mistakes occur repeatedly, steps are redundant or unnecessary, or people get frustrated.

8. *Determine why the disconnects occur.* And no, the reason is not someone in Accounting. Disconnects occur because the process breaks down.

9. *Develop solutions and measures.* A few ways to come up with possible solutions include:

➤ Identify which steps add value to the materials/information flowing through the process and find ways to eliminate steps that don't.

➤ Ask if a step really needs to occur or if it could be eliminated (or if not eliminated, minimized).

➤ Consider how to change the process to control variation.

➤ Benchmark similar processes outside the organization (As B. Joseph Pine II wrote, "The objective is to redesign, not reinvent.").

➤ Identify in-process measures that those working the process can use to monitor and improve the performance of the process.

10. *Create a new process map reflecting the improvements.* Don't get attached to it. Process improvement is an ongoing effort that can quickly make process maps obsolete. However, you still need the maps to document and communicate changes to the process.

11. *Test the solutions and analyze the results.* Track the in-process measures. Compare performance on the measures to performance on customer satisfaction measures to see if both are in sync. Solicit feedback from those who work the process and from customers of the process.

12. *Deploy the improvements.* Standardize the changes. Give those working the process the information and authority to manage and improve it.

13. *Get the dots and plot the dots.* You cannot improve what you do not measure. If you're not sure what to measure, try process cycle time, which Carl Thor calls "the key measure of internal quality. Nothing else that can be measured has the comprehensive power to reflect all the forms of waste in the organization" (Thor 1994). An important part of plotting the dots is understanding variation, which we will look at below.

In the course of mapping and improving a process, it's easy to get sucked into the steps and lose sight of the whole. The authors of *Product Juggernauts* state that "A process cannot be effectively executed, nor drastically improved, until all the participants understand the whole process and are motivated to make it work well" (Deschamps and Nayak 1995). The motivation comes from a culture that promotes process thinking and continuous improvement. The holistic view requires a conscious effort to step back from the details and study the process as a whole, including the inputs of suppliers, the exchanges between functional areas, and the broader implications of the improvements being made.

Among those implications is the impact of changes on other processes, particularly management processes. For example, if a work process improvement involves empowering employees to manage the process, but a management process dictates that only managers can make decisions about changing a process, something must give. The best way to head off these conflicts is to include senior leadership representation on the process improvement team, not as the leader of the team but as an expert on management process issues.

To institutionalize process management, Geary Rummler and Alan Brache recommend in *Improving Performance* that the newly improved core process has:

> ➤ A map documenting steps and who performs them
>
> ➤ A set of customer-driven measures that drive functional measures
>
> ➤ A process owner
>
> ➤ A permanent process team
>
> ➤ An annual business plan
>
> ➤ Mechanisms for monitoring process performance
>
> ➤ Procedures and vehicles for solving process problems and capitalizing on process opportunities

■ UNDERSTANDING VARIATION

A process consists of many variables. Changes in these variables create variation in the process. The key to managing and improving a process is to understand the causes of variation and what to do about them.

There are two causes of variation: common causes and special causes. You need to understand the difference to be able to manage the process.

Common causes of variation exist in the process at all times. A common cause has little impact on the process by itself, but when it combines with other common causes, the impact can be significant.

Special causes appear sporadically from outside the process. Although they may have little impact, they usually contribute more to variation than common causes.

The first step in controlling variation is to understand what is causing it, and that begins with measurement. You cannot evaluate a process without quantifiable data on the key indicators of process performance. For example, if your process for shipping products to customers suffers from periods of mislabeled boxes and delayed shipments, you must initiate your search for the problem by analyzing the in-process data related to quality and timeliness. The normal reaction is to guess what the problem might be and attempt to fix it. This is called *tampering*, and it's almost always worse than doing nothing at all. As Brian Joiner writes in *Fourth Generation Management*, "Don't just do something—stand there!"

As you collect data points, plot them. Look for the normal boundaries of performance: a center line and normal boundaries on either side. If a data point falls outside the boundaries (control limits), it is a signal that the variation is due to a special cause.

A special cause destabilizes the process. To bring the process back into control, you need to make sure your data is timely, accurate, and plotted. When you're sure a special cause is at work, you must first contain the damage with a quick fix, then search for the special cause. Ask what changed within the process or outside the process that affected it. Identify what was different, examine how it could be eliminated, then implement a long-term fix.

Common causes also present opportunities for improvement, although the approach is quite different. Because common causes are part of the process, the only way to remove them is to fundamentally change the process. And the only reasonable approach to changing the process is to examine all relevant data for how the process works and how its pieces interact.

Joiner identifies three categories of strategies to accomplish this:

➤ *Stratify:* Sort the data into groups or categories based on different factors; look for patterns in the way the data points cluster or do not cluster.

➤ *Experiment:* Make planned changes and learn from the effects—again, by plotting the dots.

➤ *Disaggregate:* Divide the process into component pieces and manage the pieces.

You can learn which strategies to employ, how to distinguish between common causes and special causes, how to plot the dots and identify control limits, and more during a course in statistical process control. If you thought SPC was only relevant on the manufacturing floor, think again. Any process is a candidate for SPC. All you need are in-process measures and knowledge of how to use them.

■ REENGINEERING A PROCESS

There will be times when the existing process just won't cut it anymore. Think of it as entering the Indianapolis 500 car race with a brand-new subcompact car. You can improve that car all you want—beef up the engine, add high-performance tires, tighten the suspension—but the limits of the improved car will still keep it from being competitive. If you need a process that goes faster than the current one can handle, or provides a higher level of quality, or better satisfies customers than the current process, you will need to pull out a clean sheet of paper and build a new one.

The official definition of reengineering, presented by reengineering guru Michael Hammer, is: "The fundamental rethinking and radical redesign of business processes to bring about dramatic improvement in performance." Hammer and coauthor James Champy launched the reengineering craze in 1993 with their book *Reengineering the Corporation*. In the book, Hammer and Champy identify recurring themes or characteristics of the reengineered process, including these:

> ➤ Several jobs are combined into one.

> ➤ Workers make decisions.

> ➤ The steps in the process are performed in a natural order.

> ➤ Processes have multiple versions (which makes mass customization possible).

> ➤ Work is performed where it makes the most sense.

The themes sound promising. Big companies bought into reengineering because they liked the idea of throwing out old, ineffective processes in favor of new, streamlined ones. Radical redesign suggested action, change, dramatic improvement, *lower costs*. Big companies reengineered. They waited for the benefits. Most were disappointed. According to a 1994 CSC Index study, of ninety-nine completed reengineering initiatives, 67 percent were judged as producing mediocre, marginal, or failed results (Davenport 1995).

Much has been written lately about why reengineering fails. The analysis tends to settle on four primary reasons:

> ➤ *No strategic connection.* Companies reengineer for reasons that do not serve the organization's strategic plan. The reengi-

neering occurs in a vacuum; the new perspective dies when the initiative wanes.

➤ *No system connection.* No process is an island. Reengineering a process without also working on its interdependencies with other processes invites a breakdown. That includes its links to management processes which, as David Garvin notes, "are radically different in a process-oriented organization than in a functional, command-and-control organization" (Garvin 1995).

➤ *No senior management support.* An organization cannot embrace radical change unless its leaders make such change possible. Leaders gut a reengineering initiative when they delegate it to outside consultants or internal experts, then ignore it. Leaders must lead the effort for as long as it continues.

➤ *Timidity, fear, and pessimism.* Conservative, command-and-control bodies treat reengineering like a virus: They don't feel right until they kill it. Employees slow the reengineering process to a crawl, then propose Band-Aid solutions. They fear that reengineering is just another way to downsize. They worry that the new process will demand skills they don't have. They see reengineering as another management ploy to get more for less. And in most cases, they're right on all counts. If the organization treats people as commodities, no new initiative is going to convince them they're not. (In fact, CSC Index found that 73 percent of the companies in its study said they were using reengineering to eliminate, on average, 21 percent of the jobs.)

All four reasons for failure share the same root cause: The organization's management system cannot support reengineering.

To succeed, reengineering requires an environment in which senior managers are personally involved in the initiative, it supports the organization's shared vision and strategic plan, employees are given and accept responsibility for initiating change, fear and blame are minimal, and optimism prevails. Without these preconditions for success, no organization should waste its resources on reengineering.

However, if the management system provides fertile ground for such an initiative, reengineering can transform organizations and dramatically improve their performance. In his book *Process Innovation,* Thomas Davenport recommends a five-step process:

1. *Identify processes for innovation (his term for reengineering).* We discussed this process earlier in the chapter.

2. *Identify change levers.* Change levers can be technological, organizational, informational, or human. For example, information technology supports reengineering by reducing the amount of labor required in a process, improving the collection and analysis of process information, and improving the coordination between steps in a process and among processes. An example of an organizational enabler is a team-based structure that can product effective reengineering teams. Information can enable change by being well chosen and communicated, serving the reengineering effort by measuring performance and integrating across and within processes. A human enabler would be a highly trained and empowered workforce with the authority to conduct a reengineering initiative. Organizations use the change levers to provide opportunities for innovation during their reengineering initiative.

   At Marlow Industries, the implementation of a new computer system is being used as a vehicle for reengineering business processes. "It helps to have a focal point," Chris Witzke says. "People are more open to change because of the computer system."

3. *Develop a process vision.* An effective process vision: (1) serves the organization's broader strategic plan; (2) serve the process customers' performance requirements; (3) reflects the best practices of similar benchmarked processes; (4) contains specific process performance objectives; and (5) includes process attributes, a vision of how the process will operate in the future.

4. *Understand the existing process.* Davenport cites four reasons to take this step: (1) to develop a common understanding of the existing state; (2) to make it easier to migrate to the new process; (3) to avoid repeating the same mistakes in the new process; and (4) to measure the value of reengineering the process.

5. *Design and prototype the new process.* The actual reengineering process unfolds like any other improvement process: (1) identify alternatives; (2) assess the options and choose one; (3) test the new design; (4) determine if the new design will fulfill the process vision; (5) develop a strategy for implementing the new process; and (6) implement the new process.

Some companies have found that they can get many of the benefits of reengineering without all the cost and disruption by slowing down the pace of change and pulling back slightly on ambitious goals. According to a 1995 study of reengineering projects, researchers found that senior executives who did this were still able to reduce the cost of processes by 30 to 50 percent, shorten cycle times, and dramatically improve customer service. They still planned for radical redesign; those plans provided a blueprint for major change in the future (Reengineering: it doesn't have to be all or nothing 1995).

■ PROCESS THINKING AND BUSINESS EXCELLENCE

Few of the organizations featured in this book have ever had a formal reengineering initiative. All have improved their processes, some dramatically. Based on their experiences, one could conclude that smaller organizations have less need to reengineer because their processes are less complex. They are able to get their arms around a process, to understand its boundaries and steps, to initiate major changes in the process without having to throw it out and start over.

One could also conclude that, because they think in terms of processes, they will never need to reengineer. Jeff Pope describes how Custom Research began attacking problems from a process perspective by forming task forces to address cycle-time issues. "We started seeing results in two years," he says. "Now we respond to problems by asking what's wrong with the process that allows that to happen."

Process thinking fits well with the other basics of business excellence. It breaks down barriers between functions. It focuses the organization on its customers. It thrives by engaging people in process improvement. It serves the vision and strategies of the organization. It demands management by fact. And it encourages learning.

■ STRATEGIES FOR IMPROVEMENT

➤ Jump Start

➤ Assess the organizational culture and structure to determine if it will support process thinking. A strong functional orientation, management by command-and-control, or a focus on products rather than customers inhibit process thinking. If your culture and structure work against process thinking, you will need to make it more process-friendly (see Chapters 2–6) or people will continue to slip back into their narrow, functional views.

➤ Look for enablers of process change, such as an initiative to expand the use of information technology, a movement toward broader use of teams, or a new measurement system aligned to the strategic plan. The enablers help make it possible to piggyback process change onto the other changes occurring in the organization.

➤ Identify your organization's core processes. The best way to start thinking in terms of processes is to figure out what your key processes are. Refer to earlier sections of this chapter for ideas on how to identify core processes.

➤ Work consciously to change the language of the organization to reflect process thinking. Encourage people to consider how their work contributes to the processes that serve customer requirements. Track in-process measures of quality, speed, and cost. When a problem occurs, ask what went wrong with the process and how it can be fixed.

➤ Tune Up

➤ Form cross-functional teams to tackle those core processes most in need of improvement based on customer requirements and the organization's strategic plan. Train team members in team skills, process improvement, measurement, and statistical process control. Provide clear directions and deadlines to help the teams stay on task.

➤ Train other employees whose work impacts a core process, including executives and managers, in statistical process control, then make sure they have the opportunity to apply their new knowledge. Present the training as the best way to make intelligent decisions about what's happening in a process and what to do about it.

➤ Based on the findings of the cross-functional process improvement teams, determine whether a core process can be improved or needs to be reengineered. If reengineering is necessary, prepare the organization for the radical change to come. In either case, provide whatever assistance is required to help the teams get information, make decisions, and implement changes.

➤ Involve customers in the process changes. Ask for their input on what would best serve their requirements. Invite their feedback on proposed process changes. Measure their satisfaction with products/services/relationships before and after the process changes.

➤ Pull Away

➤ Reorganize around core processes. Custom Research does this through account teams that handle all aspects of market research projects for their customers. The entire market research process unfolds within each account team.

➤ Benchmark similar processes at companies that excel in those areas. This is not an easy task. The most similar processes are those of competitors, but few competitors will give you the kind of access required to understand their processes. Instead, you must look hard to find a similar process outside your industry, then determine if you can learn from it, then figure out how to apply what you learn to your process. Despite the difficulty, however, benchmarking can dramatically accelerate process improvement, initiating changes that will lift the entire process to new levels of performance.

➤ Get the dots and plot the dots. Continuous process improvement depends on continuous process measurement.

Chapter 8

Manage by Fact

Wainwright Industries manages by fact. One visit to Mission Control and you believe it.

Wainwright dedicates one conference room at its headquarters in St. Peters, Missouri, to displaying the information and analysis that drives its award-winning continuous improvement efforts. It calls the room Mission Control.

The walls display a plethora of charts and graphs, including trends for quality and performance indicators and, for each customer, monthly satisfaction index scores, trends for quality measures, stretch targets for exceeding customer expectations, and weekly customer feedback reports.

Wainwright developed five key strategic indicator categories from its strategic business planning process: safety, internal and external customer satisfaction, Six Sigma quality, and business performance. "We focus on safety first and making money last," says plant manager Mike Simms. And the focus has paid off. "We went from $100,000 in Workers Compensation claims in 1991 to zero in 1994," Simms says, "and our number of recordable accidents dropped from 66 to 12." At the same time, putting business performance last did not mean it suffered. Over the same time period, Wainwright's gross profit as a percent of sales jumped from 8.7 to 14.2 percent.

Mission Control displays key quality indicators for each of the five categories, all of which link to the company's mission, vision, values, and objectives. The Mission Control indicators are recordable accidents, associate suggestion rate, internal and external customer satisfaction, internal parts per million, sales, and net income. Trends are updated and reviewed regularly. "I go into Mission Control every day," says Don Wainwright, chairman and chief executive officer. "With a glance I can tell how all of our customers are doing, both internal and external."

To keep the focus on serving its customers, the company created a flag system. If Wainwright is on track to meet its stretch goals for a customer, it hangs a green flag next to that customer's satisfaction rating. It uses a red flag when potential problems could prevent it from achieving its goals. The appearance of a red flag leads to the formation of an action team that works with the customer to study the problem and implement a solution. Action teams are also formed when any customer satisfaction index score drops below 95 percent. At any given time, 95 percent of the flags in Mission Control are green.

Of course, the conference room still serves as a conference room. Wainwright conducts all in-house training, staff meetings, and presentations to customers and suppliers in the room, where they can't help but soak up the myriad quality messages surrounding them.

Mission Control is one-stop shopping for those curious about the condition of the company and involved in improving it. It doesn't replace having key indicators posted near those employees who can affect them, nor does it segregate quality from the rest of the organization. What it does is communicate the big picture in a powerful way.

Collecting the right information is critical. Communicating it is essential. Margaret Wheatley writes that "information is an organization's primary source of nourishment; it is so vital to survival that its absence creates a strong vacuum. If information is not available, people make it up." They start rumors. They make assumptions. They invent information. They eavesdrop on conversations. They read supposedly confidential memos and faxes. They pump their peers for the inside scoop. All to satisfy the craving for information, a craving that our hierarchical organizations are not designed to serve.

"We have lived so long in the tight confines of bureaucracies," writes Wheatley, "that we need to learn how to live in a conscious organization, how to facilitate intelligence. This requires an entirely new relationship with information, one in which we embrace its living properties. If we are seeking resilient organizations, a property prized in self-organizing systems, information needs to be our key ally" (Wheatley 1992).

As Wainwright Industries has shown, information becomes an ally when it is collected, analyzed, and communicated religiously. Only then can an organization claim to manage by fact.

■ THE NEED TO MANAGE BY FACT

If you were to pick one basic of business excellence at which American companies consistently stink, it would have to be managing by fact. Curt Reimann, former head of the Baldrige program, has often said that the category with the weakest responses from Baldrige Award applicants is the information and analysis category. We think we know what's going on, but if you look for the facts to support our thinking, you often come up empty.

Peter Senge calls this a leap of abstraction. "Leaps of abstraction occur when we move from direct observations to generalizations without testing," he writes (Senge 1990). Your company is operating on leaps of abstraction:

> ➤ If you assume you know exactly what your customers require but have never formally asked them or checked your assumptions with them

> ➤ If you fix a problem without identifying the source of the problem or measuring the process

> ➤ If you reengineer without assessing the need for radical change or the effects of such change on the organization

> ➤ If you blame people for mistakes without understanding the system or measuring the process

> ➤ If you develop a strategy with little knowledge of competitors or the market or risks or internal capabilities

> ➤ If you reach out for any new initiative in the hope that it might turn your organization around

Most leaders and managers are so used to mistaking leaps of abstraction for truth that they feel very comfortable with their view of the organization. Asked to support that view with information and data, they tell stories. Pressed for proof, they point out that it's their job to know. Suggest that they are managing by assumption rather than fact and they claim their assumptions *are* the facts.

How do you know if you're making leaps of abstraction? First, according to Senge, ask yourself "what you believe about the way the world works—the nature of business, people in general, and specific individuals. Ask 'What is the data on which this generalization is based?' Then ask yourself, 'Am I willing to consider that this generalization may be inaccurate or misleading?' It is important to ask this last question consciously because, if the answer is no, there is no point in proceeding."

For most leaders and managers, the transition to managing by fact begins with the admission that that's not how things are currently done. Very few organizations have sound measurement systems in place. Very few organizations know exactly what their customers require, know exactly how satisfied customers are with the organization's performance, know exactly how their processes are performing, know exactly how their people are performing, know exactly how their suppliers are performing, know exactly how well leadership is performing, or know exactly if they are making progress toward their vision.

Why does knowing exactly matter? It's almost an embarrassing question, as if running an organization on intuition, guesswork, and assumptions is acceptable. Managing by fact through a solid measurement system:

➤ Enables leaders, managers, work units, and individuals to identify opportunities for improvement

➤ Focuses attention on areas that are critical to the organization's success

➤ Helps in the prioritization of issues to address and the allocation of resources

➤ Aligns all activities with the organization's goals

➤ Shows progress toward achieving those goals

➤ Provides a common language for the entire organization

Companies that excel in these areas are moving toward measurement systems that tell them in real time how well they are meeting customer requirements. This doesn't mean the measurements are limited to external indicators such as customer satisfaction and retention, although they are part of the measurement system. *A world-class measurement system is a comprehensive set of performance indicators focused on customer-driven improvements.*

One of the clearest examples is the measurement system of AT&T Universal Card Services (UCS), which won the Baldrige Award in 1992. At the top of UCS's measurement system are primary customer satisfiers, which the company identified through surveys, focus groups, and phone interviews of more than 100 customers per day. UCS knows that, if it excels in these areas, it will have satisfied and loyal customers.

Each primary satisfier has secondary satisfiers that further define customer requirements. For example, one primary satisfier is customer service. A secondary satisfier that further defines customer service is professionalism.

Each secondary satisfier has tertiary satisfiers that measure internal performance; courtesy is an internal measure linked to professionalism. At this level, the external customer measures are linked to internal performance measures. UCS knows that if it improves performance on these tertiary satisfiers, it will improve performance on its primary customer satisfiers. Each of the tertiary satisfiers has many more key measures under it that UCS uses to diagnose the performance of its processes.

With this measurement system, UCS aligns all activities with its customers' requirements, which is the essential purpose of any measurement system.

Leaders and managers who are not used to managing by fact resist the idea of a measurement system because:

> ➤ *It takes too much time.* Identifying the right measures takes time. Actually getting the dots and plotting the dots takes a little time. Analyzing the information to identify opportunities for improvement can take time. If the time spent results in continuous improvement of the processes that are being measured, is it too much time? Besides, the time saved by improving the processes will quickly exceed the time spent measuring and analyzing.

> ➤ *It's measuring for measuring's sake.* Not if the system is set up right. If measures exist that no one is using to monitor key processes and identify areas for improvement, they are worthless. A solid measurement system contains only those measures that contribute to customer-driven improvements.

➤ *You can't measure critical steps in what we do.* Baloney. I remember Patrick Mene, Ritz-Carlton's director of quality, telling me that "people who haven't measured haven't even tried. They're making excuses." We'll look at how to develop a measurement system later in this chapter.

➤ *I'll get hammered if my measures go south.* If that's true, leadership needs to realize that the organization will never excel in a culture of blameology, for two reasons: (1) nearly all problems are problems with the system, not with people, and (2) employees cannot succeed—nor can the organization— when fear rules. Leaders and managers must address this issue at the same time they are developing a measuring system or the system will fail.

Leaders also resist measurement systems, managing by fact, and sharing information because they desperately need to maintain control. A measurement system like the one used by AT&T Universal Card Services is effective only if people throughout the organization are responsible for measuring and improving key processes. That's empowerment, and that's a threat to command-and-control leaders. Managing by fact implies that leaders and managers have been making plans and decisions on little or no relevant factual information, an implication most leaders and managers have trouble accepting. And sharing information disperses power throughout the organization, because the more people know, the more involved they become in acting on their knowledge.

Leaders who value empowerment, who see the communication of information as the key to being fast and flexible, welcome the sharing of all types of information, including financial information. Honeywell Solid State Electronics Center shares all of the division's financial numbers with employees and trains them in how to understand and use the numbers to improve. While some leaders quake at the thought, organizations that have practiced open-book management have achieved impressive results.

The best-known example is Springfield Remanufacturing Corporation (SRC). Its president and CEO, Jack Stack, wrote a book about SRC's experience, *The Great Game of Business.* Stack writes, "The more people know about a company, the better that company will perform. This is an ironclad rule. You will *always* be more successful in business by sharing information with the people you work with than by keeping them in the dark. Let your people know whatever you know about the company, the division, the department, the particular task at hand. Information should not be a power tool—it should be a means of education. Don't use information to intimidate, control, or manipulate people. Use it to teach people how to work together to achieve common goals and thereby gain control over their lives."

The ideas behind open-book management are not new; Peter Drucker wrote about them in 1954. According to Drucker, an employee needs "enough information to control, measure, and guide his own performance." The employee "should know how he is doing without being told," "how his work relates to the work of the whole," and "what he contributes to the work of the enterprise and, through the enterprise, to society" (Case 1995). Organizations that make this basic information available to their employees put those employees in position to make daily, continuous contributions to the organization's vision and goals. "The payoff," Stack writes, "comes from getting the people who create the numbers to understand the numbers. When that happens, the communication between the bottom and the top of the organization is just phenomenal."

■ MANAGING BY BALANCED SCORECARD

Although managing by financial numbers is a fairly recent phenomenon (circa 1950), financial measures dominate the business landscape. Business magazines rank companies according to profits, revenues, stock prices, and other financial indicators. Executives are deemed successes or failures based on these indicators. Companies evaluate their performance using these indicators. Financial measures are so pervasive they have become the language of business. But that language is changing.

And business is driving the change. Top performers recognize that financial measurements tell only part of the story—and that the numbers can be manipulated to make that story very appealing. They seek a measurement system that accurately reflects the companies' performance: the strength and flexibility of their processes, the satisfaction of their customers, the quality and innovation of their employees.

They also seek a measurement system that helps them act instead of react. Some people have equated managing by financial numbers only with driving by looking in the rearview mirror. Don Wainwright likes to use a tennis analogy. "If we're playing tennis, you watch the scoreboard and I'll watch the ball and we'll see who wins. The scoreboard represents the bottom line. I used to look at the financials thinking I could control something, but all those numbers are yesterday's."

Organizations that wish to manage by fact need a more balanced measurement system. One way to create such a system is through a balanced scorecard.

Robert Kaplan and David Norton introduced the balanced scorecard in a 1992 article in *Harvard Business Review.* The idea is to organize all key performance measurements into primary "buckets," such as the financial bucket, the customer bucket, the internal operating bucket, and the innovation and learning bucket. These four perspectives were identified by Kaplan and Norton in their article. Your organization may choose different ones. For each of these perspectives, strategic goals are set and corresponding measurements and targets established (Kaplan and Norton 1992).

Diane Schmalensee of Schmalensee Partners has been helping companies develop measurement systems since 1990. "A company's measures should be determined by the company's strategies," she says. "Whatever a company decides it needs to do to be successful should be reflected in its balanced scorecard."

For high-tech businesses, which were the audience for the Kaplan-Norton article, innovation is critical to success, so innovation became one of the four buckets. Schmalensee's work with service companies has produced a different set of buckets: customer, operational, employee, and results. "Employees are particularly important to service companies, so they have their own bucket. I call the fourth bucket 'results' rather than 'financial' because it includes nonfinancial results such as market share, new product development, and share of business from new products."

At the 1996 national conference of the American Society for Quality Control, Hay Wun Wain described her company's development of a balanced scorecard. AMETEK, a manufacturing company located in Paoli, Pennsylvania, formed a measurement system team in 1992 with the goal of implementing a measurement system starting in 1994. The team decided to use Kaplan and Norton's balanced scorecard approach. Team members brainstormed performance categories, surveyed internal management for input, and benchmarked other measurement systems, then developed a key performance indicator measurement system.

The team identified seven buckets:

➤ External customer satisfaction—external measurement (i.e., customer rating/auditing, customer satisfaction team survey, net new customers, percent market share)

➤ External customer satisfaction—internal measurement (i.e., on-time delivery, customer complaints, responsiveness to customers)

➤ Cost of quality—all (i.e., prevention costs, appraisal costs, internal failure costs, external failure costs)

➤ Productivity (i.e., value added per colleague, yields, physical output per colleague, inventory turns)

➤ Cycle time of key processes (i.e., new product development cycle time, order-entry-to-ship cycle time, material procurement cycle time, customer complaint resolution cycle time)

➤ Innovation and learning (i.e., rate of new product introduction, percent of sales from new product introduced in last three years, resources devoted to technological leadership)

➤ Human resource excellence (i.e., development of managerial and leadership talent, colleague satisfaction)

All AMETEK divisions had to select at least one key performance indicator (KPI) to measure in each category, with the exception of the cost of quality category, where all four components are measured. Each division/plan is responsible for monitoring performance. The KPIs and method and frequency of measurement are approved by the appropriate executive. The executive reviews performance on the division's/plant's balanced scorecard with corporate executives annually. The next step for AMETEK is to develop a predictive model for forecasting the impact of KPIs on financial performance.

AMETEK's process for developing a measurement system parallels the four stages Schmalensee sees in developing and implementing a balanced scorecard approach:

➤ Stage 1: Enlightenment

Senior executives come to believe that the path to solid, long-term profitability isn't a one-dimensional, slash-and-burn approach. They recognize that the organization needs to understand customer requirements and meet them. They realize that the organization needs to understand employee requirements in order to reduce turnover, improve processes, and provide better service. They know the organization needs to understand operational processes and costs to discover how to become faster and more flexible. With this realization, leaders seek measurements that will tell them how the company is doing in each of these areas. Better yet, they want a measurement system that shows the connection between these vital areas. They are enlightened. The need for a balanced scorecard is born.

➤ Stage 2: Identification

The organization initiates a systemwide effort to identify existing measures and to create needed measures where none exist. It begins to track performance on these measures, to report progress to employees, and to reward them for meeting performance goals.

➤ Stage 3: Refinement

The reaction to the measurements, progress, reports, and rewards suggests that people respond to what is measured. This leads to greater refinement of the measures. For example, since daily performance measures receive more attention than annual customer surveys, leadership may decide it should have more frequent customer measures and establish interim performance indicators tied to the less frequent surveys.

➤ Stage 4: Integrated analysis

The organization's measurement system is linked to the organization's vision with goals for key indicators. Results are recorded and communicated regularly. Employees understand through the measurement system what the company is trying to achieve. The final stage is to understand cause and effect using integrated databases, modeling, statistical work, and other methods of predicting which areas provide the best leverage for achieving the company's vision.

How long does it take to develop an effective balanced scorecard? Assuming that Stage 1 is complete and that leadership wants a holistic view of the organization, Stage 2 can take from three to six months depending on what measurements the company has in place. Developing the right measures and the ability to report them can take another year. "At this stage, you have to do a lot of work on the infrastructure of the organization," Schmalensee observes. "When I work on this I get to know the information services, survey, and customer service people well."

It takes another year or so to have enough data to begin doing statistical analysis and modeling, for a total of 2.5 to 3 years from leadership enlightenment to balanced scorecard bliss.

The bliss comes from the consistent, focused communication that occurs in companies using a balanced scorecard. "Everybody in the company knows where the company is going and understands its strategies, values, and mission," says Schmalensee. "It all becomes clear if they've done a good job on their balanced scorecard. Better yet, people's behavior changes rapidly because they can see the payoff of what they are doing."

The best way to see the payoff of what you are doing, especially in organizations that are driven by short-term financial results, is to make financial information one of your buckets, then to communicate it throughout the organization. "Business information—financial data—is particularly powerful because it shows people the reasons for doing something," writes John Case. "And when people see a reason, they're likely to act." The right information, according to Case, includes key operational numbers and "the financial measures that are critical to your business. The income statement, of course. The cash-flow statement and its 'second bottom line,' operating cash flow. The balance sheet when it's appropriate" (Case 1995).

Leaders who have always protected financial information cringe at the thought of making it available to employees. They fear that the numbers will be used against them, especially if they are constantly doing battle with their own employees. And they're right. They worry that people will figure out how much they are being paid. And they will. They dread the thought that competitors could get their hands on the numbers. And they will.

What leaders need to determine is whether, if all of these fears are realized, the negative impact will outweigh the positive effects of sharing financial information. The leaders who have embraced open-book management will tell you that it does not. The authors who are writing about open-book management can show you its benefits. For example, after opening its books to employees and training them in how to understand and improve the company's financial performance, SRC's annual sales grew from $16 million to $83 million and a share of stock worth 10 cents in 1983 was worth more than $20 in 1993.

Every organization must be profitable to exist. For years, leaders have used every trick imaginable to get people to increase profits without actually focusing on profits. They've threatened, demanded, and controlled. They've reorganized, reengineered, and redesigned. They've established quality circles, task forces, and teams. They've created visions, plans, and goals. They've offered awards, incentives, and bonuses. In every case, leaders claim they are acting to improve quality and increase customer service, when what they *really* want is to boost the bottom line.

And their employees know it. They see through all the tricks. They know that "Quality Is Job One" is a lie. They laugh when they hear "The Customer Comes First." Making money is job one. Profitability comes first. Leaders who make everyone in the organization responsible for financial performance by opening the books eliminate the dishonesty, erode the cynicism, and unite the organization.

Which is not to say that being responsible for financial performance means your attention is always focused on the bottom line. As the leaders of the organizations featured in this book have discovered, the best way to improve financial performance is to excel at providing value to your customers. Serve customers well and the numbers will follow.

■ DEVELOPING A MEASUREMENT SYSTEM

The balanced scorecard is one approach to serving customers well through an effective measurement system. There are others. AT&T Universal Card Services used customer satisfiers as the focal point of its measurement system. Wainwright Industries developed five key strategic indicator categories, which could easily be considered balanced scorecard buckets.

Granite Rock Company went from one measure—profit—to twelve baseline goals in the first year of its measurement initiative to its current focus on 58 measures for nine corporate objectives. It took the company nine years to reach this point. "When we went from one to twelve it felt like we were swallowing a gorilla," says Bruce Woolpert. "We weren't smart enough to get to 58 in the first year. It took us this long to figure out how to measure things."

To develop a measurement system for your organization, consider the following process:

1. *Organize a team to spearhead the development.*   The team should include representatives from different parts of the organization, such as marketing, production, finance, and human resources.

2. *Identify key performance indicators (KPIs).*   There are several ways to do this:

   ➤ The nominal group technique "is a structured brainstorming approach that's useful for resolving any open-ended question where there may be strong differences in opinion and preference among the members of a group that needs to reach a consensus" (Thor 1994). Team members meet to nominate what Thor calls "a family of measures." They think of ideas independently, then nominate their ideas during a round-robin. The list is pared down by eliminating redundancies, then each member votes by secret ballot for a certain number of ideas. For example, you can have each participant choose eight ideas by giving eight points for the best, on down to one point for the eighth best. The top ten finishers overall are then debated and the list is refined.

   ➤ Companies such as AT&T Universal Card Services begin the process by identifying the KPIs for their customers. The best way to do this is to ask customers how they measure and assess your effectiveness, what they require and how they would prioritize their requirements, and what it would take to delight them. The resulting KPIs focus the organization on what must be done to satisfy and retain customers.

   ➤ The flip side of this approach is to involve the people who are doing the work in developing the measurements. A system still needs to organize and align these measures, but that system may just be vague buckets in the beginning, such as cycle time, customer satisfaction, employee development, and financial results. The benefit of inviting the people who are responsible for improving the measures, whether they are managers, supervisors, or frontline workers, to choose the measures is that they are in the best position to know what the key indicators of performance are for their processes.

➤ A fourth approach is to develop a measurement system using all three of the previous approaches. The measurement team determines the buckets, one of which is customer satisfaction. A part of the team and/or marketing and customer service identify KPIs for key customer groups. These KPIs are tied to the customer satisfaction bucket and to others, such as operational performance, to keep the organization focused on its customers. At the same time, divisions, departments, and work units develop measures that feed into the general categories. The measurement team coordinates the effort, works with groups to develop and align measures, and continues to refine the system.

3. *Set clear and accurate baselines.* The only way to measure improvement is to know where you're starting from. This is not as easy as it sounds. In those cases where a new measure is created, it will take time to establish a baseline, since the first measurement may not be an accurate reflection of the "normal" result. When the measurement has been taken for a period of time, it can be difficult to decide which period is the best indicator of normal times. "The safest strategy," according to Thor, "is to present a great deal of data in graphical form and let each person draw his or her own conclusion." Yet this may not work if the measurement is new and there is immediate pressure to improve it. In this case, the baseline will have to be one of the first measurements taken.

4. *Analyze the results.* At the work unit level, the analysis involves studying the numbers and, more importantly, the variation in numbers. Before employees can use the measurements wisely, they need to understand the sources of variation and what to do about them. Otherwise they are tampering, which often makes the problem worse (see Chapter 7).

At the company, division, and department levels, the goal of the analysis is to show overall progress. Thor recommends using an objectives matrix to accomplish this. An example of such a matrix is shown in Figure 8-1. The buckets are shown at the top. Under each is current performance. A scoring system identifies levels of performance in each column. A weighting system indicates how much

Customer Satisfaction	Employee Development	Cycle Time	Error Rate	Operating Profit	
91	4.5	12.2	0.1	3.3	Actual Performance
100	8	2	0.01	6	10
99	7.5	3.3	0.02	5.5	9
98	7	4.7	0.03	5	8
97	6.5	6	0.04	4.5	7
96	6	7.3	0.05	4	6
95	5.5	8.7	0.06	3.5	5
94	5	10	0.07	3	4
93	(4.5)	11.3	0.08	2.5	3
92	4	12.7	0.09	2	2
(91)	3.5	14	(0.1)	1.5	1
25	20	20	15	20	Weight
1	3	2.4	1	4.6	Score
25	60	48	15	92	Value
				Total:	240

Figure 8-1. Sample Objectives Matrix

relative value each bucket has. The matrix is ready for use when all rows are completed except the actual performance, score, and value rows. The actual performance row is completed at the conclusion of a measurement period. The ovals indicate where actual performance was on the scoring matrix; the score is written in the score row. The score times the weight produces the numbers in the value row, which are added together to get a total.

The objectives matrix can be used by departments, divisions, and companies to track progress. With input from customers and employees, leaders decide what the scoring ranges are and what weights to assign to each category. The matrix is completed on a regular basis, with monthly being the most common frequency. It provides leadership with a comprehensive snapshot of how things are going without the detail needed to make improvements. "As with most measurement," Thor writes, "it identifies where the problem appears but not necessarily what caused it. Nonetheless, it is a starting point for identifying the root causes of organizational problems."

5. *Communicate results.* Wainwright has its Mission Control. Custom Research Inc. communicates all results as they are available, but it also communicates them formally every quarter through its quarterly quality report. The report includes a quality index for the company and by account team, primary and secondary measures of accuracy and timing, cycle time, client satisfaction, supplier ratings, and performance measures for internal departments. What's important is that you collect data, analyze it, and report it on a regularly scheduled basis. That means graphing results and posting them where the people who can change them will see them.

The result of this process will be a measurement system that focuses on those activities that are most important to your organization. Thor refers to the system as a family of measures, the characteristics of which are:

➤ It must be linked to the appropriate level of the strategic plan and expressed in that level's language.

➤ It must be well communicated throughout the organization.

➤ It must be made up of enough members to ensure completeness but not so many that the organization loses its focus.

➤ It must be technically sound.

➤ It must be taken and reviewed as often as appropriate.

➤ It must provide information on both level and trend.

➤ It must be consistent with rewards, recognition, and management style (Thor 1994).

The measurement system is the brain center of the organization, which means it must link with and help align all of the organization's activities. Thor refers to some of those links—the strategic plan, rewards, recognition, and management style—with the implication that it also connects with customer requirements and satisfiers, operational and financial performance, and employee development and satisfaction. Such a pervasive, well-constructed measurement system can be a powerful tool for aligning the activities of everyone in the organization. It can also become a force for improving communication throughout the organization.

■ COMMUNICATING INFORMATION

Leaders intent on making their organizations faster and more flexible quickly realize that they need better methods of communication. In a command-and-control structure, leaders and managers know what is going on because people report to them and defer to them for all decisions. In less hierarchical organizations, leaders know what is going on because they track key performance indicators, as Don Wainwright does with Mission Control. In a command-and-control structure, employees know what to work on because managers tell them. In less hierarchical organizations, employees know what to do because of the information and data available to them.

To become faster and more flexible, organizations must change their relationship with information. Hierarchies tend to protect information, releasing bits and pieces to those people on the leaders need-to-know list. Frontline employees have little exposure to big picture information.

An effective measurement system demands a new approach to communication. Management experts with very different backgrounds sound very much alike when they write about the need for communication:

➤ From a humanistic standpoint, Stephen Covey writes, "I say keep involving people in the raw data. People are basically proactive—they have the capacity to respond. When you share raw, unfiltered data, trust goes up and people move fast. There is no dependence. [These types of] stakeholder information systems keep people focused on the mission and the vision—not on the leader" (Spears 1995).

➤ From a management perspective, Christopher Bartlett and Sumantra Ghoshal write, "Executives have been rethinking their role in managing organizational information. Instead of building systems to collect data solely to help them make top-level decisions, they now realize that they must ensure that all employees have access to information as a vital organizational resource. In the information age, a company's survival depends on its ability to capture intelligence, transform it into usable knowledge, embed it as organizational learning, and diffuse it rapidly throughout the company" (Bartlett and Ghoshal 1995).

➤ From a scientific standpoint, Margaret Wheatley writes, "An organization can only exist in such a fluid fashion if it has access to new information, both about external factors and internal resources. It must constantly process this data with high levels of self-awareness, plentiful sensing devices, and a strong capacity for reflection" (Wheatley 1992).

➤ From a financial perspective, John Case points out, "Opening the books means a whole lot more than just announcing quarterly results the way publicly traded companies do. It means communicating *all* the relevant information, monthly or weekly or daily, to people in every plant or department or store or unit within a company. Business management, whatever else it may mean, means trying to reach certain objectives. And the point of getting the data out there is so that people can work together in pursuit of those objectives" (Case 1995).

No matter what your perspective, communicating information makes good business sense. The people closest to the process need timely information they can use to improve the process. Leaders and managers need complete information they can use to evaluate opportunities, make decisions, allocate resources, and think strategically about the direction of the organization. Everyone's needs can be served by effective measurements that are well communicated.

To make such communication possible, consider these approaches:

➤ *Encourage the proliferation of charts and graphs.* When I visit an organization that values information, I'm frequently impressed by the number of charts and graphs exhibited throughout its facilities. A sure sign that you are managing by fact is evidence that the people who are responsible for improving a measure are tracking that measure, and that their progress is shown on a graph posted in their area. A sure sign that an organization is managing by fact is a measurement system that can be seen in trends that roll up into more inclusive trends that roll up into even more inclusive trends that leaders use to run the organization—and all of these trends are up-to-date and posted where employees, managers, and leaders can track them.

➤ *Create a Mission Control.*   Some organizations, like Wainwright Industries, choose to pull together all key indicators into a central location where everyone can see at a glance how the organization is doing. Wainwright uses a conference room. I've seen similar presentations in lunchrooms, reception areas, and main hallways. The goal of this scoreboard approach is to make all essential information available to all employees in a form that tells people how the organization is doing and how they can help it improve.

➤ *Make managing by fact an essential part of every company/ division/department/work unit/team meeting.*   If you are tracking the right numbers, the numbers will tell you how you are doing and what needs to be done. By reviewing the critical numbers at every meeting, you are reinforcing your organization's commitment to managing by fact.

➤ *Share information across functions.*   If your organization is still organized functionally, identify opportunities to communicate information horizontally, such as cross-functional meetings, cross-functional teams, and cross-functional newsletters.

➤ *Develop a communication plan.*   As your organization makes the transition from closely held to openly shared information, you may want to develop an annual communication plan that "identifies what information is to be shared, who it is to be shared with, when it is to be shared, and how it is to be shared" (Ashkenas et al. 1995).

The more ways you can find to communicate information and data, the more engaged employees will be in improving those areas that are important to the organization. As Carl Thor writes, "Voluntarily providing information for everyone on workplace results is one of the most trust-generating actions that an organization can take. Not coincidentally, it's also one of the most cost-effective improvement actions available because the provided information ultimately becomes the basis for voluntary improvement activity" (Thor 1994).

■ OBSTACLES TO AN EFFECTIVE MEASUREMENT SYSTEM

We looked at a few of these obstacles earlier in the chapter, but a complete list may help you anticipate, recognize, and deal with them as they appear.

> ➤ *The absence of an overall vision and strategies for the organization.* Without such direction, you will not know if the measurement system is helping you get where you need to go.

> ➤ *A weak development effort.* People will resist measuring what they do. They will claim it can't be measured. They will stall. The absence of executive champions and/or a measurement system team will make such waffling possible.

> ➤ *A lack of leadership commitment.* If leaders continue to place more emphasis on financial performance than the other key performance indicators, or if they fail to align the rest of the system with the measurement system, or if they let the initiative die, the measurement system will fail.

> ➤ *A lack of appropriate measures.* What you currently have is only part of what you will need.

> ➤ *A missing link between key measurements and rewards.* "This is where the ugliest fighting comes," says Diane Schmalensee. She suggests having a hypothetical reward and recognition system in place parallel to the existing system for at least six months to help prepare people for the new system.

> ➤ *Partial deployment.* Everyone at every level of the organization must focus on the same measurement system.

> ➤ *A hierarchical, command-and-control structure.* Information is slowed every time it butts up against another layer of management or another policy or rule.

➤ *Losing sight of the whole system.* As organizations develop their measurement systems, they must also create processes for monitoring and communicating the measurements, identifying problems and opportunities, preparing action plans to address them, and allocating resources. This must be done at every level of the organization.

None of these obstacles is insurmountable. In fact, all of them can be addressed at once through the development and deployment of an effective measurement system, and through leadership's long-term commitment to managing by fact.

■ THE LINK BETWEEN MEASURING AND PLANNING

An effective measurement system helps align activities among functions by having individual departments and teams measure what is important to the organization, what feeds the organization's key performance indicators. But it cannot and does not move the organization toward those goals and objectives that promise long-term success.

A strategic plan puts measurement in the context of longer-term perspective. As we'll see in the next chapter, the best plans identify objectives for the organization and how performance on those objectives will be measured. Organizations that use a balanced scorecard approach align their buckets with their key business drivers. Other organizations identify the key indicators for each strategic objective, then ask departments and teams to measure those areas that contribute to the key indicators.

With a sound measurement system and comprehensive strategic plan in place, an organization is prepared to focus its resources on those few areas that promise the greatest success.

■ STRATEGIES FOR IMPROVEMENT

➤ Jump Start

➤ Determine what information people need to do their jobs, such as the organization's vision and values, internal and external customer requirements, process measures, financial performance, and human resources measures. The best way to do this is to clarify expectations for an employee or for groups of employees, then ask them what data and information they would need to meet those expectations.

➤ Identify the obstacles to managing by fact that exist in your organization. Again, the best way to do this is to ask. When I conduct a quality assessment, I ask every executive and manager how they determine the performance of their division or department and what measures they look at on a regular basis. You quickly learn how the organization views measurement and where the most obvious obstacles lie.

➤ Examine how communication occurs in your organization and where barriers to communication exist. This is another place where an organizational assessment can help. Asking people what they know and how they know it is always a very revealing exercise.

➤ Organize a team to develop a measurement system. Use the process described earlier in this chapter to identify key performance indicators and deploy them throughout the organization.

➤ Tune Up

➤ Question your assumptions. Organizations that have not done this for a while often discover that they are leading and managing by their leaps of abstraction. Ask what you believe about the way the world, your industry, and your organization work, and if you would be willing to consider that these beliefs may be wrong. Then seek information and data that can be used to develop a factual portrait of your world.

➤ Refine your measurement system. The first measurement system is never the best. As leaders, look at the key performance indicators for the organization to see if they are moving, if their movement is a true indication of the organization's performance, and if you can lead and manage using the measurement system.

➤ Make financial measures *one* of your key indicators. The most effective measurement systems include a balance of indicators that capture the organization's most critical areas of performance. Every organization must be profitable, so financial performance is critical. Most organizations stop there, as if the measurement of profitability tells you all you need to know about how the organization is working. You may want to explore a balanced scorecard approach to elevating the importance of performance in such key areas as customer satisfaction, quality, cycle time, innovation, and employee development.

➤ Pull Away

➤ Develop processes to integrate and analyze information and data from all parts of the organization. As the Baldrige Award criteria advise: "Despite the importance of individual facts and data, they do not usually provide a sound basis for actions or priorities. Action depends upon understanding cause/effect connections among processes and between processes and business results. Process actions may have many resource implications; results may have many cost and revenue implications as well. Given that resources for improvement are limited, and cause/effect connections are often unclear, there is a critical need to provide a sound analytical basis for decisions."

➤ Develop and implement a systematic approach to benchmarking. Benchmarking offers three benefits: (1) it tells you how well/poorly you are doing; (2) it tells you how well/poorly your competitors are doing; and (3) it helps you understand and improve your processes. Without benchmarking, you have no way of knowing how good you are. It's like a friend telling you he averages twenty points in his basketball league: That's great if you find out nobody's averaging more, not so great if you find out everybody on the team is averaging at least twenty points. You need to know where you stand before you can decide what and how to improve. For advice on benchmarking, see *Benchmarking for Best Practices* by Christopher Bogan and Michael English.

Align through Planning

Destiny is not a matter of chance, it is a matter of choice; it is not a thing to be waited for, it is a thing to be achieved.

WILLIAM JENNINGS BRYAN

Organizations that master the basics of business excellence put themselves in the best position to achieve their destinies. Leaders serve the needs of all stakeholders. A shared vision focuses the energy of the organization. Engaged employees transform the vision into action. Customer requirements drive the organization, including how it is designed. Key processes are identified and continuously improved. Decisions at every level are based on accurate and timely information. And all decisions and activities are guided by and aligned through a strategic plan.

Not everyone warms to the idea of strategic planning, usually because urgent, immediate problems demand total attention. Leaders who have never done strategic planning look at it as an exercise in wishful thinking. They have a business plan that lays out what can be spent and what must be earned. They have identified strategies to help them reach their financial goals. They have quarterly financial reports to monitor their progress. That's enough planning to keep them busy.

Such leaders have never participated in a systematic strategic planning process, nor have they benefited from the plans that result. Without this experience, it's easy to believe that strategic planning is for leaders who have the luxury of gazing into the distant future, imagining scenarios likely never to occur, devising plans that have no bearing on reality. These misinformed leaders need to talk to their peers who champion a strategic planning process and who align their organizations through the plans that result.

The purpose of strategic planning is to:

1. Understand how the requirements of key stakeholders (customers, employees, owners, community), the forces that impact the organization (competitive, industry, market, technological, regulatory), and the capabilities of the organization and its suppliers affect the organization's ability to achieve its short- and long-term goals.

2. Optimize the use of resources to leverage the organization's core competencies for both immediate and long-term success.

3. Align the efforts of everyone in the organization with the goals and objectives that the organization has determined will produce customer-driven quality, operational performance excellence, and financial success.

The strategic plan integrates quality and business planning into a single road map for the organization. Without such a plan, companies spend their time reacting to change, responding to problems, and regretting hasty, uninformed decisions. The strategic planning process provides an organization with the opportunity to translate its vision into objectives and actions that will help it achieve the vision. The strategic plan captures the best thinking in the organization about the current and future environment and about how the organization can capitalize on its strengths and address its weaknesses. For those organizations that want to move as one toward their visions, strategic planning is the tool of choice.

■ THE STRATEGIC PLANNING PROCESS

All of the organizations featured in this book conduct strategic planning. They typically develop short-term plans and objectives for the coming year and long-term plans for the next three to five years. "We look five years out," says Marlow's Chris Witzke, "but not beyond that. Since we can't predict what's going to happen, we're building a company that can adapt to any future."

The typical annual planning processes take from six to eight months to complete. The process is led by a team, i.e., the steering committee at Custom Research Inc., the strategic planning group at Wainwright Industries, and the executive staff and product line teams at Honeywell SSEC. A visual summary of the key elements in their planning processes is shown in Figure 9-1.

➤ Stage 1: Inputs

The quality and value of the final plan is directly related to the quality of the inputs to the planning process. "We think the most important first step in strategic planning is to figure out what your company is good at and what you're not good at," says Lyondell's Bob Gower. "This honest appraisal is critical. The second step is to figure out where the industry is going. Then we look for which of our strengths we can capitalize on and which weaknesses we can turn into strengths."

In those organizations that use planning teams, team members share responsibility for acquiring information about the general areas shown in Figure 9-1, usually with one person in charge of one area. The information comes from logical sources, such as industry/trade associations, competitive comparisons and information, human resources for employee issues, marketing for customer requirements, and purchasing for supplier capabilities. In other cases, such as clarifying organizational capabilities and reviewing the vision and key business drivers, the team member responsible for the area may facilitate brainstorming sessions with executives and managers to collect timely information from key sources.

This is not the only way to gather information. To avoid the leaps of abstraction that plague those closest to an area, you may want to shuffle responsibilities so that no team member is in charge of an area he or she works in every day. For example, you may want to have a human resources team member learn about customer requirements or a marketing team member look into organizational capabilities.

You may also want to encourage interviewing people outside the organization as an input to the process. Key customers and sup-

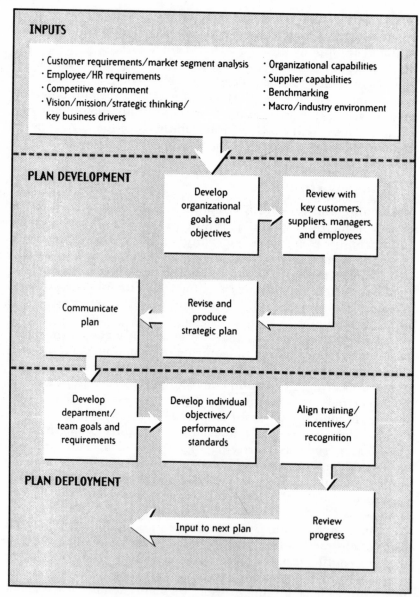

Figure 9-1. Strategic Planning Process

pliers can provide valuable perspectives on their needs and your organization. Although benchmarking is listed separately in the chart, it can also be part of several other areas including benchmarking competitors, processes, employee training and development, and supplier relationships.

The final step in the first stage could also be considered the first step in the planning process: revisiting the organization's vision, mission, key business drivers, and strategic thinking/scenarios. If these do not exist, the step will focus on developing them, although the strategic thinking part can wait (see Chapter 3 for more information on this process).

The reason an organization must be clear about its vision and drivers is that it cannot do everything. Resources are limited. Time is critical. Competition is growing. Mass customization is expanding. "Companies are much more focused today," writes Rosabeth Moss Kanter, "and focus is considered an important element of business strategy. It is important in a world of change to pick only those areas in which you can be excellent on all dimensions, or you lose the new game" (Kanter 1995). In other words, an organization's answer to "Who am I?" has never been more important.

The subject is rife with leaps of abstraction. Very few organizations devote time to the thoughtful examination of who they are. Even fewer would admit that they don't really know. Instead, they push ahead in the hope that the road they are taking goes up and not down, and that the vehicle they are riding will not collapse anytime soon.

The strategic planning process replaces hope with knowledge. The inputs to the process provide the information an organization needs to understand where it is, where it needs to go, and how it can get there. A shared vision captures the aspirations of the people, while the key business drivers represent the areas of performance most critical to the organization's success. *If an organization made sure it had a truly shared vision, an accurate list of key business drivers, a rock-solid understanding of customer group and requirements, and a strategic plan that linked all three, it would be in prime position to separate itself from its competitors.*

None of these components is difficult to develop. All require timely and accurate information and the relentless pursuit of unchallenged assumptions. To stimulate thinking about these core issues, consider the following questions:

➤ Who are our customers?

➤ Who should our customers be?

➤ What unique value do we provide these customers?

➤ What capabilities do we have that no competitor can match?

➤ How can we build on those capabilities?

➤ How can we develop new capabilities that will bring us new customers and help us retain our current ones?

➤ Where can we improve to bring new customers and retain current ones?

➤ If we were to join forces with another organization, including a customer, supplier, or competitor, how would it impact our ability to gain and retain customers?

➤ Why are we doing what we're doing?

➤ Why are we doing it this way?

➤ What do we believe about our organization/customers/competitors/industry that cannot be supported by facts?

➤ How do we know employees share the organization's vision?

➤ On what do we base our belief that our key business drivers represent those areas most critical to our success?

Another way of looking at key business drivers is to compare your organization's capabilities with your customers' key requirements. In *Whole System Architecture*, Lawrence Miller presents a strategy matrix for this purpose. Figure 9-2 is an example of a strategy matrix for a fictional organization; key words are used to represent customer requirements. As you can see, completing the matrix requires thorough knowledge of customer requirements and the organization's true capabilities. You will want to develop a strategy matrix for each customer group. You may also want to plot key competitors on each matrix for a visual comparison of strengths and weaknesses.

The strategy matrix reveals which capabilities are responsible for your current market success and which capabilities your organization needs to work on. The leadership team will need to use this and other inputs to identify those areas most critical to the organization's success, which may or may not mean focusing resources on the high-priority items. In most cases, an organization is wise to raise its performance on all key customer require-

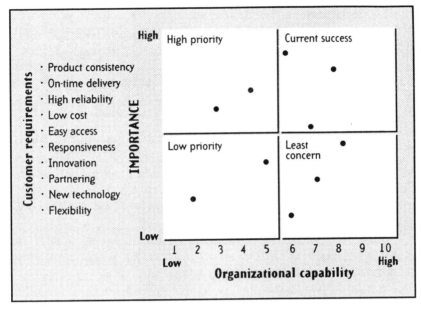

Figure 9-2. Strategy Matrix

ments to threshold levels—say, 5 on the strategy matrix—at the same time it is working to excel in one or two areas, which may be areas where it is already a leader. Organizations that are close to their customers and to their own processes are in the best position to identify their key business drivers.

Honeywell Solid State Electronics Center lists its key business drivers in a matrix that also shows the short-term performance requirements and benchmarks for each goal, the long-term requirements, and the primary strategies SSEC will use to meet each goal. SSEC's key business drivers are:

➤ On-time delivery with short lead times

➤ World-class product quality and reliability

➤ Leader in product value with best-in-class service

➤ Meet SSEC business/financial goals

➤ Continuously improve business and operational processes

➤ Provide effective leadership and a positive work environment that empowers and motivates

Custom Research Inc. developed a similar matrix that ties its key business drivers to the points on a star icon, which visually represents CRI's management system:

➤ *People:* Developing competent and empowered people

➤ *Processes:* Managing work through technology-driven processes

➤ *Requirements:* Meeting or exceeding unique client requirements and expectations

➤ *Relationships:* Building partnering relationships with major clients and suppliers

➤ *Results:* Producing growth and profit

CRI's matrix identifies key measurements for each driver, current performance on each measure, short- and long-term goals for each measure, and benchmarks.

As a leadership tool, such a matrix has no peer. Both SSEC's and CRI's matrices clearly communicate what is important to the organization and how it intends to improve. Key business drivers are shown. Key measurements are identified. Short- and long-term goals exist. Benchmarks provide context. The people at SSEC and CRI know the strategy they are pursuing.

"Knowing what strategic area drives your organization and the areas of excellence required to support that strategy is akin to understanding what the strategic weapon is that will give you a distinct and sustainable advantage in the marketplace," writes Michel Robert. "Our experience has clearly shown that any strategy can work, but that no company can pursue two strategies simultaneously. No organization has the resources to develop excellence in several areas concurrently" (Robert 1993).

For an organization to identify its strategy for success, it must know itself, its customers, and its industry extremely well. Such knowledge is also a prerequisite for entering the next stage of the strategic planning process.

➤ Stage 2: Plan Development

With your homework completed, it's time to develop a strategic plan. The first order of business is to decide who will be involved in the development.

The most obvious choice is senior executives, especially in smaller organizations. They tend to have the broadest perspective and the greatest interest. However, they are not the only group with contributions to make. Many organizations are expanding the list of participants to include management and other employee groups. The reasons for involving a broader spectrum of employees are twofold, according to Michel Robert:

1. People don't implement properly what they don't understand.
2. People don't implement what they are not committed to.

"We know that the best way to build ownership is to give over the creation process to those who will be charged with its implementation," writes Margaret Wheatley. "We are never successful if we merely present a plan in finished form to employees. It doesn't work to just ask people to sign on when they haven't been involved in the design process, when they haven't experienced the plan as a living, breathing thing. People can only become aware of the reality of the plan by interacting with it, by creating different possibilities through their personal process of observation" (Wheatley 1992).

Some organizations are even going so far as to delegate the responsibility for strategic planning to frontline managers. The trend was reported by Christopher Bartlett and Sumantra Ghoshal after a study of twenty large, successful companies. They found that "top-level managers still influence long-term direction, but they recognize that they have their greatest impact by working internally to develop the organization's resources, knowledge, and capabilities as strategic assets" (Bartlett and Ghoshal 1995). My experience with smaller organizations is that top-level managers remain intimately involved in the planning process—*and* in developing their organizations' resources, knowledge, and capabilities.

Another trend for organizations of all sizes is the involvement of key customers and suppliers in the strategic planning process. For example, Honeywell SSEC invites major customers representing more than 50 percent of its business to participate in its planning process. Internal teams interview customers to clarify their requirements, expectations, and perceptions of SSEC. After the first draft of the plan is produced, SSEC asks the customers to review it to see how well the plan addresses their needs. Customer participation in the process ensures that SSEC will remain customer focused.

Organizations involve key suppliers in the planning process when supplier capabilities are critical to the organization's success. For example, organizations that rely on suppliers for technological expertise and innovation benefit from their input into the strategic plan. The suppliers learn what their customer wants to accomplish and how they can contribute. They learn what will be expected from them in the years ahead. And they improve the plan by bringing their knowledge and experience to the table.

Once the participants in the planning process have been determined, the next step is to develop short- and long-term organizational goals and objectives. This is often done by a planning team. The goals/objectives are reviewed with key constituencies, both internal and external, to gain some consensus about the direction of the organization. With input from these constituencies, a final strategic plan is produced.

The strategic plan can take whatever form best serves the organization. In their book *Return on Quality*, authors Rust, Zahorik, and Keiningham recommend a plan of twenty to fifty pages organized in the following sections:

➤ Executive summary

➤ Historical update (the year in review; trends; progress on key strategies)

➤ Situation analysis (an explanation of the key inputs to the process)

➤ Objectives (what the organizations needs to accomplish in the coming year)

➤ Strategies and program details (how the organization will accomplish its objectives)

➤ Financial statements (what resources will be available to accomplish the objectives)

➤ Monitors and controls

➤ Contingency plans

"A well-crafted plan should have clearly defined areas of responsibility and deadlines, so that sources of shortfalls or unexpectedly effective performance can be identified," write Rust, Zahorik, and Keiningham. "Measurements to be tracked should be clearly specified in the plan itself, since in many cases they provide the operational definitions of what is expected of employees."

One method of translating objectives into actions is through action plans. A sample action plan summary, which is a modified version of plans used by Southern Pacific Railroad, is shown in Figure 9-3. The benefit of including such plans in the strategic plan is that critical actions are defined, ownership is taken, measurements are determined, and a process for proceeding is described.

Key Business Driver:		
Problem/Opportunity Statement (Gap):		
Root Cause:		
Improvement Objective:		
Measurements (including targets and baselines):		
Objective Owner:		
Action Plan (What, Where, How)	Completion Date (When)	Accountable (Who)

Figure 9-3. Action Plan Summary

For the strategic plan to be acted upon, it must be communicated to everyone vested in its implementation. Those organizations that use the plan to align the activities of departments, teams, and individuals communicate it through the deployment process.

➤ Stage 3: Plan Deployment

As with other initiatives, most plans bog down when it comes to implementation. Interviewing customers, researching competitors, analyzing capabilities, brainstorming strategies, devising plans—none of this is as hard as deploying the strategic plan throughout the organization.

Organizations master deployment through processes that require departments, teams, and individuals to align their activities with the organization's objectives. A summary of these processes is shown in Figure 9-1.

The first step in deployment is to translate the organization's plan into department and team goals and requirements. For example, at Custom Research Inc., all departments and teams (which account for everyone in the company) develop plans and goals that will support the company's goals and present them to senior leadership for review and alignment. Marlow Industries' seven departments develop implementation plans that include key goals and indices, required improvements, and prioritized action plans. At Honeywell SSEC, each functional department and team develops its own requirements and strategies to support the division's objectives.

The department/team plans align the activities of the departments and teams with the organization's strategic plan. They translate the key business drivers and objectives into bite-sized steps the department or team can accomplish. In this way, strategies become concrete action plans designed to lead to their implementation.

Some organizations take deployment another step, translating department/team plans into individual objectives and performance standards. For example, every CRI employee develops individual plans to meet his or her team's or department's goals. The individual plans feed into the department/team plans, which feed into the company's strategic plan, aligning the activities of every employee with the company's goals and objectives.

The power of such alignment epitomizes the *focused* organization, from key business drivers to plans to strategies to objectives to department/team plans to individual plans. Everyone pulling in the same direction. Every resource directed at the same goals. Every decision supporting a shared vision. Every part in step with the whole.

The alignment extends to those areas that support the organization, including training, incentives, and recognition. For example, every CRI employee has a development plan. Employees work with their managers to create the plan, making sure individual, team/department, and company goals are in alignment.

While the verdict is out on how much incentives and recognition boost performance, no one argues that they can harm it. If a strategic plan calls for improvements in customer and employee satisfaction, quality, productivity, and profitability, but the incentive system only rewards profitability, guess which part of the plan will be achieved? If a strategic plan outlines a process for becoming team based, but the recognition program only rewards individual accomplishments, guess what the response will be to teams? Once the strategic plan is in place, these other, vital elements of the management system must be reviewed and aligned for the plan to be successful.

The final step in the planning process is to review progress to plan. Since the objectives, strategies, and action plans represent the areas most critical to the organization, reviews of progress to plan tend to occur at weekly or monthly staff meetings and at regular department meetings and team and task force meetings. Organizations also post the key elements of the plan, and trends showing progress on key measures, in high-traffic areas. For example, Wainwright Industries displays progress to plan in its Mission Control conference room. The goal of the reviews and communication of progress is to keep employees focused on the path ahead and informed of where they are in the journey.

■ THE ATTRACTION OF ALIGNMENT

In a letter to the editor of *Harvard Business Review,* David Simon, group chief executive and deputy chairman of the British Petroleum Company, stated, "In my view, more wealth can be created by aligning purpose, process, and people within an organization than most of us realize. Competitors may understand a company's products, technology, and finances, but they cannot easily replicate management processes that are deeply embedded in a company's traditions and culture."

A shared vision and a strategic plan enable an organization to align purpose, process, and people. BP's shared vision is called a statement of purpose; it consists of six declarations of priorities and goals. The shared visions of the organizations featured in this book are presented in Chapter 3. Guided by a shared vision, an organization can shift its energy from controlling people to helping them contribute. Leaders can stop worrying about employees acting against the organization's best interests and start thinking about removing obstacles to performance.

A strategic plan translates the shared vision into milestones that will move the organization toward the vision. As with the shared vision, the best strategic plans involve employees in their development in order to, as Simon writes, align "the motivation and commitment of individuals to those of the company." Sure, senior executives are perfectly capable of creating a terrific strategic plan, but creating the plan is only part of the process. Until it is fully deployed throughout the organization, the plan is little more than vanity publishing. And it won't be fully deployed unless employees are committed to acting on it—a condition that is hard to achieve when the plan is conceived without their help and dumped in their laps for implementation.

As the organizations featured in this book have discovered, mastering the basics of business excellence makes it possible for them to gain control of their activities, while alignment makes it possible to focus those activities on a shared vision. Focused, fast, and flexible, they distinguish themselves from their competitors in an area that is almost impossible to copy: the quality of their management systems.

■ STRATEGIES FOR IMPROVEMENT

➤ Jump Start

➤ Commit to strategic planning as the organization's primary method of setting priorities, allocating resources, and reviewing performance. Leaders can act on their commitment by participating in the planning process or in the input stage and plan-review step of the process, then reviewing performance to plan at regular staff meetings.

➤ Refer to Chapter 3 for ideas on how to develop and communicate a shared vision. Since the vision guides the strategic plan, it is important to have the vision nailed down before completing the plan.

➤ Form a strategic planning team. Select team members from different functions and levels within the organization. Encourage them to develop a planning process that includes the elements in Figure 9-1. Make sure to give the team enough time (six to eight months is ideal) to complete and communicate the plan and allow departments, teams, and individuals to develop their own objectives and plans.

➤ Tune Up

➤ Expand participation in the planning process. The planning team can improve the quality of the plan dramatically by soliciting ideas and feedback from more employees and from key customers and suppliers. The ideas come during the input stage of the process, while feedback is sought on the first draft of the plan.

➤ Challenge your assumptions. If you have not looked for leaps of abstraction lately, take time to ask the simple questions about who your customers are and what they want, what business you are in, what value you provide your customers, what unique capabilities your organization possesses, and how you distinguish your organization from your competitors'. If you cannot support a position with information and data, look for the proof or rethink the position.

➤ Clarify your leverage points, those "steps, pieces, or components that, when improved, substantially improve the performance of the system as a whole" (Joiner 1994). "Organizations that can focus on the one, two, or perhaps three most important leverage points have much more success," Joiner writes. And those leverage points become key strategies in your strategic plan.

➤ Pull Away

➤ Benchmark other planning processes. The fastest way to create a world-class planning process is to learn from the world-class processes of others. These may not be easy to find, but you can always start with Baldrige Award winners (and possibly state quality award winners), then contact the administrators of your state quality award for suggestions or a benchmarking council, such as The Council on Benchmarking of the Strategic Planning Institute or The International Benchmarking Clearinghouse of the American Productivity and Quality Center.

➤ Align measures throughout the organization with those in the plan. If your organization developed a measurement system separate from its strategic planning process, chances are the system and plan are not in sync. Your strategic plan should have key performance indicators for every objective, which are then cascaded throughout the organization, meaning departments and teams should have their own indicators that line up with the organization's KPIs. These indicators should be the most important indicators in the organization. If they are not, either the measurement system or the plan must change.

➤ Verify deployment of the plan by establishing regular performance reviews during which progress on every objective and performance on every key indicator are reviewed. Get out of the habit of focusing on financial performance in favor of analyzing those indicators that predict financial performance, because those are the areas you can still improve.

Chapter 10

Mastering Change

For the first eighteen years of my life I was insulated from change. My hometown—Pomeroy, Iowa, population 830 at the time— flowed with the seasons, but it never seemed to change.

I knew who lived in every house in town. At one time or another I delivered newspapers to homes on every block. When I was nine I sat on the floor at Meyer's Rexall Drug Store and read the new comic books within a week of their arrival. I shagged foul balls at town team baseball games, earning a nickel for each ball I returned. As a teen I cut through McCarty's grocery store to reach the pool hall, the only entertainment center in town. When I wasn't helping my father put out the town's weekly newspaper, I baled hay and shelled corn and pulled weeds from the bean fields.

For eighteen years change treated Pomeroy and me kindly. A few stores closed, but a few others opened. My family moved twice, but the new house was always bigger and better. Change invited, never threatened. It did not intimidate. I would wish such safe, slow, simple times for everyone.

In a way we are all lulled into believing that change is no big deal. The sun rises and sets. Seasons arrive in order. Democrats revile Republicans, and vice versa. Rush hour traffic crawls. The monthly bills must be paid. We eat. We sleep. We look in the mirror and see the same face, the same eyes and nose with a few more wrinkles and a little less hair.

It is an illusion, of course. Physician Deepak Chopra likened us more to a river than to anything "frozen in time and space." Our skin is new every month, our liver every six weeks. Our brain changes its contents of carbon, nitrogen, and oxygen about every twelve months. With every breath, we inhale the elements we need to create new cells and exhale what were our cells. As Margaret Wheatley writes, "Although we experience ourselves as a stable form, our body changes frequently" (Wheatley 1992).

For the most part, change is what happens when you're not looking. The way to master change, then, is first to be conscious of it, then to learn about it, to treat it as an ally and not a foe. As much as we would like to return to the good old days, we cannot. New challenges confront us. A new century calls. A new relationship with change is required.

■ A PHILOSOPHY OF CHANGE

As the pace of life late in the twentieth century has quickened and become more complex, the issue of change has attracted a following. Management experts write about total transformation, radical redesign, upheaval, and fundamental change. Businesses look to transform themselves through reengineering, restructuring, mergers, networking, downsizing, and a steady stream of initiatives. Leaders discuss whether change should be fast or slow, whether to motivate by crisis or vision, whether to be hard-nosed (if you're not with us, you're against us) or supportive (we're all in this together). This obsession with change has produced a kind of consensus on mastering it, although the approaches vary considerably.

People who talk and write about change agree that the ability to master change has become an organizational necessity and, in some cases, a competitive edge. In an article in *Fortune* magazine, Johnson & Johnson CEO Ralph Larsen said, "If we can manage a high level of complexity coupled with a tolerance of ambiguity, that would be an important competitive advantage" (O'Reilly 1994).

Organizations like Johnson & Johnson welcome change because they know they cannot control it. "Circumstances change faster than we can plan for them," says Randy Berggren, general manager of the Eugene, Oregon, Water & Electric Board. "We have to come to grips with the fact that we are not in control" (Stewart 1994).

Not being in control of change doesn't equate with not being in control of the organization. Just look at Johnson & Johnson, which has made change part of its strategy to succeed. Organizations that have broken down their command-and-control structures in the pursuit of speed and flexibility become more adaptable, more fluid, more tolerant of ambiguity. When they have also mastered the basics of business excellence, they are in position to initiate changes that serve them and to respond positively to changes that affect them.

Marlow Industries was in such a position when a historical change occurred: the fall of the Berlin Wall. At the time, 70 percent of Marlow's business was military and 30 percent was commercial. Marlow's leaders understood that the end of the cold war could mean a decline in the company's military business. It targeted commercial opportunities. As a result, the company now does 70 percent of its business in the commercial area and 30 percent in the military (even though the volume of military business has not declined) because it had a management system in place that allowed it to control its actions even if it couldn't control the change.

Marlow's senior leaders talk about change constantly. At every opportunity they describe how their customers' needs are changing and what the company must do to satisfy them. Each month they hold company meetings for all employees at which Ray Marlow communicates any ongoing or foreseeable changes in speed, quality, the organization, and the company's efforts to make its customers successful (which is Marlow's corporate mission). Such communication, which is a key characteristic of the company's management system, has helped Marlow continue to improve performance on all of its key indicators since winning the Baldrige Award in 1991.

Another key characteristic of Marlow's management system is its core values: making customers successful; employee satisfaction; loyalty to customers and employees; honesty; trustworthiness; responsibility; market leadership. The shared values define how the people at Marlow behave, what they work for, why they make the decisions they make. When the fall of the Berlin Wall demanded change, Marlow's core values gave direction through uncharted territory. James Collins, coauthor of *Built to Last,* has found that the best companies have one thing in common: "They have successfully adapted over the decades to a changing world without losing their core values" (Collins 1995).

Not only have they not lost them, successful companies depend on their core values to guide them. The scientific term for this is *self-reference,* which means that as a system changes it refers to itself, so that the new form is consistent with the old. "Self-reference is what facilitates orderly change in turbulent environments," writes Margaret Wheatley. "In human organizations, a clear sense of identity—of the values, traditions, aspirations, competencies, and culture that guide the organization—is the real source of independence from the environment. When the environment demands a new response, there is a reference point for change. This prevents the vacillations and the random search for new customers and new ventures that have destroyed so many businesses over the past several years" (Wheatley 1992).

Leaders who know their organizations must change to compete in turbulent environments would love it if the change were orderly. They would be less anxious if they knew that changes could be made at all levels of the organization, and that those changes would be consistent with the direction the organization was taking. Self-reference provides such assurance. "Instead of whirling off in different directions," Wheatley adds, "each part of the system must remain consistent with itself and with all other parts of the system as it changes."

The reference point for change is the system itself. If that system has no core, shared values, the people in the system base their actions on what they assume the organization wants. The assumptions vary. The actions are misguided. Mastering change becomes impossible.

"The culture must all be of a single fabric," the late Thornton Bradshaw, president of ARCO, once said. "From the company's social posture, through the way it treats its employees, to the care it takes in the artistic decor and style of its building—everything must manifest a commitment to quality, to excellence, to service, and to meeting the aspirations of our owners, workers, customers, and the broader society" (O'Toole 1995).

We explored the creation of a shared vision in Chapter 3. The degree to which a shared vision captures the culture of an organization depends on whether it is a vision that employees can embrace, support, and act upon. For change to be effective, employees must want to contribute to the common good even when that common good forces them outside their comfort zones. They will not do this without a clear sense of direction—core values, a shared vision—and trust in the people around them.

"I think of change management as providing relationships you can fall back on when all else fails," says Berggren. "Even if you don't know what will happen next, you can trust in the people you're working with." Wainwright Industries recognized the need for trust when, in 1991, it decided to make "a sincere trust and belief in people" the foundation of the organization. As it acted on this philosophy, the organization changed. "Organizations are webs of participation. Change the patterns of participation, and you change the organization," write John Seeley Brown and Estee Solomon Gray in an article in *Fast Company*. Break down the hierarchy and change will follow. Form teams and change will follow. Focus people on processes rather than functions and change will follow. Do any of these with a well-communicated, shared vision as your guide, and the change that follows will move the organization toward its vision.

Trust and a shared vision are two characteristics of a culture that supports change. Another is communication. Key information is continuously spread throughout the organization. Decisions that affect the group are not made without dialogue among the group members. All subjects, no matter how sacred, are open for discussion. Knowledge is valued and shared through electronic networks. In these and other ways, free, open, and frequent communication support change.

Yet communication, trust, and a shared vision cannot produce a culture that supports change without a fourth characteristic: leadership.

■ LEADING CHANGE

John Kotter, in an article in *Harvard Business Review,* states, "Change, by definition, requires creating a new system, which in turn always demands leadership." When does leadership step in? Based on his observations, Kotter believes it happens "when about 75 percent of a company's management is honestly convinced that business-as-usual is totally unacceptable" (Kotter 1995).

Who steps in? Senior executives participate by establishing the purpose and scope of the change, communicating about it, staying involved at key decision points, and giving people permission to create the changes. They also model the behaviors they wish to see in the new organization.

Jeanie Daniel Duck helps companies change. She talks about seeing the same hard truth again and again: "When it comes to change, people don't believe in a new direction because they suspend their disbelief. They believe because they're actually seeing behavior, action, and results that lead them to conclude that the program works" (Duck 1993). In other words, people will not believe a shared vision, they will not trust the motives of leaders or a change initiative, unless they see the vision reflected in their leaders' behavior.

"The first change in behavior should be that of the top executives," Duck writes. "Leaders need to ask themselves, 'If we were managing the way we say we want to manage, how would we act? How would we attack our problems? What kind of meetings and conversations would we have? Who would be involved? How would we define, recognize, compensate, and reward appropriate behavior?' "

Asking these questions and taking responsibility for changing behaviors based on the answers is more personal than many leaders want change to be. Most leaders, like most everybody, resist change. As Woody Boyd said on the last episode of *Cheers,* "Why do things have to change? *I* don't want to change! I *hate* change!"

So why do leaders change? What drives them to venture away from the security of what they know to the uncertainty of what they hope is better? In some cases, it is pain. In others, faith. A few change because they know the same-old, same-old won't cut it anymore. One of the most popular reasons to change, although leaders use it as a reason everyone else in the organization needs to change, is a crisis.

In business circles, this last reason is known as the burning platform, after a popular story about a North Sea oil rig worker who, when faced with certain death on a burning platform or probable death jumping into the frigid sea, chose to jump. He lived. Leaders like the story because it provides a rationale for revolutionary change: *Our company stands on a burning platform. If we stay here, we will not survive. If we jump, we have a long plunge to freezing waters with no assurance that we will live. Certain death or probable death? We choose probable death* (although 5,000 of you will need to be sacrificed to the layoff troll under the platform).

Command-and-control leaders rely on crises to promote change because they can't find a better way to do it. They can't see outside their top-of-the-pyramid box. They could not conceive of the notion that, if everyone in the company fully understood its financial problems or quality problems or customer satisfaction problems and felt responsible for their solution, employees would see change as a natural response to the situation. Leaders can't imagine how, if everyone in the company felt a personal commitment to the company's shared vision, they would accept changes that moved them closer to achieving that vision.

Not only do command-and-control leaders lack these options, most of them believe that people change *only* in times of crisis. Peter Senge and Fred Kofman call it "the most pervasive leadership strategy in America—create a crisis, or at least a perception of a crisis." The worst part, according to Senge and Kofman, is that "management by fear and crisis becomes a self-fulfilling prophecy. Because it *does* produce short-term results, managers see their crisis orientation as vindicated, people in the organization grow accustomed to 'waiting for the next crisis,' manager belief in the apathy of the troops is reinforced, and they become predisposed to generate the next crisis" (Spears 1995).

Can we change without a crisis? Can you? If the answer is yes for each of us individually, it must surely be yes for all of us collectively.

Another reason leaders like a crisis is because it gives them a chance to really *lead*. Sit tall in the saddle. Command the troops. Outmaneuver the opposition. Lead the charge. It's a heroic image to be sure, but it may not be the best way to lead.

In the 1970s, NASA put three-person crews into flight simulators and measured their effectiveness in dealing with computer-generated crises. The pilots reacted in one of two ways: most took command and started giving out orders, but a few consulted with their copilots and engineers before making a decision. As James O'Toole reports, "the researchers generally found that the pilots who 'took charge' were less likely to arrive at a safe and valid response to the crisis than those who sought more information and advice before deciding what action to take" (O'Toole 1995).

Not many executive decisions must be made in seconds, yet few executives are able to give others a voice in important decisions. The very idea clashes with the notion that the leader knows best.

Studies contradict that notion. One study asked the chief executives of two dozen leading U.S. and European companies about the problems they had with their senior staffs. According to the CEOs, the biggest problem was the inadequacies of individual executives, primarily their shortsighted behavior in order to boost financial performance. If leaders are judged inadequate and shortsighted, how can we then expect them to have all the answers?

Doesn't it make sense that a more collaborative decision-making process is preferable to the Lone Ranger approach, especially when the Lone Ranger couldn't hit a target if his silver bullets had guided missile technology?

The second most serious problem identified by the CEOs was a mismatch between new competition or market requirements and senior executives who had developed their skills under different conditions. In a rapidly changing marketplace, their leaders fell behind. Which is only bad if we then look to them to make informed decisions. Which is what command-and-control leadership is all about.

The worst examples of executive decisions gone awry have been the multitude of recent failures at transforming a company through reengineering. Thomas Davenport, who wrote about reengineering before Hammer and Champy popularized it, cautions leaders, "When the Next Big Thing in management hits, try to remember the lessons of reengineering. Don't drop all your ongoing approaches to change in favor of the handsome newcomer. Don't listen to the new approach's most charismatic advocates, but only to the most reasoned. Talk softly about what you're doing and carry a big ruler to measure real results. And start with a question: Would I like this management approach applied to me and my job? If the answer is yes, do it to yourself first. You'll set a great example" (Davenport 1995).

To change a command-and-control organization, leaders must take the call to change personally. They must assess and change their own behaviors, including their willingness and ability to trust and believe in employees. And they must be open to leading by serving, as described in Chapter 2. In *Reflections on Leadership*, several of the contributors suggest that organizations that want to create meaningful change are best served by starting with servant-leadership as the foundational understanding (Spears 1995). Peter Block, author of *Stewardship*, agrees:

> *Our task is to create organizations that work, especially in a world where everything constantly seems up in the air. We know that fundamental change is required. We keep talking about cultural change, but this will not be enough if we stay focused on changing attitudes and skills. No question that beliefs and attitudes need to change, but unless there is also a*

*shift in governance, namely, how we distribute power, and
privilege, and the control of money, the efforts will be more
cosmetic than enduring.*

Now *that's* change.

I'd like to touch on a similarly radical notion, courtesy of Mike
Simms and Wainwright Industries. Mike doesn't believe anyone
ever changes; they adapt. He also doesn't believe senior executives
lead the transformation of an organization; middle management
does. "You always read that middle managers can be the roadblock
to the change process," says Mike. "That means they control it.
We're the only ones to make or break it. The top can't do it.
Employees can't do it. It cost us four years waiting for our leaders
to lead change. It just doesn't happen that way in the real world.
The top's role is to support change, not to drive it. The middle managers have to drive change while top leadership sits in the back supporting and pushing it. They don't have the constant focus on trust
and belief in people on the floor."

When Mike and Don Wainwright told their story at the Minnesota Quality Conference in 1995, they used the analogy of driving a bus. Don's role is to sit in the back of the bus and watch the
road markers (all of which are posted in Mission Control; see
Chapter 8). Mike's job, and that of Wainwright's other managers, is
to drive the bus, to take care of the good and the bad, to lead the
change. I think Mike's message is empowering for middle managers, but I've never seen an organization yet where significant
change occurred without senior executives' full support. Any manager who has lobbied long and hard for change only to be stifled by
autocratic leaders would probably disagree with Mike's view.

As for the notion that nobody changes, Mike remembers an
earlier effort when "we took all the tools and techniques and went
out and tried to change our people. That's why we failed. Now we
choose to play the game accepting it for what it is. We give people
the things they need to make a better world. We train to help them
become better people." They act on their sincere trust and belief in
people, accepting that people are what they are.

In the process, of course, people learn more, assume more
responsibility, initiate more improvements, participate, contribute,
communicate, enjoy. You can call that adapting if you like, but it
sounds like people changing to me.

■ RESISTANCE TO CHANGE

As Wainwright discovered, people resist change. We resist trying new foods. We take the same way to work every day. We hold tightly to jobs, homes, and relationships even when we're miserable in them. We defend opinions we barely believe anymore.

Anyone who has ever tried to lead or facilitate a major change knows that resistance is a natural part of the process. "Resistance to change is neither capricious nor mysterious," Peter Senge writes. "It almost always arises from threats to traditional norms and ways of doing things" (Senge 1990). Margaret Wheatley describes the science of resistance: "It is natural for any system, whether it be human or chemical, to attempt to quell a disturbance when it first appears. But if the disturbance survives those first attempts at suppression and remains lodged within the system, an iterative process begins. The disturbance increases as different parts of the system get hold of it. Finally, it becomes so amplified that it cannot be ignored" (Wheatley 1992).

The resistance to change is often strongest among those in power. As James O'Toole writes in *Leading Change*, "Nothing is more certain to stir up resistance to change than a challenge to the psychological comfort of the powerful." Another formidable source of resistance is the successful organization. For one thing, they do not endorse the need to change. For another, they cannot let go of the behaviors that have created success in the past.

Few organizations have been as successful as Levi Strauss & Co. Yet in 1995, after nine years of record sales, the company embarked on the largest change program in the history of the company. It did so because its customers were telling it that quality wasn't great and service was slow. The change effort is documented in an excellent article, "Levi's Changes Everything," written by David Sheff, in the June-July 1996 issue of *Fast Company*.

Levi's initiated the process by organizing 200 of its best people into 20 teams and charging them with reinventing the supply chain. Levi's relies on 600 contractors in 50 countries to provide the 65,000 different combinations of brand, design, fabric, color, and size that it sells. The leader of the change process is Tom Kasten, who was the subject of Sheff's interview. Kasten describes his three rules about resistance: expect it, don't take it personally, and understand that resistance comes in code. Few people come right out and say they don't want to change. Instead, they offer arguments against the change. "I've made a list of the codes I hear again and again," Kasten says. " 'Our customers haven't asked for this level of service.' 'Our customers don't want what they say they want.' 'Our competitors aren't doing what they say they're doing.' 'This makes sense for the company, but it won't work in our division.' 'Our performance is good enough—we don't need to turn the place upside down.' Whenever I hear these statements, I know what's going on. I've cracked the code."

Asked how Levi's is managing the resistance, Kasten offers the three "i" words: information, involvement, intervention.

You cannot provide too much information. Paul Allaire, Xerox chairman and CEO, points out, "Every time we make one of these changes, we find that we undercommunicate it. After four or five times repeating the same message, we assume that it has been heard. In reality, many people have not absorbed the information. It takes a lot of time to win understanding and acceptance of major changes" (Garvin 1995). You can do a better job of informing people of the reasons for the change, the nature of the change, the effects of the change, and their roles in the process by developing a communication plan early in the change process, then taking advantage of every opportunity to talk about the process as it proceeds. Emily Morgan, one of Tom Kasten's change agents at Levi's, cites three lessons related to information and involvement:

1. Context is king. "People can learn to deal with ambiguity; they may even learn to prefer it," Morgan says. "But they need a clear picture of the end goals."

2. Check in early and often. "Implementing change is a dynamic process. You always have to worry about how far and fast people can move."

3. Be a catalyst, not a controller. "Let the people who are going to do the work fill in the blanks between the 'big concepts' and what's happening on the ground" (Sheff 1996).

Involvement means everyone. "Your change agents, the people who really see the future, pull the organization along," Kasten says. "But if they get too far out, if they don't circle back, they lose people." Shooting the stragglers is unacceptable in the new leadership model. The alternative is to circle back to pick up the stragglers, progressing toward the goal in concentric circles rather than a straight line.

Intervention is necessary for those who persist in resisting. As Kasten says, "There comes a point where you have to be very clear where you're going. The boat is leaving the dock. There are plenty of seats for everyone, but you have to choose whether you're going to get on board. Everyone has a voice. Not everyone has a vote."

It's important to remember that intervention may also reveal a need for additional information, training, or a different position in the company. Firing should be a last resort, after every other option has been tried, because it's the right thing to do for the individual and for the organization. You are trying to establish a culture of trust. Nothing destroys trust quicker than a callous approach to employees.

■ THE SPEED OF CHANGE

Experts disagree on this. Most advocate total, rapid change. Others argue for slower, less disruptive change.

Rapid change is the only route, its supporters say, because its blasts people out of their business-as-usual mindset. If you make a little change here, pilot another change there, look for small successes to build on, the whole process may stall or never get enough momentum to achieve the significant results you need. "Piecemeal programs are not good enough," writes Rosabeth Moss Kanter. "Only total transformation will help companies—and people—change" (Kanter 1995).

The problem with rapid change is that it is extremely disruptive. Even if people know it's coming, agree with its goals, and support the process, they will not be able to change their behaviors or the ways they relate to other groups in the organization as quickly as the change process requires. Rather than people walking in step with the changes, the change process will pull most of the people along, and the disruption that results will scuttle all but the hardiest process.

The solution seems to be to design an ambitious change process but be patient with its implementation. Reengineering provides many examples of radical change processes. According to a 1995 study of such projects, "the process of planning for radical change provides these organizations with a blueprint for long-term transformation." The study concluded that "all successful reengineering projects began with radical designs." It also revealed that organizations could gain the full benefits of the project even if their leaders managed the pace of change slowly (Reengineering: it doesn't have to be all or nothing 1995).

Managing the pace of change is no small task. Bruce Woolpert claims that Granite Rock did not get half of its people on board until the end of the third year of its change process. At that point, the company's employee survey indicated that 51 percent of employees felt free to make decisions that made their jobs better. That figure now stands at 96 percent. "People have to hear it, see other people do it, see other people succeed, then try it themselves," Bruce says.

In a study of companies involved in transforming themselves, John Kotter quantified the amount of change that occurred each year over a seven-year period. "The peak came in year 5, fully 36 months after the first set of visible wins," he writes (Kotter 1995).

"If you aren't willing to be relentless and persevere, don't even think about launching a change process," says Craig Weatherup, president and CEO of Pepsi-Cola North America. "It takes years of hard work, and you have to be the one driving it forward" (Garvin 1995).

The secret to significant, lasting change, according to those who have succeeded at it, is to be radical in design, relentless in implementation, patient in the pursuit, and supportive of the journey everyone must take. It also requires an awareness of the reasons a change process may fail. In *Whole System Architecture*, Lawrence Miller identifies a dozen reasons for failure, most of which we've discussed in this chapter:

➤ Lack of strategic linkage
➤ Inadequate readiness
➤ Past and present successes
➤ Past and present failures
➤ Short-term business focus
➤ "Piecemeal" approach
➤ Externally driven initiatives
➤ Inadequate commitment

➤ Activity versus results focus

➤ Poor change management

➤ Insufficient training

➤ Little positive reinforcement

The best way to address the causes of failure is to develop and follow an effective change process.

■ THE CHANGE PROCESS

Whether the change involves the entire organization, a division or department within the organization, or a major process, consider the following steps:

1. Determine the organization's readiness to change.
2. Commit to change.
3. Form a guiding change team.
4. Create a vision and objectives for the change process.
5. Develop a comprehensive, holistic change plan.
6. Prepare people for change. Communication, example, training.
7. Engage employees in the process.
8. Build on early successes.
9. Align the system with the vision.
10. Institutionalize new approaches.

Determine the Organization's Readiness to Change

In their book *The Wisdom of Teams,* Jon Katzenbach and Douglas Smith propose four questions to help determine an organization's readiness to change:

➤ Does the organization have to get very good at one or more basic things it is not very good at now?

➤ Do large numbers of people throughout the entire organization have to change specific behaviors?

➤ Does the organization have a track record of success in changes of this type?

➤ Do people throughout the organization understand the implications of the change for their own behaviors and urgently believe that the time to act is now?

As pointed out earlier, some believe an organization is ready to change when at least 75 percent of its leaders believe it must.

Commit to Change

In *Leading Change,* James O'Toole talks about the leaders of change in several major organizations, including Girl Scouts, Herman Miller, Corning, Motorola, SAS, Polaroid, and MasterCard. He concludes, "In each case, the process began with a sine qua non of change: a clear, long-term, top management commitment to the hard work of altering corporate culture, beginning with themselves as leaders."

Form a Guiding Change Team

Jeanie Daniel Duck calls it the Transition Management Team (TMT), consisting of eight to twelve leaders "who commit all their time to making the transition a reality" (Duck 1993). The team must have the power and authority to fund the process, align the projects, and contribute to the evaluations of performance. The senior leader of the organization champions the transformation; the TMT leads it.

Duck suggest eight primary responsibilities for the TMT:

➤ *Establish context for change and provide guidelines.* One of the best ways to do this is open houses, town meetings, focus groups, and as part of the agenda of department meetings.

➤ *Stimulate conversation.* The focus here is on cross-functional discussions that begin to break down functional boundaries.

➤ *Provide appropriate resources.* The TMT has the authority to allocate resources and kill projects that are no longer needed.

➤ *Coordinate and align projects.* The proliferation of change programs, teams, and projects can create confusion. The TMT makes sure all projects are aligned with the goals of the transformation and communicates how they fit throughout the organization.

➤ *Ensure congruence of messages, activities, policies, and behaviors.* "The TMT's job is to be on the lookout for inconsistencies that undermine the credibility of the change effort," Duck writes.

➤ *Provide opportunities for joint creation.* This means making sure everyone in the organization has the training, information, and responsibility to create their future together.

➤ *Anticipate, identify, and address people problems.* We talked about resistance to change in the previous section.

➤ *Prepare the critical mass.* Asked what steps Levi's was taking to ensure the success of its change program, Tom Kasten described a meeting of seventy veteran managers to review every major change program in the company's history. The meeting produced two conclusions. First, Levi's was better at initiating change than at finishing it. Second, it did a poor job of preparing people for change. To address this, the change team "created a collection of resources to help people move forward: videos, seminars, workbooks, self-diagnostics. You can't expect people to change if you don't give them the tools" (Sheff 1996).

"The real contribution of leadership in a time of change lies in managing the dynamics, not the pieces," Duck writes. "The fundamental job of leadership is to deal with the dynamics of change, the confluence and congruence of the forces that change unleashes, so that the company is better prepared to compete."

Create a Vision and Objectives for the Change Process

The vision must be shared, specific, and actionable. The objectives must translate the vision into timely, tangible, and measurable or observable results. The authors of *The Boundaryless Organization* describe how researchers at Harvard, after studying dozens of corporations engaged in major change, "have concluded that the successful companies had an unrelenting focus on results while the less successful companies focused on activities that kept people busy but were aimed at changing intermediate variables rather than bottom-line results" (Ashkenas, Ulrich, Jick, and Kerr 1995).

Develop a Comprehensive, Holistic Change Plan

The creation of such a plan requires a complete and realistic understanding of how the current management system works, what strengths the organization can leverage and what weaknesses it must overcome, what the organization will look like when the transformation is complete, how other successful change programs have progressed, the steps in this process, milestones, measurements, risks, and potential problems. The plan must also consider pacing; too many initiatives from too many directions confuse and overwhelm people, which then slows or stops the change process.

Finally, the plan should be flexible, more iterative than grand in scale. One way to build in flexibility is for the planning group to consider the most likely "what if" possibilities. In *Whole System Architecture,* Lawrence Miller proposes using the S.P.I.N. model for this purpose:

> ➤ Situation: What are some possible situations that might impact your implementation efforts?
>
> ➤ Problem: What problems would this situation cause?
>
> ➤ Implications: If not addressed, what would be the effect of this problem on the implementation process?
>
> ➤ Need: What needs to be done to prevent or fix the situation?

Prepare People for Change

As Kasten said, you can't expect people to change without giving them the tools. And you can't overcommunicate. Use every vehicle possible to communicate the vision, objectives, and plan. Leaders and change team members should model the new behaviors that people will need in the "new" organization. The change plan should identify the training people will need to participate in the change process and function successfully when the change is complete.

At the same time, the focus is on preparing people for change, not changing them. "We create opportunities for people to change," Kasten says, "but we can't change them. They have to change themselves."

Engage Employees in the Process

Remove obstacles to change. Encourage action, risk taking, learning. Invite participation on teams and in discussions. Recognize and reward individuals and teams for contributions to the process. Keep everyone informed. Margaret Wheatley writes about seeing leaders "make great efforts to speak forthrightly and frequently to employees about current struggles, about the tough times that lie ahead, and about what they dream of for the future. These conversations fill a painful period with new purpose" (Wheatley 1992).

Build on Early Successes

Initiate the change process in those areas most likely to succeed. Communicate to the rest of the organization how these pilot areas proceeded and the results they achieved. Incorporate the lessons learned from the pilots into the subsequent rollout of the change plan. Encourage the leaders of change in the pilots to share what they learned with other leaders and to participate on other change teams.

Align the System with the Vision

The old system was designed to support the old way of doing business. The transformed organization will require a new approach to such things as employee satisfaction, customer focus, measurements, planning, recognition, process thinking, and compensation. You can begin to manage from this holistic perspective by mastering the basics of business excellence presented in this book.

Institutionalize New Approaches

The change is not complete until the new behaviors and practices are institutionalized, which most agree is at least a three-year process. You institutionalize change by preaching a consistent vision, acting in step with the vision, deploying successful strategies and approaches throughout the organization, aligning the system, and ensuring that the transformation will continue even if its leadership changes.

The flip side of the steps to success is the reasons for failure. John Kotter notes eight crucial mistakes organizations make:

➤ Not establishing enough of a sense of urgency

➤ Not creating a powerful enough guiding coalition

➤ Lacking a vision

➤ Undercommunicating the vision by a factor of ten

➤ Not removing obstacles to the new vision

➤ Not systematically planning for or creating short-term wins

➤ Declaring victory too soon

➤ Not anchoring changes in the corporation's culture (Kotter 1995).

I would add a ninth: Leaders don't understand the basics of business excellence, the fundamentals of their business, or the commitment required to change. As with the other eight mistakes, all of these can be anticipated and overcome by thoughtful planning, a willingness to learn and grow, and the realization that leaders cannot be isolated from the change.

■ THE PROMISE OF CHANGE

Change is getting so much press these days, you feel like a piker if you're not busy transforming something. Even worse, the business media implies that if you haven't transformed yet, you're so far behind that you'll never catch up. How many times have you heard that some characteristic or other is "the ticket into the game?" As in, quality is the ticket into the game, the implication being that, unless you have pretty high quality, you can't compete. I disagree. If quality is the ticket into the minivan game, for example, the molding on my new Dodge Caravan wouldn't fall off less than a month after I bought it and the transmission wouldn't have to be replaced at 40,000 miles. Yet the Chrysler minivans are considered the best of the crop. *Motor Trend's* car of the year. If quality were the ticket to that game, I believe Chrysler would still be looking for the ticket line.

The ticket to the game claims are the worst kinds of lies, packaged with enough truth to deceive. We all know that the stakes for "the game" have grown. We realize that quality, innovation, value, or other dimensions of excellence are imperative. Not possessing them in sufficient degrees, we feel condemned to mediocrity and failure.

The assumption triggers sudden and costly decisions. Pick your program of the month—TQM, reengineering, self-directed teams, core competencing, value disciplining—and you will find a host of leaders who bought this ticket because they feared being left behind. They had no plan. No idea what the ticket actually bought. Pretending movement is progress and any change is a positive change.

Everybody worries about being left behind, unable to get into the game. The truth is, you're already in. If you believe your organization must have some preordained level of performance and you don't find out what that level is for yourself, you are setting your organization up for failure.

The companies featured in this book are not perfect. No organization is. But they are steadily, systematically improving their organizations. Their total business management approach is the remedy for the ticket to the game deceit. It is an approach you can adapt to your organization with immediate and long-term results. And it begins by mastering the basics of business excellence.

Such mastery will not come easily. It will require an examination of where you are and where you want to be, both personally and as an organization. It will require patience and perseverance and a commitment to improve and grow. And it will require change.

The change holds a promise, however, an opportunity to burst from the box of tired habits and rigid rules and concrete expectations to reach for new challenges. The opportunity to learn. The opportunity to feel part of something greater than yourself.

Margaret Wheatley describes the impact of change in *Leadership and the New Science:*

I, too, can feel the ground shaking. I hear its deep rumblings. Any moment now, the earth will crack open and I will stare into its dark center. Into the smoking caldera, I will throw most of what I have treasured, most of the techniques and tools that have made me feel competent. I cannot do that yet; I cannot just heave everything I know into the abyss. But I know it is coming. And when it comes, when I have made my sacrificial offerings to the gods of understanding, then the ruptures will cease. Healing waters will cover the land, giving birth to new life, burying forever the ancient, rusting machines of our past understandings. And on these waters I will set sail to places I only now imagine. There I will be blessed with new visions and new magic. I will feel once again like a creative contributor to this mysterious world.

The Management System Analysis

The Management System Analysis can help you assess the current condition of your organization's management system and understand the requirements for world-class performance. Adapted from the criteria for the Malcolm Baldrige National Quality Award, the analysis focuses on improving your competitiveness by delivering value to customers while improving overall company performance and capabilities. **It is not intended to replace a formal, documented assessment, but rather to provide a snapshot of your management system.**

You can use the assessment to:

➤ Identify strengths and areas for improvement

➤ Determine the overall health of your management system

➤ Establish a benchmark for future comparisons

➤ Understand the elements common to all management systems

■ HOW TO ASSESS YOUR ORGANIZATION

The analysis consists of seventy-seven statements. The statements are organized to lead you through the entire management system, beginning with understanding customer requirements, translating those requirements into products and services, designing and managing the processes that produce those products and services (and all other key processes in the company), and improving supplier performance. Attention then turns to the information and data used to drive improvement and develop strategic plans, the business planning process, and human resource plans and approaches, including high-performance work systems, training, and employee satisfaction. The analysis closes the loop by assessing how you determine customer satisfaction, then concludes by focusing on the organization's leadership and management. The final eighteen statements assess the results of the approaches addressed in the first fifty-nine statements.

To produce the most valuable assessment, read each statement carefully, determine the extent to which what your company does compares to what the statement addresses, then score your response based on these guidelines:

Approach refers to how you do something—the method and/or process you use. For each statement (1–59), determine whether your methods are systematic, integrated, and consistently applied, and whether they are based on objective, reliable data and information. On the scoring continuum, a 0 means no systematic approach is being used, while the highest score (either 5 or 7, depending on the statement) means a systematic, integrated approach is consistently applied. *For each scoring dimension (approach, deployment, refinement, or results),* your score may be the lowest or highest score or some number between them.

Deployment refers to the extent to which your approach is applied to all the requirements in the statement. On the scoring continuum, a 0 means major gaps exist in deployment that would inhibit progress in this area, while a 3 means the approach is fully deployed with no significant weaknesses or gaps in any areas or work units.

Refinement refers to the presence of a formal process for evaluating and improving your approach. On the scoring continuum, a 0 means no improvement cycle exists, while a 2 means a strong, fact-based improvement process is a key management tool, with continual refinement of your approach supported by excellent analysis.

Results refers to the outcomes of your approaches and deployment. For statements 60–77, you will be asked to determine if you can chart results for the key measures and/or indicators, the extent to which you can show improvement trends and/or good performance levels, and how your trends or levels compare to those of key benchmarks. Unlike scoring in the *Approach and Deployment* section, the scoring in the *Results* section often depends on previous statements. For example, if you determine that you have only half the results you should have to measure performance in a particular area, you cannot award yourself more than half the possible points for subsequent statements asking about performance levels or comparisons to key benchmarks. The scoring guidelines in the *Results* section explain how to do this.

■ BEFORE YOU START

To produce the most accurate and beneficial assessment, follow these guidelines:

➤ **Think in terms of processes.** The Baldrige criteria are very process-oriented, repeatedly asking *how* areas are addressed. A process orientation focuses on continuous improvement using the P-D-C-A cycle: Plan–Do–Check–Act, then repeat the cycle. The degree to which this process orientation and approach to improvement is embedded in your company's culture determines how well you will score. If you have sound, systematic processes in place for the statements that follow, if those processes are fully deployed in all areas and to all work units, and if you can show excellent results depicting the payoff of your efforts to continuously improve, you will score well. If you have few processes in place, if your processes are not widely deployed, or if you cannot show the results of your efforts to improve, you will not score as well.

➤ **Evaluate each statement carefully.** Many statements ask you to evaluate your organization's performance in more than one area. For example, statement 6 says: "We follow up with customers on products, services, and recent transactions to determine satisfaction, resolve problems, seek feedback for improvement, and build relationships." To evaluate your company's performance for this statement, you need to identify your approach for following up with customers on products to determine satisfaction, your approach for following up with customers on products to resolve problems, etc., then how well each approach is deployed and the extent to which it is refined. You must then do the same evaluation for services and recent transactions. Every aspect of every statement must be evaluated to produce an accurate score.

➤ **Be able to prove your score.** A fact-based assessment is based on proof. Before assigning a score to a statement, make sure you understand the reality of the situation. Check with internal experts in the process. Determine the extent to which an approach is used, evaluated, and improved. Not only will you improve the accuracy of your scoring, but you will also begin to identify strengths and areas for improvement. In addition, seeking proof will help you avoid one of the greatest obstacles to an accurate assessment: the example. Most people can think of a good story or anecdote to demonstrate how their company excels in a particular area. However, if you ask these people for the process that produced the example, few can identify one. The analysis rewards sound, systematic approaches. "Anecdotal information," according to the Baldrige scoring system, scores 0 percent.

➤ **Results must reflect key measures and/or indicators.** The measures or indicators should represent the factors that lead to improved customer, operational, and financial performance. Many of these measures or indicators appear in statements in the Approach and Deployment section. For example, statements 8 and 12 refer to the measures used to maintain and improve key production and delivery processes for each of your products and services. You should assess the results on these key measures for statements 60–63.

For an accurate assessment, each result requires data to demonstrate progress, achievement, and breadth of deployment. Evaluation of achievement is usually based on two factors: (1) that the performance level has been sustained or is the current result of a favorable trend; and (2) that the performance level can be compared with those of other appropriate organizations. If you were to depict your results, the ideal graph for each would include the elements shown in the Figure A-1.

➤ **Use the 50% line.** Baldrige Award examiners use percent ranges when assigning a score to an item. Many begin at the

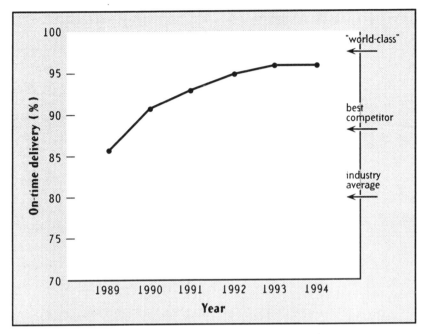

Figure A-1. Performance Level Graph

50% line. For an approach/deployment statement, 50% means your company's approach meets the basic objectives of the statement and is deployed to the principal activities covered by the statement. For a results statement, 50% represents clear indication of improvement trends and/or good levels of performance in the principal results areas covered by the statement. Once you determine which side of the 50% line your company falls on, you can zero in on an accurate score for the statement.

➤ **Be realistic.** Very few Baldrige Award applicants score more than 500 points out of a possible 1,000. The highest scoring applicant in any year scores around 700 points. The goal is not to squeeze out the highest possible score, but to identify those areas of greatest leverage, where intense focus and strong improvement will result in better value to customers and improved company performance.

■ USING THE ASSESSMENT TO IMPROVE

This is a tool for identifying strengths and areas for improvement in your total business management system. To get the most out of the tool, you will need to translate the findings of the assessment into objectives and action plans, a process that can be wrapped into your strategic planning process, addressed by your senior management team, or assigned to a cross-functional team or teams for analysis and action.

The purpose of the assessment is to help your company enhance its competitiveness by focusing on dual, results-oriented goals:

➤ Delivery of ever-improving value to customers, resulting in marketplace success; and

➤ Improvement of overall company performance and capabilities.

Your company can move toward these goals by using the assessment to identify and prioritize opportunities for improvement, develop action plans with measures and targets, implement the actions and measure progress, and evaluate and improve the process. It can also use the assessment to improve understanding of the basics of business excellence that are the foundation for integrating customer and company performance requirements.

■ APPROACH AND DEPLOYMENT

1. Our process for determining customers'
   requirements (including unarticulated needs)
   is fed by timely, reliable, and accurate
   information on:
   - Current customers
   - Potential customers
   - The customers of competitors
   And includes other key information such as:
   - Complaints
   - Gains and losses of customers
   - The performance of our products and services

   Approach (0-5): ☐
   Deployment (0-3): ☐
   Refinement (0-2): ☐
   TOTAL: ☐

2. We anticipate our customers' future
   requirements through a process that includes
   such key listening and learning strategies as:
   - Working closely with customers
   - Rapid innovation
   - Closely monitoring industry factors and trends
   - Won/lost analysis relative to competitors
   - Post-transaction follow-up to solicit customer
     feedback

   Approach (0-5): ☐
   Deployment (0-3): ☐
   Refinement (0-2): ☐
   TOTAL: ☐

3. Our process for translating customer
   requirements into specific product and service
   features includes:
   - Reviews by, and feedback from, customers
   - A determination of the relative importance of
     these features
   - The identification of those features that
     differentiate our products and services from
     those of our competitors

   Approach (0-5): ☐
   Deployment (0-3): ☐
   Refinement (0-2): ☐
   TOTAL: ☐

4. We have performance measures and service
   standards for communicating with customers
   and providing them with easy access to
   information and assistance, including processes
   for evaluating and improving how we manage
   customer relationships.

   Approach (0-5): ☐
   Deployment (0-3): ☐
   Refinement (0-2): ☐
   TOTAL: ☐

5. Our complaint management process ensures that:
   - All formal and informal complaints are resolved effectively and promptly
   - Customer confidence is recovered
   - Customer requirements for complaint resolution are met
   - The causes of the complaints are eliminated

   Approach (0-5): ☐
   Deployment (0-3): ☐
   Refinement (0-2): ☐
   TOTAL: ☐

6. We follow up with customers on products, services, and recent transactions to:
   - Determine satisfaction
   - Resolve problems
   - Seek feedback for improvement
   - Build relationships

   Approach (0-5): ☐
   Deployment (0-3): ☐
   Refinement (0-2): ☐
   TOTAL: ☐

7. We follow a formal process for translating customer requirements into design requirements for our products and services.

   Approach (0-5): ☐
   Deployment (0-3): ☐
   Refinement (0-2): ☐
   TOTAL: ☐

8. We follow a formal process for translating product/service design requirements into efficient and effective production and delivery processes. The processes include measurement plans that:
   - Spell out what is to be measured
   - Identify how and when measurements are to be made
   - Set performance levels or standards to ensure that the results can be used to control and improve the processes

   Approach (0-5): ☐
   Deployment (0-3): ☐
   Refinement (0-2): ☐
   TOTAL: ☐

9. Early in the design of our products, services, and production/delivery processes, all appropriate company units, suppliers, and partners address all requirements to ensure integration, coordination, and capability.

   Approach (0-5): ☐
   Deployment (0-3): ☐
   Refinement (0-2): ☐
   TOTAL: ☐

10. We follow formal processes for reviewing and/or testing the designs of our products, services, and production/delivery processes to ensure trouble-free launch.

Approach (0-5): ☐
Deployment (0-3): ☐
Refinement (0-2): ☐
TOTAL: ☐

11. We have identified the key processes we use to produce and deliver our products and services and the key requirements for each process.

Approach (0-7): ☐
Deployment (0-3): ☐
TOTAL: ☐

12. We use measurements defined by our measurement plan to maintain the performance of our key product and service production/delivery processes.

Approach (0-7): ☐
Deployment (0-3): ☐
TOTAL: ☐

13. We continually improve our operational performance by continually evaluating and improving our key product and service production/delivery processes.

Approach (0-7): ☐
Deployment (0-3): ☐
TOTAL: ☐

14. To improve these processes, we use process analysis and research, benchmarking, alternative technologies, and information from internal and external customers of the processes.

Approach (0-7): ☐
Deployment (0-3): ☐
TOTAL: ☐

15. We have identified the key processes for our support services (those services that support product and service design, production, and delivery, such as finance and accounting, sales, marketing, information services, personnel, and administrative services) and the key requirements and measurement plans for each process.

Approach (0-7): ☐
Deployment (0-3): ☐
TOTAL: ☐

16. We use measurements defined by our measurement plan to maintain the performance of our key support service processes.

Approach (0-7): ☐
Deployment (0-3): ☐
TOTAL: ☐

17. We continually improve our operational
    performance by continually evaluating and
    improving our key support service processes
    using:
    • Process analysis and research
    • Benchmarking
    • Alternative technologies
    • Information from internal and external
      customers of the processes

    Approach (0-7): ☐
    Deployment (0-3): ☐
    TOTAL: ☐

18. For those key suppliers that provide the most
    important products/services to our business,
    we have identified and communicated to them:
    • Our principal requirements
    • The measures and/or indicators for each
    • The expected performance levels

    Approach (0-7): ☐
    Deployment (0-3): ☐
    TOTAL: ☐

19. We have formal processes for determining
    whether or not suppliers are meeting our
    requirements and for communicating such
    performance information to suppliers.

    Approach (0-7): ☐
    Deployment (0-3): ☐
    TOTAL: ☐

20. We continually evaluate and improve our
    supplier relationships and performance and
    our own procurement processes, including the
    use of such actions and plans as:
    • Customer-supplier teams and planning
    • Rapid information exchanges
    • Use of benchmarking
    • Training
    • Recognition

    Approach (0-7): ☐
    Deployment (0-3): ☐
    TOTAL: ☐

21. We have identified the information and data
    needed to drive improvement of our company's
    overall performance and can relate each type
    of information and data to one or more of our
    key business drivers (the areas of performance
    most critical to our success; see No. 30 for
    further description).

    Approach (0-7): ☐
    Deployment (0-3): ☐
    TOTAL: ☐

22. We evaluate and improve the selection,
    analysis, and integration of information and
    data, aligning them with our business priorities
    and taking into account:
    - The scope of the information and data
    - How they are used to support process
      management and performance improvement
    - Feedback from users of the information and data

    Approach (0-7): ☐
    Deployment (0-3): ☐
    TOTAL: ☐

23. We have identified our needs and priorities for
    competitive comparisons and benchmarking
    information and established criteria for
    seeking this information from within and
    outside our industry.

    Approach (0-5): ☐
    Deployment (0-3): ☐
    Refinement (0-2): ☐
    TOTAL: ☐

24. We use competitive comparisons and
    benchmarking to drive improvement of overall
    company performance, including improving
    the understanding of our processes, setting
    stretch targets, and encouraging breakthrough
    approaches.

    Approach (0-5): ☐
    Deployment (0-3): ☐
    Refinement (0-2): ☐
    TOTAL: ☐

25. We integrate and analyze information and
    data from all parts of the company to better
    understand our customers and markets; such
    analysis includes:
    - Trends
    - Projections
    - Cause-effect correlations
    - The search for deeper understanding to set
      priorities and allocate resources

    Approach (0-5): ☐
    Deployment (0-3): ☐
    Refinement (0-2): ☐
    TOTAL: ☐

26. We integrate and analyze information and
    data from all parts of the company to better
    understand our operational performance
    and company capabilities.

    Approach (0-5): ☐
    Deployment (0-3): ☐
    Refinement (0-2): ☐
    TOTAL: ☐

27. We integrate and analyze information and
    data from all parts of the company to better
    understand our competitive performance.

    Approach (0-5): ☐
    Deployment (0-3): ☐
    Refinement (0-2): ☐
    TOTAL: ☐

28. To set priorities for improvement, we relate customer and market data and improvements in product/service quality and operational performance to changes in financial and market indicators of performance.

Approach (0-5): ☐
Deployment (0-3): ☐
Refinement (0-2): ☐
TOTAL: ☐

29. We use these different types of analyses plus information about the competitive environment, risks, company capabilities, and supplier capabilities to develop strategies and business plans aimed at strengthening our performance and improving our competitive position.

Approach (0-7): ☐
Deployment (0-3): ☐
TOTAL: ☐

30. We translate our strategies and plans into actionable key business drivers (including customer-driven quality requirements and operational requirements such as productivity, cycle time, employee productivity, etc.) which include key measures we use to track progress in deploying our business plan.

Approach (0-7): ☐
Deployment (0-3): ☐
TOTAL: ☐

31. We formally evaluate and improve our strategic planning process and the process for deploying the plan, including how well strategies and requirements are communicated and understood and how well key measures are aligned.

Approach (0-7): ☐
Deployment (0-3): ☐
TOTAL: ☐

32. We have:
   • Identified our key business drivers, the key performance requirements for each, and the associated operational performance measures for each
   • Deployed the plan and requirements to work units and suppliers and aligned their efforts with the plan
   • Included productivity and cycle time improvement and waste reduction in the plan
   • Committed resources to accomplishing the plan

Approach (0-5): ☐
Deployment (0-3): ☐
Refinement (0-2): ☐
TOTAL: ☐

33. When we compare our expected performance on these key measures over the next two to five years to the expected performance of our key competitors and key benchmarks, we can show how our company will strengthen its competitive advantage.

Approach (0-5): ☐
Deployment (0-3): ☐
Refinement (0-2): ☐
TOTAL: ☐

34. Our process for translating our business plan into specific human resources plans includes plans for:
    • Changes in work design to improve flexibility, innovation, and rapid response
    • Employee development, education, and training
    • Improvements in compensation, recognition, and benefits
    • Recruitment

Approach (0-7): ☐
Deployment (0-3): ☐
TOTAL: ☐

35. We evaluate and improve our human resources planning and practices and their alignment with our business plan and strategies, including using employee-related data and company performance data to:
    • Assess the development and well-being of all employees
    • Assess the linkage between human resources practices and key business results
    • Ensure that reliable and complete human resources information is available for strategic and business planning

Approach (0-7): ☐
Deployment (0-3): ☐
TOTAL: ☐

36. Our work and job design promote high performance by creating opportunities for initiative and self-directed responsibility for all employees.

Approach (0-5): ☐
Deployment (0-3): ☐
Refinement (0-2): ☐
TOTAL: ☐

37. Our work and job design promote high performance by fostering flexibility and rapid response to changing requirements and ensuring effective communications across functions and units.

Approach (0-5): ☐
Deployment (0-3): ☐
Refinement (0-2): ☐
TOTAL: ☐

38. Our company's approach to *compensation* for individuals and groups reinforces the effectiveness of our work and job design.

Approach (0-5): ☐
Deployment (0-3): ☐
Refinement (0-2): ☐
TOTAL: ☐

39. Our company's approach to *recognition* for individuals and groups reinforces the effectiveness of our work and job design.

Approach (0-5): ☐
Deployment (0-3): ☐
Refinement (0-2): ☐
TOTAL: ☐

40. Education and training serve as a key vehicle for building company and employee capabilities.

Approach (0-7): ☐
Deployment (0-3): ☐
TOTAL: ☐

41. Education and training address the company's key performance objectives (including those related to enhancing high performance work units) and the progression and development of all employees.

Approach (0-7): ☐
Deployment (0-3): ☐
TOTAL: ☐

42. Employees and line managers contribute to or are involved in determining specific education and training needs and designing education and training.

Approach (0-7): ☐
Deployment (0-3): ☐
TOTAL: ☐

43. We follow formal processes to design, deliver, reinforce, evaluate, and improve our education and training, including reinforcing knowledge and skills through on-the-job application.

Approach (0-7): ☐
Deployment (0-3): ☐
TOTAL: ☐

44. We have identified the factors that contribute to a safe and healthful work environment and have principal improvement requirements, measures, and targets for each factor.

Approach (0-5): ☐
Deployment (0-3): ☐
Refinement (0-2): ☐
TOTAL: ☐

45. We offer a wide variety of services, activities, and opportunities to employees to support their well-being and satisfaction and to enhance their work experience and development potential.

Approach (0-5): ☐
Deployment (0-3): ☐
Refinement (0-2): ☐
TOTAL: ☐

46. We use specific methods such as employee surveys and measures of safety, absenteeism, and turnover to determine employee satisfaction, well-being, and motivation, and we use the information from these methods to improve.

Approach (0-5): ☐
Deployment (0-3): ☐
Refinement (0-2): ☐
TOTAL: ☐

47. Our customer satisfaction measurement systems (for each customer group and/or market segment) give us reliable information about customer ratings of specific product and service features and the customer's likely future market behavior.

Approach (0-7): ☐
Deployment (0-3): ☐
TOTAL: ☐

48. We determine customer satisfaction relative to that for competitors through company-based comparative studies and comparative studies or evaluations made by independent organizations and/or customers.

Approach (0-7): ☐
Deployment (0-3): ☐
TOTAL: ☐

49. Our process for evaluating and improving our customer satisfaction measurement system includes other indicators (such as gains and losses of customers) and indicators of customer dissatisfaction (such as complaints, claims, and warranty costs).

Approach (0-7): ☐
Deployment (0-3): ☐
TOTAL: ☐

50. Our leadership system, management, and organization focus on customers and high-performance objectives.

Approach (0-5): ☐
Deployment (0-3): ☐
Refinement (0-2): ☐
TOTAL: ☐

51. We use several methods to communicate and reinforce our company's values, expectations, and directions throughout the entire workforce.

Approach (0-5): ☐
Deployment (0-3): ☐
Refinement (0-2): ☐
TOTAL: ☐

52. We use the results of key performance measures and indicators, and the analysis of these results, to review company and work unit performance and to improve performance.

Approach (0-5): ☐
Deployment (0-3): ☐
Refinement (0-2): ☐
TOTAL: ☐

53. These reviews include measures of the company's public responsibilities, including legal requirements, public concerns, and legal and ethical conduct.

Approach (0-5): ☐
Deployment (0-3): ☐
Refinement (0-2): ☐
TOTAL: ☐

54. Our company is a leading corporate citizen through its efforts to strengthen areas such as community services, education, health care, environment, and the practices of trade or business associations.

Approach (0-5): ☐
Deployment (0-3): ☐
Refinement (0-2): ☐
TOTAL: ☐

55. Senior executives (the highest-ranking official and those reporting directly to that official) actively create and reinforce our company's values and expectations throughout our leadership system.

Approach (0-5): ☐
Deployment (0-3): ☐
Refinement (0-2): ☐
TOTAL: ☐

56. Senior executives actively contribute to setting our company's directions and performance excellence goals through strategic and business planning.

Approach (0-5): ☐
Deployment (0-3): ☐
Refinement (0-2): ☐
TOTAL: ☐

57. Senior executives lead and are involved in reviews of company performance, including customer-related and operational performance, and use those reviews to focus on key business objectives.

Approach (0-5): ☐
Deployment (0-3): ☐
Refinement (0-2): ☐
TOTAL: ☐

58. Senior executives enhance the effectiveness of their leadership through activities such as:
    • Mentoring other executives
    • Benchmarking
    • Employee recognition
    • Interacting with customers, employees, and suppliers

Approach (0-5): ☐
Deployment (0-3): ☐
Refinement (0-2): ☐
TOTAL: ☐

59. Senior executives use tools such as employee surveys and assessments by peers, direct reports, or a board of directors to evaluate and improve the effectiveness of the company's leadership system and organization.

Approach (0-5): ☐
Deployment (0-3): ☐
Refinement (0-2): ☐
TOTAL: ☐

■ RESULTS

Product and Service Quality Results

60. We have trends and current levels for all key measures and/or indicators of product and service quality. These are the key internal measures and/or indicators derived from translating customer requirements into product and service features, design requirements, and production and delivery processes (see Nos. 3, 7, 8, 11, and 12 for an overview of how this translation occurs). These measures and/or indicators predict customer satisfaction and retention.

30 points possible. Determine what key measures/indicators you have, then what percent that is of the key measures you should have. The percent multiplied by 30 gives you the ...

TOTAL: ☐

61. All key measures/indicators show positive trends (three or more years) and/or consistently positive levels.

20 points possible. Multiply 20 by the percent determined for No. 60 above. Multiply the new total by the percent of key measures you have that also show positive trends or consistently positive levels to arrive at the...

TOTAL: ☐

62. All key measures/indicators include comparisons with industry best, best competitor, industry average, and other appropriate benchmarks.

20 points possible. Multiply 20 by the percent determined for No. 60 above. Multiply the new total by the percent of key measures you have that also show comparisons to arrive at the...

TOTAL: ☐

63. All key measures/indicators compare favorably with those benchmarks.

10 points possible. Multiply 10 by the percent of key measures you have that show comparisons (determined in No. 62). Multiply the new total by the percent of key measures you have that compare favorably with the benchmarks to arrive at the...

TOTAL: ☐

Company Operational and Financial Results

64. We have trends and current levels for all key measures and/or indicators of company operational and financial performance. These key measures and/or indicators should address the following areas:
    • Productivity and other indicators of effective use of manpower, materials, energy, capital, and assets
    • Cycle time and responsiveness

5 points possible. Multiply 5 by the percent of key measures you have that show comparisons (determined in No. 70). Multiply the new total by the percent of key measures you have that compare favorably with the benchmarks to arrive at the...

TOTAL: ☐

- Support service measures (see Nos. 15 and 16 for description)
- Financial indicators such as cost reductions, asset utilization, and benefit/cost results from improvement efforts
- Human resources indicators such as safety, absenteeism, turnover, involvement, recognition, training, and satisfaction
- Public responsibilities such as environmental improvements
- Company-specific indicators such as innovation rates

65. All key measures/indicators show positive trends (three or more years) and/or consistently positive levels.

30 points possible. Multiply 30 by the percent determined for No. 64 above. Multiply the new total by the percent of key measures you have that also show positive trends or consistently positive levels to arrive at the...

TOTAL: ☐

66. All key measures/indicators include comparisons with industry best, best competitor, industry average, and other appropriate benchmarks.

30 points possible. Multiply 30 by the percent determined for No. 64 above. Multiply the new total by the percent of key measures you have that also show comparisons to arrive at the...

TOTAL: ☐

67. All key measures/indicators compare favorably with those benchmarks.

20 points possible. Multiply 20 by the percent of key measures you have that show comparisons (determined in No. 66). Multiply the new total by the percent of key measures you have that compare favorably with the benchmarks to arrive at the...

TOTAL: ☐

Supplier Performance Results

68. We have trends and current levels for all key measures and/or indicators of supplier performance (see Nos. 17 and 18).

15 points possible. Determine what key measures/indicators you have, then what percent that is of the key measures you should have. The percent multiplied by 15 gives you the...

TOTAL: ☐

69. All key measures/indicators show positive trends (three or more years) and/or consistently positive levels.

10 points possible. Multiply 10 by the percent determined for No. 68 above. Multiply the new total by the percent of key measures you have that also show positive trends or consistently positive levels to arrive at the...

TOTAL: ☐

70. All key measures/indicators include comparisons with industry best, best competitor, industry average, and other appropriate benchmarks.

10 points possible. Multiply 10 by the percent determined for No. 68 above. Multiply the new total by the percent of key measures you have that also show comparisons to arrive at the...

TOTAL: ☐

71. All key measures/indicators compare favorably with those benchmarks.

5 points possible. Multiply 5 by the percent of key measures you have that show comparisons (determined in No. 70). Multiply the new total by the percent of key measures you have that compare favorably with the benchmarks to arrive at the...

TOTAL: ☐

Customer Satisfaction Results

72. We have trends and current levels for all key measures and/or indicators of customer satisfaction for all customer groups.

40 points possible. Determine what key measures/indicators you have, then what percent that is of the key measures you should have for all customer groups. The percent multiplied by 40 gives you the...

TOTAL: ☐

73. All key measures/indicators of customer satisfaction show positive trends (three or more years) and/or consistently positive levels.

20 points possible. Multiply 20 by the percent determined for No. 72 above. Multiply the new total by the percent of key measures you have that also show positive trends or consistently positive levels to arrive at the...

TOTAL: ☐

74. All key measures/indicators of customer satisfaction include comparisons with competitors, including gains and losses of customers. The results may include objective information from independent organizations, including customers. All key measures/indicators compare favorably to competitors.

30 points possible. Multiply 30 by the percent determined for No. 72 above. Multiply the new total by the percent of key measures you have that also show comparisons. Multiply the new total by the percent of key measures that compare favorably to competitors to arrive at the...

TOTAL: ☐

75. We have trends and current levels for all key measures and/or indicators of customer dissatisfaction for all customer groups.

25 points possible. Determine what key measures/indicators you have, then what percent that is of the key measures you should have. The percent multiplied by 25 gives you the...

TOTAL: ☐

76. All key measures/indicators of customer dissatisfaction show positive trends (three or more years) and/or consistently positive levels. These are the most relevant and important indicators for the company's products and services.

15 points possible. Multiply 15 by the percent determined for No. 75 above. Multiply the new total by the percent of key measures you have that also show positive trends or consistently positive levels to arrive at the...

TOTAL: ☐

77. We have trends in gaining or losing market share to competitors, and the trends are positive.

30 points possible. Determine the percent of markets for which you have market share trends and multiply that percent by 30. Multiply the new total by the percent of trends that are positive to arrive at the...

TOTAL: ☐

Total Score: _____   **Year:** _____

Point at which a company begins to break away from the competition:
500 points

Highest scoring Baldrige applicant in 1994:
625 points

Resources and Bibliography

■ RESOURCES

Contacts at organizations featured in this book:

Custom Research Inc.
Contact: Jeff Pope or Judith Corson, Partners
PO Box 26695
Minneapolis, MN 55426
(612) 542-0800

Granite Rock Company
Contact: Bruce Woolpert, President and CEO
PO Box 50001
Watsonville, CA 95077-5001
(408) 761-2300

Honeywell Solid State Electronics Center
Contact: Jay Schrankler, Director, Quality and Information Systems
12001 State Hwy. 55
Plymouth, MN 55441-4799
(612) 954-2662

Lyondell Petrochemical
Contact: Jackie Wilson, Director, Public Affairs
PO Box 3646
Houston, TX 77253-3646
(713) 652-4596

Marlow Industries
Contact: Ray Marlow, President
10451 Vista Park Road
Dallas, TX 75238-1645
(214) 340-4900

Wainwright Industries
Contact: Michael Simms, Plant Manager
PO Box 640
St. Peters, MO 63376
(314) 278-5850

To contact the author:

Stephen George
3381 Gorham Ave., Ste. 203
Minneapolis, MN 55426
(800) 605-4193
Fax: (612) 927-0206

■ BIBLIOGRAPHY

Ackoff, Russell L. 1994. *The democratic corporation: A radical prescription for recreating corporate America and rediscovering success.* New York: Oxford University Press.

American Society for Quality Control (ASQC). 1996. *Quality, the future, and you.*

Ashkenas, Ron, Dave Ulrich, Todd Jick, and Steve Kerr. 1995. *The boundaryless organization: Breaking the chains of organizational structure.* San Francisco: Jossey-Bass.

Bartlett, Christopher A., and Sumantra Ghoshal. 1994. Changing the role of top management: Beyond strategies to purpose. *Harvard Business Review,* November-December, 79.

Bartlett, Christopher A., and Sumantra Ghoshal. 1995. Changing the role of top management: Beyond systems to people. *Harvard Business Review,* May-June, 132.

Bemowski, Karen. 1995. What makes American teams tick. *Quality Progress,* January, 39.

Block, Peter. 1993. *Stewardship: Choosing service over self-interest.* San Francisco: Berrett-Koehler Publishers.

Bogan, Christopher E., and Michael J. English. 1994. *Benchmarking for best practices: Winning through innovative adaptation.* New York: McGraw-Hill.

Bowles, Jerry. 1995. Quality happens through people. *Fortune* (September advertising section): 51.

Brown, John Seeley, and Estee Solomon Gray. 1995. The people are the company. *Fast Company,* premier issue, 78.

Can't anybody here play this game. 1995. *Fast Company,* premier issue, 18.

Case, John. 1995. *Open-book management: The coming business revolution.* New York: HarperBusiness.

Chaleff, Ira. 1995. *The courageous follower: Standing up to and for our leaders.* San Francisco: Berrett-Koehler.

Chawla, Sarita, and John Renesch, eds. 1995. *Learning organizations: Developing cultures for tomorrow's workplace.* Portland, Oreg.: Productivity Press.

Collins, James C. 1995. Change is good—but first, know what should never change. *Fortune,* 29 May, 141.

Corporate survey finds fewer layoffs. 1995. The Wall Street Journal (23 October): 2.

Davenport, Thomas H. 1993. *Process innovation: Reengineering work through information technology.* Boston: Harvard Business School Press.

Davenport, Thomas H. 1995. The fad that forgot people. *Fast Company,* premier issue, 69.

Deschamps, Jean-Phillippe, and P. Ranganath Nayak. 1995. *Product juggernauts: How companies mobilize to generate a stream of market winners.* Boston: Harvard Business School Press.

Do managers care about their workers? 1995. *Quality Progress,* July, 14.

Donkin, Richard. 1995. Loyalty bonus should not be devalued. *The Financial Times,* 1 November.

Downsizing: How quality is affected as companies shrink. 1995. *Quality Progress,* April, 23.

Drucker, Peter. 1995. Information tools executives truly need. *Harvard Business Review,* January-February.

Duck, Jeanie Daniel. 1993. Managing change: The art of balancing. *Harvard Business Review,* November-December, 109.

Dumaine, Brian. 1994. Why do we work? Fortune (26 December): 196.

Galbraith, Jay R. 1995. *Designing organizations: An executive briefing on strategy, structure, and process.* San Francisco: Jossey-Bass.

Garvin, David A. 1995. Leveraging processes for strategic advantage. *Harvard Business Review,* September-October, 76.

George, Stephen. 1992. *The Baldrige quality system: The do-it-yourself way to transform your business.* New York: Wiley.

George, Stephen, and Arnold Weimerskirch. 1994. *Total quality management: Strategies and techniques proven at today's most successful companies.* New York: Wiley.

Grant, Alan W. H., and Leonard A. Schlesinger. 1995. Realize your customers' full profit potential. *Harvard Business Review,* September-October, 59.

Hamel, Gary, and C. K. Prahalad. 1994. *Competing for the future: Breakthrough strategies for seizing control of your industry and creating the markets of tomorrow.* Boston: Harvard Business School Press.

Hammer, Michael, and James Champy. 1993. *Reengineering the corporation: A manifesto for business revolution.* New York: Harper-Business.

Hammer, Michael, and Steven A. Stanton. 1995. *The reengineeiing revolution: A handbook.* New York: HarperBusiness.

Heifetz, Ronald A. 1994. *Leadership without easy answers.* Cambridge, Mass.: Belknap Press.

Helgesen, Sally. 1995. *The web of inclusion: A new architecture for building great organizations.* New York: Currency Doubleday.

Howard, Alice, Joan Magretta, and John Sawhill. 1995. Surviving success: An interview with the nature conservancy. *Harvard Business Review* (September-October): 108.

How a little company won big by betting on brainpower. 1995. *Fortune,* 4 September.

Jacob, Rahul. 1995. The struggle to create an organization for the 21st century. *Fortune,* 3 April, 90.

Joiner, Brian L. 1994. *Fourth generation management: The new business consciousness.* New York: McGraw-Hill.

Jones, Thomas O., and W. Earl Sasser Jr. 1995. Why satisfied customers defect. *Harvard Business Review,* November-December, 88.

Kanter, Rosabeth Moss. 1995. *World class: Thriving locally in the global economy.* New York: Simon & Schuster.

Kaplan, Robert, and David Norton. 1992. The balanced scorecard—Measures that drive performance. Harvard Business Review (January-February): 71.

Katzenbach, Jon R., and Douglas K. Smith. 1993. *The wisdom of teams: Creating the high-performance organization.* New York: HarperBusiness.

Kessler, Sheila. 1995. *Total quality service: A simplified approach to using the Baldrige award criteria.* Milwaukee: ASQC Quality Press.

Kotter, John P. 1995. Leading change: Why transformation efforts fail. *Harvard Business Review,* March-April, 59.

Labich, Kenneth. 1994. Why companies fail. *Fortune,* 14 November, 52.

Lane, Rhodes. 1996. Laughter is good for business. Business Week (Summer): 15.

Latzko, William J., and David M. Saunders. 1995. *Four days with Dr. Deming: A strategy for modern methods of management.* Reading, Mass.: Addison-Wesley.

Loeb, Marshall. 1994. How to Grow a New Product Every Day. *Fortune,* 14 November, 269.

Loeb, Marshall. 1995. Jack Welch lets fly on budgets. . . . *Fortune,* 29 May, 145.

Lorenz, Christopher. 1995. Management: Disarray in the executive suite. *The Financial Times* (28 July): 8.

Making perfect harmony with teams. 1995. ASQC's *Journal of Record,* November.

Malone, Michael S. 1995. Killer results without killing your self. *Fast Company,* premier issue, 124.

Miller, Lawrence M. 1994. *Whole system architecture.* Atlanta: Miller Howard Consulting Group.

Morin, William J. 1995. *Silent sabotage: Rescuing our careers, our companies, and our lives from the creeping paralysis of anger and bitterness.* New York: Amacom.

O'Reilly, Brian. 1994. J & J is on a roll. *Fortune* (26 December): 178.

Orsburn, Jack D., Linda Moran, Ed Musselwhite, and John H. Zenger. 1990. *Self-directed work teams: The new American challenge.* New York: Irwin.

O'Toole, James. 1995. *Leading change: Overcoming the ideology of comfort and the tyranny of custom.* San Francisco: Jossey-Bass.

Paré, Terence. 1995. The new champ of wealth creation. *Fortune* (18 September): 131.

Parker, Glenn M. 1994. *Cross-functional teams: Working with allies, enemies and other strangers.* San Francisco: Jossey-Bass.

Perkins, Anne G. 1994. Product variety: Beyond black. *Harvard Business Review* (November-December): 13.

Pine II, B. Joseph. 1993. *Mass customization: The new frontier in business competition.* Boston: Harvard Business School Press.

Reengineering: It doesn't have to be all or nothing. 1995. *Harvard Business Review,* November-December, 16.

Regeneration, not downsizing, is the key to success. 1995. *Quality Progress,* April, 17.

Report finds that managers who don't share power with employees lose competitive advantage. 1995. *Quality Progress,* November.

Rheem, Helen. 1995. Performance management. *Harvard Business Review* (May-June): 11.

Robert, Michel. 1993. *Strategy pure & simple: How winning CEOs outthink their competition.* New York: McGraw-Hill.

Ross, Gerald, and Michael Kay. 1994. *Toppling the pyramids: Redefining the way companies are run.* New York: Times Books.

Rummler, Geary A., and Alan P. Brache. 1990. *Improving performance: How to manage the white space on the organization chart.* San Francisco: Jossey-Bass.

Rust, Roland T., Anthony J. Zahorik, and Timothy L. Keiningham. 1994. *Return on quality: Measuring the financial impact of your company's quest for quality.* Chicago: Probus.

Ryan, Kathleen D., and Daniel K. Oestreich. 1991. *Driving fear out of the workplace: How to overcome the invisible barriers to quality, productivity, and innovation.* San Francisco: Jossey-Bass.

Scholtes, Peter R. et al. 1988. *The team handbook.* Madison, Wis.: Joiner.

Schwartz, Peter. 1991. *The art of the long view: Planning for the future in an uncertain world.* New York: Currency Doubleday.

Senge, Peter. 1990. *The fifth discipline: The art and practice of the learning organization.* New York: Doubleday.

Sheff, David. 1996. Levi's changes everything. *Fast Company,* June-July, 65.

Sherman, Strat. 1995. Stretch goals: The dark side of asking for miracles. *Fortune* (13 November): 231.

Spears, Larry C., ed. 1995. *Reflections on leadership: How Robert K. Greenleaf's theory of servant-leadership influenced today's top management thinkers.* New York: Wiley.

Stack, Jack, with Bo Burlingham. 1992. *The great game of business: Unlocking the power and profitability of open-book management.* New York: Currency Doubleday.

Stewart, Thomas A. 1994. How to lead a revolution. *Fortune,* 28 November, 48.

Thor, Carl G. 1994. *The measures of success: Creating a high performing organization.* Essex Junction, Vt.: Oliver Wight.

Treacy, Michael. 1995. Face to face. *Inc.,* April, 27.

Treacy, Michael, and Fred Wiersema. 1995. *The discipline of market leaders: Choose your customers, narrow your focus, dominate your market.* Reading, Mass.: Addison-Wesley.

Weiser, Charles R. 1995. Championing the customer. *Harvard Business Review,* November-December, 113.

Wheatley, Margaret J. 1992. *Leadership and the new science: Learning about organization from an orderly universe.* San Francisco: Berrett-Koehler.

Index

Page numbers referring to figures appear in italics.

NOTES

NOTES